The Making
of the Presidential
Candidates 2020

The Making
of the Presidential
Candidates 2020

Edited by Jonathan Bernstein
and Casey B. K. Dominguez

ROWMAN & LITTLEFIELD
Lanham • Boulder • New York • London

Published by Rowman & Littlefield
An imprint of The Rowman & Littlefield Publishing Group, Inc.
4501 Forbes Boulevard, Suite 200, Lanham, Maryland 20706
www.rowman.com

6 Tinworth Street, London SE11 5AL, United Kingdom

British Library Cataloguing in Publication Information Available

Library of Congress Cataloging-in-Publication Data Available

ISBN 978-1-5381-3107-7 (cloth : alk. paper)
ISBN 978-1-5381-3108-4 (pbk. : alk. paper)
ISBN 978-1-5381-3109-1 (electronic)

♾™ The paper used in this publication meets the minimum requirements of American National Standard for Information Sciences—Permanence of Paper for Printed Library Materials, ANSI/NISO Z39.48-1992.

Contents

Chapter One

Madame President?

Female Candidates, Masculine Norms of Executive Power, and the 2020 Nomination Contest

Linda Beail, Lilly J. Goren, and Mary A. McHugh

THINKING ABOUT THE OFFICE OF THE PRESIDENT

The year 2016 brought gender issues to the fore in presidential campaigning. Prior to 2009, the White House had never been occupied by a family of color; before 2016, no woman had ever won a major party nomination for president. For the first two centuries of our history, the American presidency was an office held solely by white men (who were also typically wealthy, well educated, and Protestant Christians), shaping voters' ideas about the kinds of leadership, experience, and personality traits most suitable to it. A few rare and remarkable candidates have challenged these norms, but for the most part, presidential nomination contests have been fairly monolithic. Candidates running for the White House have been elite, white statesmen with long résumés of political and (often) military experience. In modern campaigns, they have also needed to be media savvy and charismatic, be able to raise large sums of campaign cash, and fit their personal biography into a frame that draws on American ideals and narratives. As we move forward in the twenty-first century, the path to the presidency seems to be widening, at least in terms of some background characteristics, as we see more women, people of diverse races and ethnicities, and celebrities from fields outside of politics considering or entering the race.

While certainly distinct from other candidate characteristics, candidate gender and the embedded understandings of how that gender is performed and engaged has become more relevant and important as we consider nomination races and the contemporary road to the White House.[1] In 2016, both the primaries and the general election were unique in the ways that candidates' gender performances were portrayed, discussed, analyzed, and ultimately, considered by voters. But this conversation began long before 2016,

1

and as the 2018 midterm elections demonstrated, candidate gender continues to be a focal point in analyzing political events and understanding voters' attitudes and demands. In particular, political partisanship creates significantly different expectations and opportunities for candidates along gender lines. The Democratic and Republican parties have voters, issues, and candidate pools that offer quite distinct narratives for presidential campaigning. The media coverage of presidential candidates also shapes and reflects gendered ideas about the presidency and who is best suited to fill the Oval Office. This chapter will discuss the 2016 election cycle, as well as work that has assessed the role and understanding of gender within presidential politics. Many issues were considered and analyzed in the context of Hillary Clinton's historic run in 2016, which leads us to wonder how that election will shape the road to the 2020 nomination, particularly regarding this question of gender.

The United States presidency has a number of traits and norms associated with it that have long characterized the kind of power wielded in the office, and often, the unspoken expectations around the person who sits in the Oval Office. Though no woman has yet been elected president, quite a few women have run for the nomination of one of the two major parties. Hillary Rodham Clinton was the first to top the ticket when she became the Democratic nominee for president in 2016, after also running for and almost capturing the nomination in 2008. Prior to Clinton, both Congresswoman Shirley Chisholm in 1972 and Senator Carol Moseley Braun in 2004 ran groundbreaking campaigns as the first black women to seek the Democratic nomination for the White House. Republican women have also thrown their hats into the ring for their party's nomination, beginning with Senator Margaret Chase Smith in 1964, followed by Senator Elizabeth "Liddy" Dole in 2000, Congresswoman Michele Bachmann in 2012, and Carly Fiorina in 2016—though none of them were able to defeat all their primary opponents. Even before women could legally vote in U.S. federal elections, Victoria Woodhull was the first woman to run for president in the United States in 1872. She was followed by Belva Lockwood in 1884. A number of women have also run as third-party candidates, including Lenora Fulani (for the New Alliance Party in 1988), and Cynthia McKinney (2008) and Jill Stein (2012) from the Green Party.[2]

Both parties have also nominated women to the position of vice presidential candidate. In 1984, Walter Mondale chose House of Representatives member Geraldine Ferraro as his running mate on the Democratic ticket challenging incumbent president Ronald Reagan. The Mondale-Ferraro ticket went down in defeat in November of 1984. In 2008, the Republican nominee, the late Senator John McCain, chose Alaska Governor Sarah Palin as his running mate for the Republican ticket. The McCain-Palin ticket lost to Barack Obama and Joe Biden in November of 2008. While both parties have nominated women to run in the vice presidential slot, in neither instance was a woman elected to serve as vice president.[3] Indeed, the presidency and vice presidency remain the ultimate "glass ceiling" in American politics, though parts of it have certainly been cracked by the many women who have vied for those jobs in recent years.

While several have run, the only woman to capture the nomination of one of the two major parties was Hillary Clinton in 2016. She went on to win the popular vote—by 2.86 million votes—in the November election, but lost the electoral college vote 306–232 and thus did not become president.[4] Nonetheless, Clinton's primary campaign in 2008 and presidential race in 2016 have spurred debates about how women run for executive offices (governorships, mayoralties, and, ultimately, the White House) and how these are distinct from legislative offices. These differences might also suggest some challenges and opportunities for female candidates for the presidency as we are now embarking on the 2020 election cycle.

THE UNITED STATES PRESIDENCY: QUESTIONS OF GENDER AND OFFICE

The presidency, or the "chief magistrate" as titled by some of the founders in the *Federalist Papers* and at the constitutional convention, was, as noted by Alexander Hamilton in *Federalist #69*, not a king or a monarch. But that does not mean that the office itself is lacking many of the hallmarks of a monarch. The constitutional powers allocated to the presidency (and thus the person inhabiting the office) weave together aspects of a prince (in the Machiavellian context) in giving the office the power of commander in chief over the military, the absolute power of the pardon, and the treaty-making power (shared with the Senate). The president has a host of powers, some explicitly noted in the Constitution, many acquired over the stretch of history and due to the strategic disposition of the United States in the contemporary environment.

The office itself is, in many ways, gendered. That's because of the way in which the office was originally structured, the functional power of the presidency, the solitary nature of the position (even as the president is in charge of the largest branch of the United States federal government), and because of the way in which U.S. citizens, allies, and adversaries think about the president and the presidency. The solitary and separate power and position of the American president is distinct from its modern counterparts in parliamentary—especially Westminster style—systems where the prime minister is the "first among equals," and while situated in the position of executive, is also part of the legislature.[5] Fundamentally, the office is perceived and inhabited in a way that reflects a conceptualization of masculine power and function. Aiden Smith notes that not only is the presidency the "most gendered institution in the American political system" but that it is also the "ultimate symbol of masculine power."[6] Linda Horowitz and Holly Swyers have also explained the masculine expectations that color our imagining of what the president is and how the person in the position should look and be:

> American history is still told as a story of "founding fathers," and the idea of a patriarch as president has a firm hold in the American imagination. The result is that the notion of what a president should look like, of what is presidential, is fundamentally masculine.[7]

Voters respond by preferring stereotypical masculine qualities in potential presidents over feminine ones. As Meredith Conroy explains, studies repeatedly show that voters have a "bias that favors masculine traits in candidates (a preference for strong, assertive, aggressive, tough candidates over compassionate, warm, cautious, and compromising or consensus-building candidates). This had led the contemporary political science scholarship to suggest that women are at a disadvantage due to their presumed association with femininity."[8] Conroy's analysis, which incorporates a study of how the media contributes to the way that masculinity maps onto an understanding of the presidency, also highlights the gendered expectations of the office and thus how candidates are evaluated as suitably electable. As Rosenwasser and Seale found in their classic study of attitudes toward hypothetical male and female presidential candidates, potential voters rate men candidates higher on "masculine" leadership qualities and duties, while rating women candidates higher on "feminine" traits and tasks. Most significantly, though, they rated the masculine presidential duties (such as dealing with terrorism) as more important than feminine ones (such as solving problems for the disabled).[9] Thus while women are given positive credit for some tasks and traits, they are not the ones most valued in the presidency specifically. Researchers find that gender-trait stereotyping still holds up remarkably well in the twenty-first century: men are still expected to be decisive, daring, strong, self-reliant, authoritative, competitive, and driven, while women are assumed to be compassionate, sensitive to others, affectionate, and warm. However, as roles in both public and private life have shifted in the past few decades, women face a bit of a conundrum. In addition to traditionally feminine traits of nurture and emotion, expectations are that women should also be independent, intelligent, strong, and enjoy a challenge.[10] Women candidates need to demonstrate both competence and likability, and are punished by voters if seen as unlikable, not sharing credit for accomplishments, or being too "loud"; men candidates need to be perceived as qualified but are not dependent on being liked to win votes.[11] So the boldness, authoritativeness, and independent decision making prized in the presidency are also things that make women disliked, and even voted against. Tessa Ditonto finds this double-bind working against women in another way: in her experimental study, women candidates were more vulnerable than men to information that casts doubt on their competence, making them less liked and also less qualified.[12] Women candidates, especially for the highest executive office, face a high bar of proving their competence in a masculine realm and also remaining "likable" and recognizably feminine enough to not alienate voters.

This conceptualization of the presidency, with the masculine definition and expectations of power, became an overt narrative framing the 2016 campaign. This masculine understanding has long been the subtext of presidential campaigns, especially in critiques of candidates who may not "present" as aggressive or sufficiently tough. Conroy notes that "our cultural expectations of leadership [are] masculine, expressing feminine traits is to be a weak leader."[13] These cultural understandings of performed political power have become more explicit in campaigns, especially those for executive positions. In 2008, Senator Hillary Clinton attempted to work around these gendered expectations with her "3 a.m." ad, stressing her preparedness in foreign policy and national security while also casting her as a calm and decisive leader. This ad, aired during the early primary season in 2008 and discussed extensively by television media, featured audio of a phone insistently ringing in the middle of the night over visuals of children sleeping soundly in their beds. Viewers were asked to consider who they would want to answer the phone in the White House when an emergency struck somewhere around the globe. The thrust of the ad was to define Clinton as resolute, responsible, and seasoned, knowing how to deal with adversaries and crises firmly and without "feminine" hysteria. Without explicitly mentioning gender, the ad addressed voters' desire for a candidate with extensive leadership experience, the strength to make an independent decision in reacting to crisis, and masculine steadiness rather than an excess of emotion: all things voters might attribute as lacking in a stereotypical female candidate. Not only did Clinton think she had to make an argument for her capacity to do a "man's job," but she also had to distinguish her ability to act in an executive rather a legislative context, as other presidential candidates running from the Senate have also had to do. John McCain, Barack Obama, John Kerry, even John Kennedy all had to make an argument for how they possessed the qualities and traits to excel in the executive branch, despite more legislative experience of representation and collaboration.

This dynamic was also at work in the 2016 election cycle, with a variety of senators and former senators running for their party's nomination

(Clinton, Bernie Sanders, and Jim Webb for the Democratic nomination; Marco Rubio, Ted Cruz, Rand Paul, Lindsey Graham, and Rick Santorum for the GOP nomination). Though the U.S. Senate, as well as governors' mansions, has been the typical pool for finding potential presidential primary candidates, in the modern period those with high-level executive experience have been far more likely to be successful. Two thirds of major party nominees, and of those winning the White House, have been either state governors or sitting vice presidents prior to their run. Only 28 percent of nominees in the contemporary period, and two presidents (John F. Kennedy and Barack Obama) have gone from the Senate to the White House without executive experience.[14] Voters seem to prefer those possessing the kind of power and experience that is associated with the presidency, as Hamilton notes in *Federalist Paper #70*: "Decision, activity, secrecy, and dispatch will generally characterize the proceedings of one man in a much more eminent degree than the proceedings of any greater number; and in proportion as the number is increased, these qualities will be diminished." Hamilton's argument in #70 is for a vigorous and energetic yet singular executive, and he makes the case for the kinds of power that are often associated with masculinity, and that grow from the foundation of allocating responsibility to the assertive man in the office, making decisions, taking care that the laws are faithfully executed, commanding the troops, and fulfilling the requirements of the presidency. Hamilton yokes the form and expectations of the president to those of governors in *Federalist #69* where he compares the offices, powers, and election process for president, governor of New York, and the king. Hamilton, a bit disingenuously, argues that the president is much more like the governor of New York than the king of England. In all three cases, the office is one where a single individual holds the position. Thus, given recent history in the United States, voters have often preferred governors to ascend to the White House (Jimmy Carter, Ronald Reagan, Bill Clinton, George W. Bush). There are a number of reasons for this proclivity, as Ezra Klein notes in assessing the field of potential 2020 nominees: "There's a reason that, prior to Obama, the last candidate to win the White House from Congress was John F. Kennedy. Governors get to brag about what they've actually done, they get to criticize the toxicity of Washington from the outside, and they get to project an aura of executive competence that speechifying senators can only marvel at."[15]

This dynamic also has gendered dimensions, since there have been far fewer female governors in the political career pipeline than women senators.[16] Only forty-four women have ever served as governor of a U.S. state, the vast majority (thirty-seven) in just the past thirty years. In the 2018 election, a record-tying nine women were elected to fill gubernatorial positions and a very recent increase from the six women governors serving in 2018. Comparatively, there have been fifty-six female senators in the course of U.S. history, with twenty-five women currently serving in the U.S. Senate and more filling the legislative pipeline: 102 women in the House of Representatives and 28.5 percent of women state legislators across the nation, with Nevada as the first state to achieve a female-majority state legislature this year. The gains and candidate pool for women legislatures are steady and deep. However, if voters are looking for the skill set associated with executive offices, women have been at a disadvantage coming into a run for the White House since more women have more experience in legislatures than as executives.

A specific, related qualification for the job of commander in chief has historically been military service, which also served as a barrier to women. However, since the successful nominations of Bill Clinton, George W. Bush, Barack Obama, and Donald Trump, all of whom had minimal or nonexistent military careers, this requirement may have become less essential. Interestingly, many of the female newcomers running for Congress in 2018 were veterans or members of the national security establishment, including combat pilots Amy McGrath, Mikie Sherrill, MJ Hegar, and Martha McSally, who emphasized their military service in their campaigns, demonstrating their courage, patriotism, and toughness. Senators like Joni Ernst from Iowa and Tammy Duckworth of Illinois have also highlighted their combat experience in their successful campaigns. Women veterans may be proving they belong in a masculine political realm, making up for perceived deficiencies of women in the past without warrior qualities; but with their military experience, they are also opening up a more expansive notion of women's roles and abilities and normalizing power exercised in different ways by new faces.

POLITICAL PARTIES: NOMINATIONS AND GENDER

In considering the upcoming 2020 race, one needs to pay special attention to the nominating processes of both parties. While (at this writing) we don't expect the Republican nomination to be a heavily contested one, it is still important to look at the state of both of the two major political parties regarding gender and the nomination quest. It should not be surprising to anyone who follows politics that there has been and is extreme polarization of the electorate. There is a wide partisan divide between Democrats and Republicans over a variety of issues. However, there is also a partisan asymmetry that forces us to consider issues of gender differently in the parties. Matt Grossman and David Hopkins, in *Asymmetric Politics*, explain that the two parties do not operate as simple mirror images. They note that "because Democratic constituencies prioritize concrete policy change, Democratic candidates tout their ability to win elections and once in power, work within the political system in pursuit of tangible accomplishments. Republicans in contrast, resist viewing the electorate as an assortment of specific separable interests, instead, seeking support by presenting themselves as champions of an ideological cause."[17] The gendered nature of the office itself, as already discussed, becomes one of many components that shapes the nomination process and often contributes to the outcome itself. Thus, different perspectives on the powers of the office and expectations about who should or can best inhabit the presidency contribute to distinctions among the parties.

Asymmetry is not just confined to political parties. Female and male voters are also asymmetrical especially when it comes to gender and power, which further colors the expectations of what individuals expect and consider appropriate for the person sitting in the Oval Office. Monika McDermott, in her study of the impact of gendered personalities, notes some of this asymmetry in shaping political attitudes and behaviors:

> [M]asculinity (as the tough personality dimension) increases Republican Party identification and voting for Republican candidates, while femininity (the compassion profile) does the same for Democratic affiliation and voting. In addition, masculine traits boost political engagement. Individuals who are higher in masculine traits, including competitiveness, dominance, and standing up for one's beliefs, are more likely to show an interest in and knowledge of the political world.[18]

McDermott's research examines the expectations that voters have of candidates, specifically based on the voters' personality traits and how those expectations are directly connected to gendered understandings of politics. But these expectations are asymmetrical in terms of who is expected to serve in elected office. Part of this asymmetry comes out in the data about voters' willingness to cast their ballots for a candidate with children. Republican voters are less likely than Democratic voters to support a female candidate who has children. At the same time, these same Republican voters are more willing to vote for a male candidate who has children, as opposed to a male candidate who does not have children.

Since 1937 Gallup Polls have questioned voters about electing a woman to the presidency. In 1937, only 33 percent of those polled answered yes. Over the succeeding decades that number has grown. By 2015, 92 percent of those polled replied affirmatively when asked, "If your party nominated a generally well-qualified person for president who happened to be a woman, would you vote for that person?"[19] However, as 2016 has shown, there is a difference between giving a non-sexist answer to a poll versus actually casting a ballot for a female candidate. As one male voter explained, "There is a possibility that I would vote for a woman, but not her [Hillary Clinton]."[20]

There has been a consistent gender gap in the electorate. According to the Pew Research Center, women are more likely to identify with the Democratic Party. They note that among registered voters, 56 percent of women affiliate with or lean toward the Democratic Party, compared with 44 percent of men.[21] The 2016 and 2018 general elections show an even wider voting gap. In 2016 the gap between women and men was 22 points; it rose slightly in 2018 to 23 points, the highest it has been since 1992.[22] These numbers will contribute to our exploration of the differences between the two parties in the nomination process.

As we consider the presidential election cycle, we must first start with the candidates. Candidates emerge in a variety of ways (recruitment, promotion, self-selection) from within the party and also from outside the party. There does seem to be a pipeline that leads to someone deciding to run for president, although there is no straight line to the White House, but one generally does have to secure the nomination of one of the two major parties. Both parties look to their "bench" of potential candidates who have built up name recognition and experiences that might lead them to become viable candidates. In 2018, women who were Democrats outnumbered Republican women serving in legislative offices (U.S. Senate, U.S. House and State Legislatures). More Republican women held statewide executive offices (governor, lieutenant governor, and secretary of state) than Democratic women, though Democrats made gains in governorships in the 2018 midterms.[23] The events of the last few years, beginning with the election of Donald Trump and continuing through to his policies including his Supreme Court nominations, have mobilized many women to become more engaged and involved in politics, including prompting quite a few women to run for elected office. This surge of female candidates, especially over the past two years, has been mostly on the Democratic side. For example, at the time of filing deadlines in spring 2018, the number of Democratic women candidates for the House of Representatives had more than doubled from 2016, a 127 percent increase. Republican women's candidacies increased as well, but only by 28 percent.[24] Similar increases happened at the statehouse level, where candidacies by Democratic women jumped approximately 70 percent but Republican women's stayed fairly flat.[25] While the 2018 midterms were more favorable to Democrats than Republicans generally, this partisan divide was very stark among female officeholders. Women in state legislatures moved from 62 percent to 69 percent Democratic majorities, while women in Congress jumped from 74 percent Democratic to 84 percent Democratic. This partisan lean in women officeholders, even more pronounced after the 2018 midterms, means that the pipeline of future women candidates—including for the presidency, in 2020 and beyond—includes far more potential Democrats gaining electoral experience than Republicans.

2020: THROUGH THE REARVIEW MIRROR OF 2016

In considering the 2020 nominations, it might be helpful to look back at the 2016 election to see the effect gender had on the process in both parties. During the 2016 nomination cycle two women ran in their respective party primaries. On the Republican side, Carly Fiorina, former CEO of Hewlett Packard, announced her candidacy in May of 2015. She had limited success in the first few primaries and left the race in February of 2016. On the Democratic side, Hillary Clinton announced her candidacy in April of 2015 and went on to make history by becoming the first woman nominated by a major political party.

As historic as the 2016 nomination cycle was, one cannot discount the effect that gender had on both races. While Carly Fiorina was not a candidate for very long, she did compete within a very crowded Republican field that included Donald Trump, perhaps foreshadowing the general election race. She confronted gender issues on the campaign trail and during the debates. At one point she was attacked about her looks by Donald Trump in a *Rolling Stone* profile about his candidacy: "Look at that face! Would anyone vote for that? Can you imagine that, the face of our next president? I mean, she's a woman, and I'm not s'posedta say bad things, but really, folks, come on. Are we serious?"[26] When asked to respond to those comments during the next debate, Fiorina said coolly, "I think women all over this country heard very clearly what Mr. Trump said." Her rejoinder garnered praise as a "mic-drop moment" for its calm and for how it turned Trump's insult into a larger gender issue about his respect for and treatment of all women, not just Fiorina, and led to a brief surge in her popularity. While Fiorina spent most of the campaign debating on the undercard stage (those candidates who were not in the top ten of polling), Fiorina did make it to the primetime debate in September of 2015, but did not gain much traction. Her declining poll numbers kept her off the debate stage prior to the Iowa caucus and the New Hampshire primary making her less appealing to donors. After poor showings in Iowa and New Hampshire, she left the race in February of 2016.

The Democratic party nomination battle had fewer candidates but was a hard-fought race between Hillary Clinton and Bernie Sanders. Sanders, a Democratic socialist and senator from Vermont, ran an outsider campaign, challenging Clinton from the left. Sanders stayed in the race until the convention. The role of gender in this campaign cannot be ignored. Even now, as candidates are gearing up for the 2020 nomination battle, there are ongoing concerns about the sexist treatment of women who worked for the Sanders campaign.[27] There was also the rise of the "Bernie Bro" phenomena, which was another thread of sexist behavior in opposition to Hillary Clinton. The Bernie Bros often used social media to attack Clinton and Clinton supporters and often their approach in their attacks was sexist in form and rhetoric. As Dara Lind noted, "the trope of the mansplain-y, harass-y Sanders supporter who gets all up in the mentions of anyone insufficiently praiseful—is the definition of 'Bernie Bro.'"[28] John Sides, Michael Tesler, and Lynn Vavreck note that "Clinton did worse among the minority of Democratic primary voters who expressed more sexist attitudes, and especially among men. There was also a strong association between sexism and views of Clinton among Sanders supporters."[29] At the same time, it should be noted that while this dynamic was observed and analyzed during the 2016 primary cycle, "gender was not the dominant divide in the Democratic primary."[30] In anticipating the 2020 nominating cycle, this point should not be lost. While sexism and gender were at play in the Democratic primary, they ultimately did not prove to be an insurmountable barrier in terms of the nomination.

Clinton, running again after failing to gain the Democratic nomination in 2008, seemed to have a different campaign strategy in 2016. In 2008, Clinton did not integrate the distinction of her gender as a presidential aspirant, and she did little to promote her gender in her campaign. In 2016 her strategy shifted. While she did not run explicitly as a woman, she did not avoid it as she had in 2008. She did focus her framing more on her understanding of the world and of politics from the perspective of a mother and a grandmother, and "she openly embraced the historic significance of becoming the country's first woman president."[31] As one analyst described, "she mainstreamed gender in her performance, agenda, and strategy in ways that altered the image and expectation of presidential leadership, challenging masculine dominance instead of adapting to it."[32] In fact, at one early campaign stop in Ohio, Clinton said "Clearly I'm not asking people to vote for me simply because I'm a woman. I'm asking people to vote for me on the merits. I think one of the merits is I am a woman. And I can bring those views and perspectives to the White House."[33] Clinton entered the nomination race as the front runner and remained in that position throughout the race. She won more votes, delegates, and superdelegates than Sanders did, but while she was the presumptive nominee for much of the spring and summer of 2016, Sanders did not concede, taking the race all the way to the convention vote. This was very different from how Clinton had responded to Obama's accumulation of delegates and superdelegates in 2008. Analysts drew attention to the difference in approaches from the candidates and the campaigns in this regard, and speculated on whether gender played a role in how the Clinton campaign moved toward concession and unity in 2008 prior to the Democratic convention, and the Sanders campaign that took the primary fight all the way to the 2016 convention.

Hillary Clinton's path to the nomination was not an easy glide. It was a slow but steady climb to victory. She won the Iowa caucuses but lost in the New Hampshire primary. After New Hampshire she began to piece together victories and delegates. She was more successful in primaries and Sanders was more successful in caucus states. Even in the states she lost, because of Democratic primary rules, she was able to continue to pick up delegates and maintain her lead. Looking at the demographic breakdown of the voters of these races, we can see that there were some groups of voters who consistently supported Clinton; there were also clear groups who did not support Clinton. The gender gap is quite evident in the 2016 Democratic nomination results. With the exception of a few states (New Hampshire, Vermont, Wisconsin), women voted for Clinton over Sanders. The Pew Research Center found that Democratic women supported Clinton 52–39 over Sanders, and Democratic men supported Sanders 48–46 over Clinton.[34] Political scientist Kelly Dittmar, in March of 2016, did a recap of the early primaries, noting that the gender gap on the Democratic side was about 10 points, with the smallest gap, of 6 points, in the Mississippi and Tennessee results. In Arkansas, Clinton won 60 percent of the male vote but 76 percent of the female vote.[35] Clinton was able to garner a large amount of support from women, especially black women. Black female voters were a crucial part of Clinton's nomination coalition. As one reporter wrote, "This support was a critical part of Clinton's firewall against Sanders in the early voting states of Nevada and South Carolina, and made a big difference for her in the March 1 Super Tuesday states and beyond."[36] For example in Alabama, 93 percent of black women voted for Clinton. In Virginia, it was 85 percent.

Clinton did win by larger margins among women, but since women are not monolithic voters, it is important to take a closer look. Millennial women voted more often for Sanders than Clinton. This should not be surprising since Sanders captured the under thirty vote by a 3–1 margin. In fact, it was the fifty and older voters who seemed to support Clinton in the highest numbers.[37] According to Sides, Tesler, and Vavreck, "[B]eing more strongly identified with the Democratic Party, being nonwhite, and being older were all associated with support for Clinton. Identifying as liberal was associated with support for Sanders."[38] Again, demographic differences beyond voter gender and sex contributed to the voter split in the 2016 Democratic nomination race.

While African-American and white women were the backbone to the Clinton victory, men did not shy away from supporting her campaign either. For the most part, Clinton and Sanders ran even among white voters and men. However, Clinton found that she had the least amount of support among white men. As *Washington Post* reporter Philip Bump noted in May 2016, "One of the groups that votes against Hillary Clinton most consistently is white men. In 20 of 23 contests for which we have exit poll data, white men have preferred Sanders to Clinton. (The three exceptions were Alabama, Arkansas and Tennessee, all states where Clinton did very well.) White men back Sanders by 26.4 percentage points more than do white women."[39] Clinton's weakness with white men was not confined to the primary contest; it continued into the general election as well.

On the Republican side, even though Carly Fiorina was in the mix at the beginning of the race, the gender gap was smaller than on the Democratic side. After the first twenty GOP primaries, the average gender gap was 6.5. However, Donald Trump's support was heavily weighted towards male voters and the gender gap was averaging over 10 points.[40] During the primary battle, Trump "polled between five to ten percentage points better with men than with women."[41] Ultimately, Trump would go on to carry the votes of the majority of white women in the United States in the 2016 general election, outperforming "Clinton among white women, winning 53 percent of voters in that demographic. Drilling down further, he beat Clinton among white women without college degrees by 27 points."[42] Trump also was popular with married men (winning 57 percent of their votes), while extraordinarily unpopular with unmarried women (32 percent to Clinton's 63 percent of votes in this group, according to CNN exit polls). So, while there was a gender gap during the course of the Republican primary and the general election, that gap was not as distinct as other partisan, demographic, and geographic distinctions among voters.

LEGACY OF 2016—WHAT DOES 2016 TELL US ABOUT 2020?

While there is no official starting date for the 2020 presidential campaign, the beginning of 2019 brought about the first public announcements of candidates' interest in participating in the race. It has also allowed us to consider what the legacy of the 2016 election was by seeing if and how it has any effect on the 2020 Democratic and Republican contests. Hillary Clinton's 2016 campaign and Donald Trump's victory have both changed the lenses through which we view presidential campaigns and the presidency itself.

Looking forward at the 2020 campaign, there is an expectation that the Democratic nomination field will include a large field of candidates, perhaps as many as fifteen to twenty formally announcing. It seems likely that there will be an incumbent Republican president running for a second term, which will limit the number of candidates challenging him for renomination, assuming that Trump's popularity remains high among Republican voters.

Gender is now a more normal and expected part of any conversation about elections. Media and the public are not shocked by female candidates, LG-BTQ candidates, or candidates of color, and these candidates are generally not treated as total anomalies. But as the swearing in of the 116th Congress demonstrated, there are still novel participants in politics—including the first Muslim and Native American Congresswomen, the first refugee to serve, the first bisexual senator, and the youngest woman ever elected to the House, the viral Twitter star Alexandria Ocasio-Cortez—and they continue to draw media attention and analysis by scholars as they widen the spectrum of what political leadership can look like. In these cases, that leadership continues to be situated in the legislative branch, though there was also, as already noted, an uptick in the number of women now in gubernatorial positions.

Another point to note is that there seems to be a normalization of women running for and serving in the House, Senate, and governorships. Hillary Clinton's presidential candidacy showed women that they could and should run for office. Women finally had a model of a presidential candidate, someone who looked like them. Her loss and the subsequent backlash to Trump's victory sparked protest marches across the country, commonly referred to as the "Women's March," and these public protests were among the largest demonstrations ever held in the United States. (They were also not confined to the United States but were held on every continent in January 2017 following Trump's inauguration.) The question that hung over worldwide protests in January 2017 and January 2018 was whether these millions of demonstrators would actually do something beyond spending an afternoon with their friends in pink "pussy hats," marching around most of the cities and towns in the United States, and beyond. What seems to have resulted is more political engagement, following from Clinton's defeat and Trump's election; record numbers of women have harnessed their energy, become more civically involved, and even decided to run for office. A flood of more than fifteen thousand women contacted She Should Run, a nonpartisan group that helps women run for office, while over twenty thousand reached out to EMILY's List, which supports the candidacies of pro-choice Democratic women. Those campaigns may be just the tip of the iceberg, as local groups proliferate and grassroots activism is springing up all over the country in response to the Trump administration. Whether on issues of gerrymandering, education, immigration, refugees, or simply "protecting American democracy," researchers Lara Putnam and Theda Skocpol observe a wave of women—particularly white, middle-aged, college-educated suburban women who were not previously deeply engaged in politics and have been energized in response to Trump—rising to transform Democratic party politics.[43]

Women did not just settle to run for local offices. Many focused on the House, the Senate, and governors' mansions across the country, taking on incumbents and getting out the vote. In lessons learned from the women's marches and the #MeToo movement, women, instead of remaining silent, learned to use their voices to fight against what they saw as the failings of the president, or an approach to politics with which they disagreed. The success that women had in the 2018 midterm elections built upon Clinton's 2016 campaign. Even the selection of Nancy Pelosi as Speaker of the House—again—models this same idea that women can wield power successfully. Heading into the 2020 election, there are several women who are discussed as legitimate contenders for the Democratic nomination. Senators such as Elizabeth Warren (MA), Amy Klobuchar (MN), Kamala Harris (CA), and Kirsten Gillibrand (NY) are all considering a run.[44] Not only did Hillary Clinton crack open the door to women winning a major party nomination, but that door seems to be open wide enough to encourage multiple women's candidacies. As women of different ages, races, and professional backgrounds join the field of potential nominees, they make space for a variety of ways of performing gender and multiple narratives for making sense of women holding power.

These women candidates will also shape and reflect narratives about contemporary women's lives and about political power, just as vice presidential candidate Sarah Palin scrambled the traditional narratives of how to "run as a woman." Rather than downplay femininity to blend in with more masculine notions of politics, Governor Palin evoked gender narratives as a "hockey mom" surrounded by her five children, including a newborn; a frontier woman, embodying a sense of American adventure and strength without toppling traditional roles; and a beauty queen, in high heels, short skirts, and lipstick that highlighted her youth and attractiveness rather than dismissing them as frivolous and unimportant to serious political debate (admittedly, this last narrative frame quickly exceeded her control as she was labeled a "bimbo" by the left and a "MILF" by many supporters).[45] The cultural and media debates over how to understand Palin's candidacy touched off conversations, far beyond vote choice, regarding women's careers, motherhood, sexuality, and power in the twenty-first century.

Female candidates for the presidency in 2020 will have to find ways to position themselves as embodying American values, giving voters narratives they can relate or aspire to. Just as Barack Obama told an "only in America" story about his multiracial heritage that he hoped voters would understand and be inspired by, so too, Gillibrand, Warren, Harris, and others will need to find narratives that appeal to voters and make their unique candidacies intelligible. Warren is perhaps best known as a former professor and policy wonk, an expert on bankruptcy law and economics who likes to "nerd out" with policy detail. She has been viewed as ideologically similar to Bernie Sanders in pushing the party to the left, advocating for consumer protections, and fighting class inequality, and appealing to voters who disliked Hillary Clinton's more centrist stances. During debate over the confirmation of Jeff Sessions as Trump's attorney general in 2017, Warren read a letter critical of Sessions from civil rights leader Coretta Scott King on the Senate floor and was rebuked by Majority Leader Mitch McConnell. Part of his criticism, that Warren had been warned not to continue reading the letter but "nevertheless, she persisted," became a phrase that entered the cultural lexicon, and Warren became something of a feminist icon for refusing to be silenced or shamed into lady-like submission. In her late sixties and with a serious demeanor, whether talking about policy minutiae or angry about economic inequality, speculation about Warren's candidacy is also shaped by gendered questions of "likability" and feminine appeal, just as Clinton's was.[46]

New York Senator Kirsten Gillibrand, on the other hand, seems to be casting herself as the energetic "young mom" motivated by concern for all American children's futures, informed by her experience with her own two school-age sons. She is also seizing gendered narratives surrounding the #MeToo movement, defending her decision to criticize her former Democratic colleague, Senator Al Franken, for groping and sexually harassing young women years earlier and pressuring him to step down. She has been prominent in sponsoring policy to combat sexual violence in the military and on college campuses, blending her maternal appeal with feminist stances.

Kamala Harris, senator and former attorney general of California, stresses themes of populism, unity, and practical experience in the executive branch, working on criminal justice. Harris highlights her unique multiracial background (African American and South Asian) and as a woman of color, hopes to be the first intersectional candidate to win the Democratic nomination.

Many of the women who have been elected since 2016 have been members of the Democratic Party. As we look at the 2020 nominations, we need to be mindful of the asymmetry of the two parties, and the asymmetry with regard to the integration of female candidacies. The legacy of 2016 is that, in the lead up to the 2020 election, women are now an accepted part of the conversation about presidential primary candidates on the Democratic side. The Republican Party doesn't seem to have the same ease of inclusion of women in their conversations of candidates. One reason might be that President Trump is the incumbent and incumbent presidents are usually not seriously challenged.[47] Still, even in speculation about post-Trump candidates in 2024, there is a dearth of women being discussed as potential Republican candidates for the nomination. Thus, this leads to the consideration of whether the small pool of rising Republican women results from some sort of short term "Trump Effect" on the Republican Party or a larger issue. Women in the Trump cabinet have been limited to serving in less prominent offices such as the Small Business Administration (SBA), the Education Department, the Department of Transportation, and the U.N. ambassador—while the secretaries of education and transportation are cabinet-level posts, the director of the SBA and the U.N. ambassador fluctuate in terms of their cabinet status.[48] With limited cabinet appointments, and fewer women in the House and the Senate, one wonders about the Republican pipeline of candidates and whether the Trump presidency will affect the way that Republicans look at female candidates in the future. Thus, as we assess the landscape for 2020 and beyond, the question of gender and presidential politics remains complex and under consideration in a myriad of ways.

We have noted the asymmetrical position of the parties at the moment with regard to gender and elected officials. This broader asymmetry reflects recruitment, messaging, and the rank-and-file voters who make up the parties. It would be unusual to have a significant challenge to an incumbent president, so it would be unlikely to see serious women candidates in the GOP primary in 2020. The Democratic coalition has more energized women activists and voters, and more women in elected office filling the candidate pipeline at all levels. A plurality of Democratic voters was willing to cast a ballot for Hillary Clinton in the primaries, and ultimately to nominate Clinton as the Democratic standard bearer in 2016. The masculinity of the Oval Office itself made Clinton's two presidential campaigns appear like walking a tightrope of gender politics. From her 2008 campaign slogan "Tough but Caring," and confounding tears in a New Hampshire coffee shop, to the embrace of white suffragist-evoking pantsuits and the historic nature of her nomination win in 2016, Hillary Clinton's gender was always a dynamic of the race. Donald Trump's "locker room talk" explanation of sexually assaulting women and his contemptuous insults of women journalists and candidates (such as Fiorina) brought these dynamics into even more stark relief. As Trump runs for a second nomination, while women and men in the Democratic party position themselves against his policies and personality, gender is sure to be in play during the 2020 primaries. Notions of feminist change versus more traditional masculinity and femininity, the appeals to different demographics of voters, media and candidate narratives, the identities of those in each party's candidate pool, and masculine tropes of presidential power will all be a part of the unfolding nomination race. These images and ideas will not only reflect our conceptions of gendered power, but will shape what kinds of leaders, policies, and narratives of power will be normalized and legitimized for future presidential races to come.

NOTES

1. We are discussing this question in a binary context because it has generally been experienced and pursued in a gender-binary construction. That does not preclude gender non-conforming candidates, or non-binary candidates, from pursuit of the office.

2. Female Presidential Candidates

1872	Victoria Claflin Woodhull
1884	Belva Ann Bennett Lockwood
1888	Belva Ann Bennett Lockwood
1964	Margaret Chase Smith
1972	Shirley Anita Chisholm
	Patsy Takemoto Mink
1976	Ellen McCormack
1980	Ellen McCormack
1984	Sonia Johnson
1988	Patricia S. Schroeder
	Lenora Fulani
1992	Lenora Fulani
2000	Elizabeth Hanford Dole
2004	Carol Moseley Braun
2008	Hillary Rodham Clinton
2012	Michele Bachmann
	Jill Stein
2016	Carly Fiorina
	Jill Stein
	Hillary Clinton

3. Winona LaDuke was nominated twice to run as the vice-presidential candidate for the Green Party, in 1996 and again in 2000. In both instances she ran on the ticket that was headed by Ralph Nader and in both instances the ticket did not win or garner any electoral college votes.

4. https://www.nytimes.com/elections/2016/results/president

5. Gary N. Powell and D. Anthony Butterfield (2011) "Sex, Gender, and the US Presidency: Ready for a female President?," *Gender in Management: An International Journal*, 26 6: 394–407, https://doi.org/10.1108/17542411111164894

6. Aiden Smith, *Gender, Heteronormativity and the American Presidency*, Routledge, 2017, p. 3.

7. Linda Horowitz and Holly Swyers, "Why are All the Presidents Men," in *You've Come a Long Way, Baby: Women, Politics, and Popular Culture*, edited by Lilly J. Goren, University Press of Kentucky, 2009, p. 119.

8. Meredith Conroy, *Masculinity, Media, and the American Presidency*, Palgrave MacMillan 2015, p. 2.

9. Shirley M. Rosenwasser and Jana Seale, "Attitudes toward a Hypothetical Male or Female Presidential Candidate: A Research Note," *Political Psychology* 9:4 (December 1988), 591–598.

10. Deborah Prentice and Erica Carranza, "What Women and Men Should Be, Shouldn't Be, Are Allowed to Be and Don't Have to Be: The Contents of Prescriptive Gender Stereotypes," *Psychology of Women Quarterly* 26 (2002): 269–281.

11. Barbara Lee Family Foundation. "Politics Is Personal: Keys to Likability and Electability for Women." April 2016.

12. Tessa Ditonto, "A High Bar or a Double Standard? Gender, Competence and Information in Political Campaigns." *Political Behavior* 39:2 (June 2017), 301–325.

13. Conroy, p. 3.

14. In the past 50 years (1968 election onward), major party nominees have been evenly distributed between senators (6), vice presidents (6), governors (6), and incumbent presidents (7), with one having no previous officeholding experience (Donald Trump). However, in that same time period, former governors have won the White House a majority of the time (54 percent), while Obama is the only one to win from the Senate. Senators and House members vying for the presidency usually find the path to running through the vice presidency or other executive branch service (such as Hillary Clinton as Secretary of State, or George H.W. Bush serving as CIA director before also becoming Reagan's running mate).

15. "Who's overrated and who's underrated as a 2020 Democratic presidential prospect? A few of our favorite long shots." By Matthew Yglesias, Ezra Klein, and Dylan Matthews, Sept. 14, 2018, 9:40am EDT, *Vox.com*

16. Currently, 18 percent of U.S. governors are women, up from just 12 percent in 2018. In contrast, 25 percent of the current US Senate is made up of women, and that number has been steadily rising since 1992.

17. Matt Grossman and David Hopkins, *Asymmetric Politics*, p. 199.

18. Monika L. McDermott, *Masculinity, Femininity, and American Political Behavior*. Oxford University Press, 2016, pp. 5–6.

19. Justin McCarthy, "In U.S., Socialist Presidential Candidates Least Appealing," *Gallup news*, June 22, 2015, https://news.gallup.com/poll/183713/socialist -presidential-candidates-least-appealing.aspx?utm_source=Politics&utm_medium= newsfeed&utm_campaign=tiles).

20. Daniel Bush, "The Hidden Sexism that Could Swing the Election," *PBS Newshour*, 2016.

21. "Wide Gender Gap, Growing Educational Divide in Voters' Party Identification," Pew Research Center, March 20, 2018, *www.prewresearch.org*

22. Jamie Velencia, "The 2018 Gender Gap Was Huge. And It helped Democrats Win the House," *FiveThirtyEight.com*, November 9, 2018.

23. Beginning in January of 2019, there will be more Democratic than Republican female governors (6–3). Overall, Democratic women have held governor's offices 26 times out of 44 terms when the office was held by women and Republican women have held the office 18 times. With just over 40 percent of female governors being Republican, that is somewhat closer partisan parity than in other types of elected offices. See the Center for American Women in Politics, http://www.cawp.rutgers.edu/women-elective-office-2018.

24. Danielle Kurtzleben, "A Record 309 Women Are Running for the House (and 1103 Men)," NPR, April 13, 2018, accessed January 26, 2019 at https://www.npr.org/2018/04/13/601866062/there-are-a-record-breaking-309-women-house-candidates-and-1-103-men.

25. Danielle Kurtzleben, "Is the Record Number of Women Candidates a 2018 Blip—or a Lasting Trend?," NPR Morning Edition, September 25, 2018, accessed January 26, 2019 at https://www.npr.org/2018/09/25/651085628/is-the-record-number-of-women-candidates-a-2018-blip-or-a-lasting-trend.

26. Paul Solotaroff, "Trump Seriously: On the Trail with the GOP's Tough Guy," *Rolling Stone Magazine,* September 9, 2015, 3:56PM ET, https://www.rollingstone.com/politics/politics-news/trump-seriously-on-the-trail-with-the-gops-tough-guy-41447/

27. https://www.nytimes.com/2019/01/02/us/politics/bernie-sanders-campaign-sexism.html

28. "Bernie Bros, explained," Vox.com, By Dara Lind, Updated Feb 5, 2016, 9:51am EST, https://www.vox.com/2016/2/4/10918710/berniebro-bernie-bro

29. John Sides, Michael Tesler, and Lynn Vavreck, *Identity Crisis: The 2016 Presidential Campaign and the Battle for the Meaning of America,* Princeton University Press, 2018, p. 121.

30. *Identity Crisis*, p. 123.

31. *Identity Crisis*, p. 119.

32. Kelly Dittmar, "Finding Gender in Election 2016: Lessons from Presidential Gender Watch," Center for American Women and Politics.

33. Eric Bradner, "Hillary Clinton: 'One of the merits Is I am a woman'," *CNN. com*, July 23, 2015, https://www.cnn.com/2015/07/23/politics/hillary-clinton-gender-merits/index.html

34. Bruce Stokes, "Republicans, Especially Trump Supporters, See Free Trade Deals as Bad for U.S." Pew Research Center, March 31, 2016.

35. Kelly Dittmar, "Gender Matters: A Status Check on the Gender Gap in Presidential Primaries," March 17, 2016, Presidential Gender Watch 2016, Center for American Women and Politics.

36. Tamara Keith, "How Hillary Clinton Locked Up The Democratic Nomination in 10 Steps" *NPR.org,* June 7, 2016, https://www.npr.org/2016/06/07/480673009/how-hillary-clinton-locked-up-the-democratic-nomination-in-10-steps

37. Danielle Kurtzleben, "Three Things to Know about the Woman Candidate in 2016 Election," *NPR.org,* April 27, 2016.

38. *Identity Crisis*, p. 125.

39. Philip Bump, "White Male Democrats Have Disproportionately Voted against Hillary Clinton for Eight Years Running," *The Washington Post,* May 5, 2016, https://www.washingtonpost.com/news/the-fix/wp/2016/05/05/white-male-democrats-have-disproportionately-voted-against-hillary-clinton-for-eight-years-running/?utm_term=.8cc8b34ae589.

40. Kelly Dittmar, "Gender Matters: A Status Check on the Gender Gap in Presidential Primaries," March 17, 2016, Presidential Gender Watch 2016, Center for American Women and Politics.

41. https://www.theguardian.com/us-news/2016/apr/28/donald-trump-women-voters-poll-republican

42. https://www.vox.com/policy-and-politics/2017/1/20/14061660/women-march-washington-vote-trump

43. Lara Putnam and Theda Skocpol, "Middle America Reboots Democracy," *Democracy: A Journal of Ideas,* February 2018, accessed January 26, 2018 at https://democracyjournal.org/arguments/middle-america-reboots-democracy/.

44. It is interesting that these are all senators. Though recent history seems to favor candidates coming from executive branch experience a bit more, at this moment in American politics it may be more difficult for those candidates to break through all the Trump "noise" (Trump's unique ability to constantly and consistently garner the spotlight) and get media attention from outside DC in a governor's office, where individuals are focused more specifically on their particular state. The spotlight on Congress and its dealings with President Trump may give opportunities to senators hoping to prove themselves as presidential contenders. Holding hearings that grab national attention, as the confirmation hearings for Justice Brett Kavanaugh did, can offer a platform for Democratic presidential hopefuls to make speeches, ask questions, and position themselves in opposition to the incumbent. This, coupled with the Democratic legacy of the last decade of fewer governors and fewer female governors, limits the options and candidates coming from governor's mansions. Since the president's focus is on the national level, many senators find themselves in the position of fighting with the president from their perch in the Senate (this is the case with members both of the president's own party and from the opposition).

45. Linda Beail and Rhonda Kinney Longworth, *Framing Sarah Palin: Pitbulls, Puritans, and Politics*, Routledge Press, 2013.

46. Annie Linskey and David Weigel. "Before You Run against Trump, You Have to Run against Hillary (If You're a Woman)." *Washington Post*, January 3, 2019. Accessed January 26, 2019 at https://www.washingtonpost.com/politics/before-you-run-against-trump-you-have-to-run-against-hillary-if-youre-a-woman/2019/01/03/f552fc0c-0ec9-11e9-831f-3aa2c2be4cbd_story.html?utm_term=.295f3be5bb47.

47. Even so, there have been some discussions of possible challengers to President Trump in the 2020 primary, but they are almost all men. These challengers include John Kasich, former governor of Ohio, Jeff Flake, former senator from Arizona, possibly Mitt Romney, the new junior senator from Utah, but the former presidential nominee, and former governor of Massachusetts. The only woman who garners any attention in these considerations is Nikki Haley, the former governor of South Carolina who served for two years as Trump's Ambassador to the United Nations. Trump

himself has mentioned his daughter, Ivanka Trump, as a potential presidential candidate, and given her position as an advisor in the Trump White House, she is engaged in a path that could lead to electoral aspirations in the future.

48. Lilly J. Goren, "Few Women Hold Key Positions in the Trump Administration." *Brookings.edu*, May 2017. https://www.brookings.edu/blog/fixgov/2017/05/12/few-women-hold-key-positions-in-trump-administration/

REFERENCES

Beail, Linda, and Rhonda Kinney Longworth. 2013. *Framing Sarah Palin: Pit Bulls, Puritans and Politics.* New York: Routledge.

Bradner, Eric. 2015. "Hillary Clinton: 'One of the Merits Is I Am a Woman.'" CNN.com, July 23.

Clinton, Hillary Rodham. 2017. *What Happened.* New York: Simon and Schuster.

Conroy, Meredith. 2015. *Masculinity, Media, and the American Presidency.* New York: Palgrave Macmillan.

Cox Han, Lori. 2015. *In It to Win: Electing Madam President.* New York: Bloomsbury Publishing.

Cox Han, Lori, and Caroline Heldman, eds. 2007. *Rethinking Madam President: Are We Ready for a Woman in the White House?* Boulder, CO: Lynne Rienner Publishers.

Ditonto, Tessa. 2017. "A High Bar or a Double Standard? Gender, Competence and Information in Political Campaigns." *Political Behavior* 39, no. 2 (June): 301–25.

Dittmar, Kelly. 2016. "Gender Matters: A Status Check on the Gender Gap in Presidential Primaries," March 17. *Presidential Gender Watch 2016*, Center for American Women and Politics.

Goren, Lilly, ed. 2009. *You've Come a Long Way, Baby: Women, Politics, and Popular Culture.* Lexington, KY: University of Kentucky Press.

Hayes, Danny, and Jennifer Lawless. 2016. *Women on the Run: Gender, Media, and Political Campaigns in a Polarized Era.* New York: Cambridge University Press.

Hamilton, Alexander, James Madison, and John Jay. *The Federalist Papers.* http://avalon.law.yale.edu/subject_menus/fed.asp.

Hopkins, David, and Matt Grossman. 2016. *Asymmetric Politics.* New York: Oxford University Press.

Keith, Tamara. 2016. "How Hillary Clinton Locked Up the Democratic Nomination in 10 Steps." NPR.org, June 7.

Kurtzleben, Danielle. 2018. "Is the Record Number of Women Candidates a 2018 Blip—or a Lasting Trend?," *NPR Morning Edition*, September 25.

Linskey, Annie, and David Weigel. 2019. "Before You Run against Trump, You Have to Run against Hillary (if You're a Woman)." *Washington Post*, January 3, 2019.

McDermott, Monika L. 2016. *Masculinity, Femininity, and American Political Behavior.* New York: Oxford University Press.

Prentice, Deborah, and Erica Carranza. 2002. "What Women and Men Should Be, Shouldn't Be, Are Allowed to Be and Don't Have to Be: The Contents of Prescriptive Gender Stereotypes." *Psychology of Women Quarterly* 26: 269–81.

Putnam, Lara and Theda Skocpol. 2018. "Middle America Reboots Democracy." *Democracy: A Journal of Ideas,* February.

Rosenwasser, Shirley M., and Jana Seale. 1988. "Attitudes toward a Hypothetical Male or Female Presidential Candidate: A Research Note." *Political Psychology* 9, no. 4 (December): 591–98.

Sides, John, Michael Tesler, and Lynn Vavreck. 2018. *Identity Crisis: The 2016 Presidential Campaign and the Battle for the Meaning of America.* Princeton: Princeton University Press.

Smith, Aiden. 2018. *Gender, Heteronormativity and the American Presidency.* New York: Routledge.

Solotaroff, Paul. 2015. "Trump Seriously: On the Trail with the GOP's Tough Guy." *Rolling Stone Magazine,* September 9.

Stokes, Bruce. 2016. "Republicans, Especially Trump Supporters, See Free Trade Deals as Bad for U.S." Pew Research Center, March 31.

Velencia, Jamie. 2018. "The 2018 Gender Gap Was Huge. And It Helped Democrats Win the House." FiveThirtyEight.com, November 9.

Chapter Two

Money

The Resource Race

Casey B. K. Dominguez

When you run for president in the twenty-first century, you have to raise a *lot* of money. For some perspective, in 2016, the average winning U.S. Senate candidate raised and spent $10.4 million during the entire election cycle.[1] With a very competitive primary field on the Democratic side in 2020, individual candidates might need to raise *twenty times that much, just to secure their party's nomination*. In the 2020 nomination campaign, we can expect the presidential contenders to collectively raise and spend upward of half a billion dollars. The general election will probably require that the nominees raise hundreds of millions of dollars more.

Fundraising astronomical sums has not always been central to securing the party nomination for the presidency. As recently as the late 1990s, candidates for their party's nominations received federal subsidies for their campaigns and abided by legal spending limits. In 2000, the pre-convention spending limit was $45.7 million. Both contenders for the Democratic nomination, Al Gore and Bill Bradley, raised and spent about that much.[2] However, competition, the Internet, court decisions, and the professional campaign industry have made those subsidies and spending limits irrelevant, even while they are technically still legal options. Today, the competition is on to raise as much money as possible. New sources of campaign cash, including small online donations and candidate-linked SuperPACs, make raising enormous sums possible, but also probably advantage certain candidates over others.

Candidates must not just raise exorbitant sums of money. Because of campaign finance laws, each candidate must raise heaps of campaign cash on his or her own, mostly in small increments. There is no institution like a political party to help with this task because formal party organizations remain officially neutral during the primary season. Other political organizations like interest groups can only contribute small amounts ($5,000) to a candidate's coffers. The need to raise hundreds of millions of dollars in relatively small amounts shapes candidate behavior and affects the candidates who become viable contenders for the presidency.

Despite the vast sums raised, and despite the fact that the candidate who raises the most money usually wins the nomination, it would not be appropriate to say that money *buys* the nomination. Fundraising ability seems to follow campaign quality, name recognition, and popularity. The latter two seem to be especially important to a candidate's ultimate success. The need to raise large sums of campaign cash to be competitive with others forces candidates to begin their campaign early—officially in the early months after the midterm elections, but based on groundwork laid prior to that. And though it might not buy the nomination itself, money certainly buys viability, signals status to party elites, shapes the media narrative, affects the quality of the campaign, and influences the choices available to primary voters.

This chapter will explain why candidates must raise so much money today, how those demands came about, and what effects fundraising and campaign cash seem to have on the nomination contest.

WHY DO PRESIDENTIAL CONTENDERS NEED TO RAISE MONEY?

In some ways, the answer is the same for every election contest. Candidates need to raise "so much" money because campaigning costs money. Candidates for even low-level offices need to hire staff and pay their salaries, rent office space, buy pizza for volunteers, secure an Internet connection, pay for a website, and pay for the costs of print, television, and online advertising. Presidential nomination contests cost more than races at lower levels because the electorate (and the stakes) are just so much bigger.[3]

More specifically, however, presidential nomination contests cost a lot of money (and therefore require a lot of fundraising) because of the peculiarities of the presidential party nomination process itself. There are at least four explanations for why contemporary presidential nomination contests involve so much money. First, it's a national contest, and candidates need to build a positive reputation with a national audience. That requires communication with voters—and such communication usually requires money. Second, the delegate selection process is a race that takes place in a fairly short period of time because of the frontloaded primary calendar that has developed since the 1990s. That short window to reach a national audience puts a premium on *early* money. Third, the race is a highly personalized and competitive one in which candidates have structural incentives to raise and spend as much money as possible. Finally, presidential campaigns have become highly professionalized, which drives up costs for serious contenders.

National Name Recognition

A quick glance at the scholarly research on United States election campaigns in general will show that one of the main tasks for a candidate for any office is to get voters to recognize his or her name (Kam and Zechmeister 2013, Mann and Wolfinger 1980). Name recognition is an advantage to incumbents when they seek reelection, and aids political dynasties and celebrities as well. The need to build simple familiarity among voters is one reason why challengers for lower-level offices often have to outspend incumbents in order to have a chance at defeating them.

Since the McGovern-Fraser reforms of the early 1970s, and the consequent rise of highly personalized, public campaigns for the presidential party nomination, people who would like to be president have to introduce themselves to tens of millions of voters across the country on a fairly short time scale. Some candidates enter the presidential contest already well known to a national audience. George W. Bush, for example, was easily identified with his father, the former president who shared his name. Hillary Rodham Clinton, when she first ran for the presidency, was best known to the country for having been first lady, and had been a familiar presence in American homes for two decades. Upon her second run, of course, she had also been secretary of state. Donald Trump had been a nationally known celebrity and television personality for decades before he sought the office. Not all candidates are blessed with such universal name recognition. Most candidates for the presidency hold elected office at the state level as U.S. senators or governors, and are best known inside the borders of their own state. Others hold office at lower levels—as mayors or members of the U.S. House. The smaller their original constituency, the more campaigning—and therefore, the more fundraising—they might need to do to build a national reputation. The less well known the candidate is at the start of the campaign, the more money he or she probably needs to raise in order to build familiarity with primary voters and caucus-goers nationwide.

Lesser-known candidates face a catch-22, however, because a poor showing in early polling (which mainly measures national name recognition) can make it hard to raise enough money to compete effectively. Research shows that a candidate's early polling is a significant predictor of their total pre-primary fundraising (Adkins and Dowdle 2002, Mayer 1996, Norrander 2006). Most candidates with poor showing in polls don't raise enough money to be serious contenders.

For example, at the beginning of the 2016 nomination contest in early 2014, polling showed a majority of Democrats favored Hillary Clinton, while rival Democratic candidates Jim Webb and Martin O'Malley received only 1 percent support each.[4] Webb eventually raised less than $1 million, and O'Malley raised less than $5 million—relative pittances for a presidential campaign. In the first Republican polls to include Donald Trump as a 2016 contender, the leaders were Wisconsin governor Scott Walker, former Florida governor Jeb Bush, neurosurgeon Ben Carson, Texas senator Ted Cruz, and Florida senator Marco Rubio.[5] Ted Cruz raised the most money that year, followed by Trump (who started slowly but raised more by the time of the convention), Ben Carson, Marco Rubio, and Jeb Bush. Candidates who polled poorly early on, like former Hewlett-Packard CEO Carly Fiorina, former Pennsylvania senator Rick Santorum, and South Carolina senator Lindsey Graham, also raised the least amount of money. So there is at least a loose correlation between a candidate's standing in early polls and their ability to raise enough money to compete effectively for the nomination.

Some candidates defy those expectations, however, so early polling should not be seen as the only indicator of who will become a serious contender. Bernie Sanders was at 4 percent in the earliest polls of the 2016 Democratic nomination, and he eventually raised more than $235 million, nearly as much as the nominee, Clinton, who raised about $274 million.[6] In January 2007, Hillary Clinton out-polled Barack Obama nearly 2:1.[7] He eventually raised $323 million for the nomination, about $110 million more than she did.

Frontloading and Momentum

When the primary calendar is heavily frontloaded—that is, when many states hold primaries early in the election year—candidates must spend money to open offices and buy advertising space in a large number of states. That makes early fundraising—the amount raised in the year *prior* to the presidential election, all the more important (Goff 2004). Early fundraising allows candidates to establish robust campaign organizations in the early states, when media attention is highest and the campaigns have the ability to develop momentum (Bartels 1988). Early fundraising is also important because the national news media pays attention to fundraising totals as part of its horse-race coverage of the campaign. Receiving media attention for being on the leader board in fundraising can signal to voters and other donors that a candidate is viable (Mutz 1995). Additionally, as noted by the well-known advocacy group EMILY's List, "Early Money Is Like Yeast: it makes the dough rise." The more money a candidate raises early on, the more it can spend on its campaigning and its fundraising operation, which can in turn yield more donations (Hinckley and Green 1996). Early money can also allow candidates to survive a poor showing in an early state, as Bill Clinton did in new Hampshire in 1992 and George W. Bush did in New Hampshire and Michigan in 2000 (Adkins and Dowdle 2002, Mayer 1996).

Along with early polling, early fundraising often separates candidates into two groups: those that can build national campaign organizations and weather early setbacks, and those that cannot. As of December 31, 2015, Martin O'Malley's campaign had raised $4.2 million, while Bernie Sanders' campaign had raised nearly $73 million, and Hillary Clinton raised $108 million. Sanders and Clinton were clearly in the competitive class, and O'Malley and the rest of the small Democratic field were on the sidelines in the money primary. On the Republican side, Donald Trump would seem to have been in the uncompetitive camp, with only $6.7 million raised as of December 31, 2015. He was far outpaced in the fundraising game by Ben Carson, with $54 million; Ted Cruz, who had $47 million; and Jeb Bush, who had raised $31 million. Trump, however, led in the polls and in media coverage, and was already nationally well known, all of which probably contributed to his ability to overcome his early fundraising deficit.

Competition

If candidates and parties had their way, the nomination contest would be inexpensive and friendly, allowing the winning campaign to conserve resources for the general election. But nomination contests are rarely completely uncompetitive, because the presidency is a tempting prize, and even an unsuccessful presidential campaign can yield benefits. A losing presidential campaign can help its candidate advance an ideological agenda, secure a high-profile executive appointment, or even get a gig as a cable news pundit.

Since the 1970s, candidates have been free to mount a vigorous campaign for party delegates in any state in which they want to do so. Even if all the candidates would prefer to raise less money and campaign as cheaply as possible, as long as one candidate goes all out to raise campaign cash and spend it on advertising and campaign infrastructure in multiple states, the others feel compelled to do so as well. The presence of an independently wealthy candidate compounds this competitive incentive. When billionaires like Tom Steyer decide to seek the party nomination, they can spend their own fortunes past the point at which other candidates would have ceased finding willing donors among rank-and-file partisans. The potential competition from an independently wealthy candidate encourages other candidates to raise even more so they can avoid being outspent.

Incumbent presidents present a special case of nomination-period fundraising. A sitting president also gets to raise money during the nomination period, but since he usually doesn't face any competition for renomination, he gets to spend that money running against the other party, even before the out-party has chosen its nominee. That early start to the general election campaign can put pressure on the other party to wrap up its nomination process. However, the party running to unseat the president has only one mechanism to end its race: the national convention itself. While the party's national convention serves as the mechanism to force losing contenders out of the presidential race, no one in the current system can force a candidate to stop campaigning before the party nomination is official.

The competition between the candidates fuels the race for campaign cash. Even candidates who have officially secured enough pledged delegates that they are assured their party's nomination can face continued campaigning from candidates in their own party. While the runners-up continue to stay in the race, the frontrunner has to continue to raise and spend money on the nomination contest. That competition—driven by the personal choices of ambitious candidates—helps make nomination races more expensive. Ultimately, running out of money is one of the factors that drives losing nomination candidates to concede.

Professionalization

Presidential campaigns are big business for political consultants. In 2015 alone, candidates in both parties paid consultants $160 million, a 50 percent increase in the amount paid to consultants by the same time in the 2008 cycle (Sheingate 2015). Most of that money went to media-buying firms that helped candidates place ads on television or in digital media. Television ads and consultant fees soaked up the lion's share of campaign cash.

Despite the high fees, candidates cannot really avoid hiring professionals. Research shows that candidates who hire professional consultants are able to raise more money (Herrnson 1992) and win more votes (Medvic and Lenart 1997) than amateur campaigns. In addition, most high-level campaign professionals work exclusively within one party's networks, and candidates can establish credibility within the party by convincing a top campaign operative to work for their team (Bernstein and Dominguez 2003). Together, these factors suggest that every serious candidate will want to hire professional consultants to run their campaign, and that those consultants will raise the costs of campaigning in pursuit of their own bottom line.

WHO GIVES ALL THAT MONEY?
HOW HAVE DONORS CHANGED OVER TIME?

The all-out fundraising imperative in the nomination contest is a fairly recent phenomenon. As recently as the year 2000, serious contenders for the presidency opted into a voluntary system of spending caps and public campaign subsidies. Since that system collapsed, campaign spending has increased substantially. At the same time, the ability to raise money in small donations on the Internet, and the ability of the very wealthy to single-handedly support a candidate's campaign through SuperPACs, have both transformed the ways that candidates raise money for the nomination contest and have made it possible for the campaigns to become more expensive.

In 1974, Congress established two sets of rules that would limit fundraising in the presidential election. The Federal Election Campaign Act first established individual contribution limits that apply to anyone who wants to donate money to a candidate for federal office, including the presidency. The individual contribution limit was established to limit the ability of the very wealthy to use campaign contributions to buy special influence over candidates for federal office. This limit was originally $1,000, but was raised and inflation-adjusted in 2002, and is now about $2,700.[8] That means any person in America with the means to give $2,700 to a presidential candidate can do so—but they also cannot give more than that amount to the candidate's campaign.

Congress's second innovation in 1974 was that it created a public funding system for presidential campaigns. In addition to fully funding general election campaigns, primary campaigns for the presidency were partially financed by the public (through a dedicated funding stream—the "check-off" box on individual income tax returns). Candidates who wanted to receive that partial funding had to raise $100,000 under specific conditions in order to qualify. That $100,000 had to be raised in sums of at least $5,000 in twenty different states, from at least twenty different people in each of those states. Once they had passed that threshold, each candidate would receive dollar-for-dollar matching funds for every individual contribution they received (up to a contribution size of $250). That low cap for matching funds was intended to reward candidates who sought smaller donations. Any presidential candidate taking this public subsidy had to abide by both fundraising and spending limits. The candidate's funds were subject to an overall spending cap as well as a spending cap in each state. In 1976, that overall spending limit was $13 million. In 2016, it was $57.7 million. The system was not mandatory, but instead enticed candidates to accept voluntary fundraising and spending caps to serve a public interest of limiting the influence of big money and wealthy donors in presidential campaigns.

From 1976 to 1996, nearly every serious presidential contender accepted the primary election matching funds and abided by the spending limit set forth in the FECA.[9] One of the first major candidates to reject the system was Steve Forbes, an independently wealthy businessman, who sought the Republican nomination in 1996. His rejection of the system led indirectly to its demise. Forbes was able to match frontrunner Kansas senator Bob Dole's spending for the nomination contest out of his own pocket. That forced Dole, who took the public matching funds, to spend up to the legal spending limit early in the summer of 1996. On the other side of the aisle, the incumbent Democrat, President Bill Clinton, ran unopposed for his party's nomination. Clinton was able to spend money during the summer running against Dole, while Dole, having reached the limit winning the nomination, was unable to spend money in response. In the aftermath of Clinton's general election victory, some perceived that spending mismatch to have been a significant hindrance to Dole's campaign.

Four years later, when George W. Bush sought the Republican nomination in 2000, his campaign was unwilling to put itself in the same situation, especially with Steve Forbes again considering a run for the presidency. So Bush opted out of the public financing system for the presidential primaries (Connolly 1999). He was able to raise $100 million for the nomination contest, twice that of his closest Republican competitor, Arizona senator John McCain. That was also twice what his Democratic opponent, Al Gore, was able to raise and spend. Seeing an advantage in an all-out race for campaign cash, leading candidates in both parties opted out of the public financing system for the primaries beginning in 2004.

One major consequence of candidates' strategic refusal to accept matching funds is that individually they have to raise twice (or even five or six times) as much money as they would otherwise have had to. Presumably, all the candidates would prefer to raise less money if they were able to. However, the stakes of the competition mandate that if any one candidate wants to gain an advantage by raising and spending more, anyone who wants the beat that person has to enter the money race. This dynamic made the primary campaign significantly more expensive. Figure 2.1 shows that there is an enormous jump in the overall expense of the nomination contest after 2000. Between 2000 and 2008, overall federal campaign spending went up by 34 percent, but presidential nomination spending doubled (Polsby et al. 2015, 66).

There are proposals to revive the public financing system for the nomination contest. After all, it is still on the statute books and available to candidates—the most ambitious candidates just choose not to use it. Some proposals to revive the system involve increasing the amount of money available to candidates by increasing the tax return checkoff box and increasing the

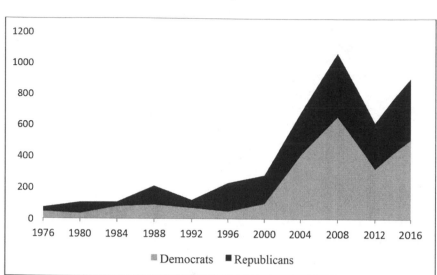

Figure 2.1. Total amount raised by all nomination candidates (in millions of dollars) including matching funds; no SuperPACs. Data from Malbin and Glavin 2018, Tables 1.1 and 1.3.

spending limit.[10] Reformers argue a system of limited spending makes the system more competitive.[11] It might also enable candidates to spend more time talking to voters and learning about policy, and less time raising money, especially from an unrepresentative pool of rich donors who can write $2,700 checks.

Large and Small Donors

Leading nomination campaigns in recent years show that attending $2,700 per plate fundraisers is not the only way to raise the large sums necessary to compete in the twenty-first century, but it is hard for any candidate to succeed without some large donations. Some candidates, including those with access to more lucrative fundraising networks, rely more on large contributions. Many candidates in the 2016 Republican field, including Jeb Bush, John Kasich, Marco Rubio, and Chris Christie, raised the majority of their campaign cash from donors who gave $1,000 or more. Bush, in particular, raised 72 percent of his campaign cash in $2,700 checks. Hillary Clinton also raised the majority of her primary funds (51 percent) in individual contributions of $1,000 or more (Malbin and Glavin 2018, table 1.04).

Internet campaigning, however, has made it possible for some candidates to raise significant amounts of money in small donations online. In 2008, Barack Obama raised $182 million, 56 percent of his primary season total, in contributions totaling $1,000 or less. He raised 29 percent of his total in contributions less than $200. In 2016, Bernie Sanders raised 82 percent of his primary funds in contributions under $1,000, and $99 million (44 percent of his total) in contributions totaling less than $200. In 2016, Donald Trump self-financed most of his primary campaign, but also raised $12 million in contributions smaller than $200. Larger donations are still part of the picture, even for insurgent candidates. Even Bernie Sanders raised $40 million in contributions over $1,000.[12]

Very Large Donors and SuperPACs

The other major change to presidential campaign finance in recent years has been the invention of candidate-aligned "SuperPACs." These have only been on the scene for two presidential election cycles, 2012 and 2016, but were a major source of campaign spending in those two election cycles. In 2012, candidate-aligned SuperPACs raised and spent $150 million during the nomination process. In 2016, they raised and spent a whopping $479 million.

Why did they suddenly become such major players in 2012? SuperPACs are formally known as "independent-expenditure-only" committees. Such committees have been legal since the Supreme Court in *Buckley v. Valeo* (1976) said that Congress could not limit campaign spending made independently of a candidate's campaign. From 1976 to 2010, very few organizations regularly raised and spent large amounts outside of candidates' and parties' formal campaign committees. In the late 1990s, political party committees began soliciting very large donations from very rich individuals. Those "soft money" donations raised reformers' ire because they created the appearance of corruption when large donors were given special perks, especially access to the White House under Bill Clinton. In response, in 2002, Congress banned parties from accepting large individual contributions. Candidates, parties, and campaigns, however, were still interested in gaining access to very large contributions. In 2004, those large individual and organizational contributions found themselves directed to other independent committees known as "527s" for the part of the tax code under which they were organized. Then, in 2010, the Supreme Court issued a series of rulings that helped to reinvigorate "independent expenditure" committees as vehicles for large campaign contributions and unlimited spending. In *Citizens United v. Federal Election Commission,* the Supreme Court said that corporations and labor unions could donate unlimited amounts out of their treasuries to these independent committees. In *SpeechNow.org v. Federal Election Commission,* the Court said that an "independent expenditure" committee that only ran uncoordinated campaigns could raise money in unlimited amounts. As the 2012 election cycle approached, allies of the major presidential candidates began to use these officially "independent" committees to raise money in very large sums from wealthy individuals in candidate-aligned SuperPACs.

These candidate-aligned SuperPACs have three notable characteristics. The first is that because they are committees organized under the auspices of federal campaign finance law, they are subject to the normal disclosure rules. According to OpenSecrets.org, all of the candidate-aligned SuperPACs in 2016 fully reported their donors to the FEC and the public.

Second, these committees should be thought of as vehicles for millionaires to support their preferred candidates. In 2012, 91 percent of the money to the SuperPAC supporting Mitt Romney came in checks over $100,000, and half of the money raised came in checks of $1 million or more. Only thirty-one individuals gave those million dollar contributions. In 2016, just fifteen individuals gave 75 percent of the money to the SuperPAC supporting Marco Rubio. Also in 2016, forty-six individuals gave more than a million dollars to the SuperPAC supporting Hillary Clinton. These SuperPACs, which can run ads and do other campaign work for candidates, are supported by only a few dozen individual wealthy people. That might not be noteworthy if these SuperPACs were truly unconnected to the candidate and the candidate's campaign, or if the donors themselves and their donations were unknown to the candidates.

However, the third characteristic of candidate-supporting SuperPACs is that the individuals who run these SuperPACs often have close ties to the candidate and their campaign staff, and are allowed to communicate to at least some degree. FEC rulings allow candidates to attend fundraisers for SuperPACs that support them, and to ask for large donations even in small, intimate settings (Gold 2015b). As noted by Michael Malbin and Brendan Glavin at the Campaign Finance Institute, well-known court decisions like *Citizens United* were not enough by themselves to bring about the candidate-aligned SuperPACs we see today. The Federal Election Commission's interpretation of the law has significantly watered down the Watergate-era rules designed to limit corruption and the influence of a few large donors over presidential candidates, and potentially their policy decisions (Malbin and Glavin 2018).

SuperPACs do not yet have a track record of appearing to determine the outcome of nomination races. Three-quarters of the SuperPAC money spent in 2016 went to support Republican candidates who did *not* win their party's nomination. Former Florida governor Jeb Bush's SuperPAC spent $121 million, on top of the Bush campaign's own $35 million, for a total of *three*

Republican convention delegates. Two of the most dramatically successful candidates in the 2016 primaries, Bernie Sanders and Donald Trump, did not have a SuperPAC supporting them when they sought the nomination. On the other hand, that is not to say that they have not had effects on the dynamics of the contests. SuperPACs have allowed a few candidates to stay in the race longer than they otherwise might have. A $10 million infusion of cash to Newt Gingrich's SuperPAC in 2012 appeared to help prolong his candidacy (Eggen 2012). Right to Rise, the SuperPAC supporting Jeb Bush, directed its considerable spending power toward positive messaging about Bush and negative attacks on Ted Cruz and Marco Rubio, but did not attack Donald Trump (Gold 2015a). It is hard to know whether the last two nomination races would have been different if SuperPACs did not exist. It is not hard to imagine that tens of millions of dollars might affect the course of a close race.

EFFECTS OF THE FUNDRAISING IMPERATIVE

That brings us to the most important question: does money buy the party nomination? In short, the evidence is mixed, and the scholarly consensus is that it does not. Usually, the person who raises the most money during the year before the election year (the so-called invisible primary) does, in fact, win the nomination. However, the ability to raise that money is closely related to other variables that scholars argue are more important to their ultimate success. Cohen et al. (2008) argue that the most important asset a presidential contender can have is broad, public support from elected officials and other established figures within their political party. Those party elites can have the biggest impact when they rally around one candidate early—and that elite support outweighs the importance of money. However, if they sit on the sidelines, other variables might be more important. Other analyses show that some combination of media coverage, candidate characteristics, elite support, and name recognition matter more to a candidate's success than spending itself (Dowdle, Adkins, and Steger 2009). Trump's success in the 2016 Republican nomination contest suggests that overwhelming media coverage might be more important than either fundraising or party support.

If money alone doesn't determine the winner of the nomination contest, that does not mean that fundraising is not important. For one, the fundraising race affects the length of U.S. presidential campaigns. People sometimes lament the length of U.S. presidential election campaigns. There are two reasons why they last at least two entire years. The first is that U.S. political parties are decentralized, and state parties select their delegates to the formal national conventions at times of their own choosing across several months in the spring. But one of the reasons the campaign stretches for another year before that is because candidates need to raise money to be able to build that national campaign, and to compete with other candidates who are also busily raising money.

Second, fundraising is important because money is required to pay for a campaign. Without it, a candidate can't compete. Money permits candidates to campaign effectively in the states that hold early primaries, as well as to weather setbacks in those early states and continue on to the rest of the contests. Research also suggests that fundraising—or the lack thereof—also helps drive some candidates out of the contest entirely (Haynes et al. 2004, Norrander 2006).[13] In 2016, Scott Walker's aggressive spending and anemic fundraising helped contribute to his early withdrawl from the race (Miller 2015).

Fundraising ability has a big effect on the types of candidates who win their party's nomination. Contrary to public belief, a candidate does not need to be personally wealthy to be a successful fundraiser. Rather, to be a successful fundraiser at the presidential level, a candidate probably needs a combination of skills and characteristics. Past fundraising ability, with ties to networks of loyal donors, is one asset. High level elected officials like senators and governors are probably more likely to have those experiences than cabinet officials or members of the U.S. House. Since fundraising networks tend to have a geographic component, deep ties to wealthy communities might help as well (Cho, Tam, and Gimpel 2007). Occupying an ideological niche or otherwise finding a way to excite and inspire the online donor base of the party might be another avenue to raising enough campaign cash to become viable.

Perhaps most importantly, though, fundraising can also be a public expression of a vast number of private conversations among the many officeholders, donors, activists, and rank and file primary voters who make up the "Expanded Party." Early in the invisible primary, a candidate will begin with their own donor base—their previous supporters and personal network. Candidates who have represented big states or wealthy areas, or have been in office a long time, might start with a bigger personal fundraising advantage. However, the challenge during the year prior to the presidential election is to expand that fundraising base, as they expand their name recognition and national stature. Whether they are successful will determine how much they are able to raise. This is why fundraising totals are interesting and instructive about the state of the competition, even in the year before voters formally cast any ballots.

Fundraising success can tell us about a candidate's ability to win over important party actors. Seen this way, different types of fundraising success send different signals about the party's support for a candidate. Personal wealth or a flush SuperPAC only communicate that a candidate has cash to spend and the ability to get more from their own bank account or from rich friends. It signals that the supported candidate can compete, but it doesn't signal anything about the candidate's actual support among party leaders, affiliated groups, officeholders, or rank-and-file primary voters. On the other hand, raising tens (or hundreds) of millions of dollars in $2,700 checks communicates that there is a lot of support for a candidate among elite donors, including those who are regular supporters of other elected officeholders in the party. Those donations aren't just cash—they tell us that there were a lot of house parties and expensive chicken dinners where well-off partisans got together and talked about why the featured candidate would be a good representative of the party, a good candidate, and a good president. Success in such venues signals widespread support among important party members. A candidate who raises tens (or hundreds) of millions of dollars in small amounts from online donors sends yet another signal—that there are many thousands of voters and potential volunteers at the grass roots of the party who support that candidate. Seen this way, all fundraising is not the same. Of two candidates—one with $100 million in a SuperPAC and a second with $100 million raised through large and small donations from active partisans—the second one is better positioned to run a successful campaign for their party's nomination, because that candidate's money is actually an expression of support from members of the party. So fundraising is important, and can teach us about the strengths of different candidates.

The fundraising imperative itself also raises questions about the types of candidates who seek and win the presidential nomination. Critics of the U.S. campaign finance system frequently note that highly qualified candidates, and those who might make especially good presidents, are turned off by the need to beg for money on a daily basis. Either by exciting the small donor masses or winning over the $1,000-a-plate elites (and probably both), a presidential candidate today must first succeed at raising money, a skill that is not necessarily related to sound executive management. On the other hand, seen as an indicator of support, a candidate who is able to raise many small and medium-sized donations from many places in the country has inspired confidence among his or her partisans, and in that way, fundraising success can be seen as an indicator of party support that is, in fact, important to governing.

WHAT SHOULD WE EXPECT IN 2020?

The 2020 nomination contest will look different in the two parties. As a sitting incumbent, Donald Trump has access to both the large-donor network at the Republican National Committee and his own base of small online donors. Any Republican challengers to his nomination will have to raise a threshold amount of money in order to be taken seriously, and will have to raise a very large amount of money to challenge the sitting president in states across the nation. Not every candidate has a reasonable chance of doing so. That is probably a task that only potential challengers with existing national name recognition have a chance of achieving. Events also matter. Only a very unpopular president will prompt donors to support a challenger for the Republican nomination.

One Republican donor class to keep an eye on in 2020 is those who give the larger individual contributions (over $1,000). During the 2016 election cycle, Trump had success with small online donors in 2016 (69 percent of his 2016 fundraising total), but less success with the $2,700 per check donor class (only 9 percent of his 2016 cycle fundraising total).[14] If a challenger were to emerge that had the support of that more elite donor class, that might indicate Trump is in for a real contest.

The "money primary" will probably be more important on the Democratic side. With a large field, fundraising prowess will probably be a significant factor in separating the serious contenders from the also-rans. In 2020 there is a large field of candidates that might be in the "serious" category because several of the candidates have already developed national fundraising networks. Bernie Sanders has one from his 2016 presidential run, for which he raised $226 million. Joe Biden might benefit from the Obama network, and he also raised tens of millions for his campaigns during his career in the Senate. Beto O'Rourke raised a record-breaking $78 million for his 2018 bid for the U.S. Senate seat in Texas. A number of U.S. senators have raised tens of millions of dollars over their careers—including Elizabeth Warren ($34 million), Cory Booker ($25 million), Kamala Harris ($21 million), and Kirsten Gillibrand ($20 million).[15] Senators and governors from smaller states might start out with smaller donor networks, but most statewide candidates have had to raise millions of dollars in the past and proven to be adept at it. On the other hand, candidates like former HUD secretary Julián Castro, who has never raised money in federal elections, and South Bend mayor Pete Buttigieg, whose 2018 PAC did not clear $1 million, might be at a disadvantage, at least initially.

We can probably safely predict that many of those with existing fundraising networks, and those who have the best national name recognition (Joe Biden and Bernie Sanders begin the 2020 invisible primary ranked highest in the name-recognition polling), will raise a lot of money during the invisible primary. This field of candidates could easily yield a large group who have enough funds to be competitive in the early states. However, the ability of a campaign to catch fire online and suddenly find itself with tens of millions of dollars makes it foolish to guess how the dynamics will play out. The emergence of online fundraising makes the money primary more unpredictable. Fundraising prowess remains, however, a reasonable indicator of a candidate's support and viability.

NOTES

1. Soo Rin Kim, "The Price of Winning Just Got Higher, Especially in the Senate." OpenSecrets news. November 9, 2016. Center for Responsive Politics. Individual races can be significantly more expensive than average. In 2018, the Florida and Texas senate races ranked as the most expensive, and in those, Rick Scott (R-FL) spent $82 million, some of which was self-financed. In Texas, Beto O'Rourke raised and spent $78 million.

2. Gore raised and spent $49.4 million and Bradley raised $42.1 million. From Michael J. Malbin and Brendan Glavin, 2018, *CFI's Guide to Money in Federal Elections: 2016 in Historical Perspective*, table 1.1. The Campaign Finance Institute.

3. According to ElectProject.org, 63.2 million people cast ballots in the 2016 presidential primaries and caucuses. That is twice the size of the population of the largest state, California.

4. Quinnipiac University Poll, February 26–March 2, 2015. N=493 registered voters nationwide who are Democrats or lean Democratic. Margin of error ± 4.4. Clinton was at 56 percent in that poll. Accessed at PollingReport.com.

5. Fox News poll conducted by Anderson Robbins Research (D) and Shaw & Company Research (R). March 29–31, 2015. N=379 likely Republican primary voters nationwide. PollingReport.com.

6. All nomination fundraising totals are through June 30 of the election year, unless otherwise noted. From Federal Election Commission June monthly presidential filings.

7. CNN/Opinion Research Corporation poll, January 19–21, 2007. N=467 registered voters nationwide who are Democrats or independents who lean to the Democratic Party. MoE ± 4.5. Accessed January 23, 2019 at PollingReport.com.

8. The contribution limit is indexed to inflation in odd-numbered years and will be slightly higher in 2020.

9. John Connally rejected public funds in 1980.

10. Congressional Research Service, *Public Financing of Presidential Campaigns: Overview and Analysis*, January 29, 2014, https://www.everycrsreport.com/reports/RL34534.html.

11. Campaign Finance Institute Task Force on Financing Presidential Nominations, 2005, *So the Voters May Choose: Reviving the Presidential Matching Fund System*, http://www.cfinst.org/president/pdf/VotersChoose.pdf.

12. Ibid.

13. Some studies argue money is not important to overall exit decisions, though it certainly seems to play a role for some candidates (Damore, Hansford, and Barghothi 2010).

14. Malbin and Glavin, *CFI's Guide to Money*, table 1.8.

15. Opensecrets, total raised 2013–2018 as of January 1, 2019.

REFERENCES

Adkins, Randall E., and Andrew J. Dowdle. 2002. "The Money Primary: What Influences the Outcome of Pre-Primary Presidential Nomination Fundraising?" *Presidential Studies Quarterly* 32 (2): 256–75.

Bartels, Larry. 1988. *Presidential Primaries and the Dynamics of Public Choice.* Princeton, NJ: Princeton University Press.

Bernstein, Jonathan, and Casey Dominguez. 2003. "Candidates and Candidacies in the Expanded Party," *PS: Political Science and Politics* 36 (April 2003): 165–69.

Campaign Finance Institute Task Force on Financing Presidential Nominations. 2005. *So the Voters May Choose: Reviving the Presidential Matching Fund System.* http://www.cfinst.org/president/pdf/VotersChoose.pdf.

Cho, Wendy, K. Tam, and James G. Gimpel. 2007. "Prospecting for (Campaign) Gold." *American Journal of Political Science* 51 (2): 255–68.

Cohen, Marty, David Karol, Hans Noel, and John Zaller. 2008. *The Party Decides: Presidential Nominations Before and After Reform.* Chicago: University of Chicago Press.

Congressional Research Service, 2014. *Public Financing of Presidential Campaigns: Overview and Analysis*, January 29, 2014. https://www.hsdl.org/?view&did=750146.

Connolly, Ceci. 1999. "Huge Money Chase Marks 2000 Race; Some in GOP May Forgo Federal Funds." *The Washington Post*, February 28, 1999. https://www.washingtonpost.com/archive/politics/1999/02/28/huge-money-chase-marks-2000-race/f22cfb82-5296-44b7-8ebb-e5e05fd439b4/.

Damore, David F., Thomas G. Hansford, and A. J. Barghothi. 2010. "Explaining the Decision to Withdraw from a U.S. Presidential Nomination Campaign." *Political Behavior* 32 (2): 157–80.

Dowdle, Andrew J., Randall E. Adkins, and Wayne P. Steger. 2009. "The Viability Primary: Modeling Candidate Support before the Primaries." *Political Research Quarterly* 62 (1): 77–91.

Eggen, Dan. 2012. "Super PACs Dominating Republican Presidential Race." *The Washington Post*, February 20, 2012. https://www.washingtonpost.com/politics/super-pacs-dominating-republican-presidential-race/2012/02/20/gIQANOaGQR_story.html.

Goff, Michael. 2004. *The Money Primary: The New Politics of the Early Presidential Nomination Process.* Lanham, MD: Rowman & Littlefield.

Gold, Matea. 2015a. "Jeb Bush's SuperPAC Burning through Money with Little to Show for It." *The Washington Post*, December 9, 2015. https://www.washingtonpost.com/politics/jeb-bushs-super-pac-burning-through-money-with-little-to-show-for-it/2015/12/09/0baaa5fe-9df8-11e5-8728-1af6af208198_story.html.

Gold, Matea. 2015b. "Now It's Even Easier for Candidates and Their Aides to Help Superpacs." *The Washington Post*, December 24, 2015. https://www.washingtonpost.com/politics/now-its-even-easier-for-candidates-and-their-aides-to-help-super-pacs/2015/12/24/d8d1ff4a-a989-11e5-9b92-dea7cd4b1a4d_story.html.

Haynes, Audrey A., Paul-Henri Gurian, Michael H. Crespin, and Christopher Zorn. 2004. "The Calculus of Concession: Media Coverage and the Dynamics of Winnowing in Presidential Nominations." *American Politics Research* 32, no. 3 (May): 310–37.

Herrnson, Paul S. 1992. "Campaign Professionalism and Fundraising in Congressional Elections." *The Journal of Politics* 54 (3): 859–70.

Hinckley, Katherine A., and John C. Green. 1996. "Fund-Raising in Presidential Nomination Campaigns: The Primary Lessons of 1988." *Political Research Quarterly* 49 (4): 693–718.

Kam, Cindy D., and Elizabeth J. Zechmeister. 2013. "Name Recognition and Candidate Support." *American Journal of Political Science* 57 (4): 971–86.

Kim, Soo Rin. 2016. "The Price of Winning Just Got Higher, Especially in the Senate." Opensecrets.org, November 9, 2016. https://www.opensecrets.org/news/2016/11/the-price-of-winning-just-got-higher-especially-in-the-senate/.

Malbin Michael J., and Brendan Glavin. 2018. *CFI's Guide to Money in Federal Elections: 2016 in Historical Perspective*. The Campaign Finance Institute.

Mann, Thomas E., and Raymond E. Wolfinger. 1980. "Candidates and Parties in Congressional Elections." *American Political Science Review* 74 (3):617–32.

Mayer, William G. 1996. "Comment: Of Money and Momentum." *Political Research Quarterly* 49 (4): 719–26.

Medvic, Stephen K., and Silvo Lenart. 1997. "The Influence of Political Consultants in the 1992 Congressional Elections." *Legislative Studies Quarterly* 22 (1): 61–77.

Miller, Zeke. 2015. "These Two Charts Explain Why Scott Walker Dropped Out." *Time Magazine*, October 15, 2015. http://time.com/4075749/scott-walker-fundraising/.

Mutz, Diana C. 1995. "Effects of Horse-Race Coverage on Campaign Coffers: Strategic Contributing in Presidential Primaries." *The Journal of Politics* 57, no. 4 (1995): 1015–42.

Norrander, Barbara. 2006. "The Attrition Game: Initial Resources, Initial Contests and the Exit of Candidates during the U.S. Presidential Primary Season." *British Journal of Political Science* 36 (3): 487–507.

Polsby, Nelson, Aaron Wildavsky, Steven Schier, and David A. Hopkins. 2015. *Presidential Elections: Strategies and Structures of American Politics*. Lanham, MD: Rowman & Littlefield: 2015.

Sheingate, Adam. 2015. "The Political Consultant Racket." *The New York Times*, December 30, 2015.

Chapter Three

How the News Media
Cover and Shape the Nomination

Kathleen Searles and Patrick Rose

As the field of primary candidates was taking shape in the summer of 2015, the *Huffington Post* announced that it would no longer cover Donald Trump's campaign in its politics section, relegating all future coverage of the candidate to its entertainment section. "Our reason is simple," the notice read. "Trump's campaign is a sideshow. If you are interested in what The Donald has to say, you'll find it next to our stories on the Kardashians and The Bachelorette" (Grim and Shea 2015). The move was almost entirely symbolic as political reporters continued receiving bylines on Trump stories. It was also a curious nod by the online-only publisher to an era of print journalism in which editorial decisions like story placement had greater influence over audience perceptions (Tewksbury and Althaus 2000; Althaus and Tewksbury 2002). HuffPost later rescinded the policy, but then days before Iowa implemented another Trump-specific policy: all articles about the candidate would include the postscript, "Note to our readers: Donald Trump is a serial liar, rampant xenophobe, racist, birther and bully who has repeatedly pledged to ban all Muslims—1.6 billion members of an entire religion—from entering the U.S." (Wemple 2016). The outlet continued that policy throughout the primary and general elections, ending it only after Trump won the general election in November of 2016 (Gold 2016).

To say this approach to covering a presidential candidate was unusual is an understatement. Media outlets like HuffPost struggled with how to cover the Trump campaign which, while proffering the conflict and scandal that incentivizes news coverage, lacked the policy substance and characteristics of traditional campaigns. The result was Trump received vastly more media coverage relative to candidates in the Republican field *and* Democratic field (Confessore and Yourish 2016; Patterson 2016a, 2016b, 2016c), an advantage some believe he was able to parlay into an electoral advantage (Patterson

2016c). In addition, the media's tendency to focus on campaign tactics and strategies over substance allowed Trump's message to be broadcast widely, and largely uncritically (Searles and Banda, 2019).

Though it is hard to dispute the unique nature of 2016 media coverage, the influence of media coverage in primary elections has long been of scholarly interest. This outsized role can be attributed to institutional characteristics of primaries in which information about candidates takes on heightened importance to voters since partisanship cues are not present (Abramowitz 1989). While media consumers today have more choices than ever (Prior 2007), mass media are the primary way the electorate learns of candidates. Often the media are instrumental in whittling down the field of possible candidates, treating some candidates as more serious than others by allocating more or less attention in their broadcasts (Polsby and Wildavsky 1976). This news exposure is vital for primary electorates, by which most delegates are selected (Coleman 2015).

Changes to the media landscape and the nomination process are fundamental to understanding the media's role in primary elections. We can think of media coverage as interacting with the delegate-selection process in ways that shape the nomination. Candidates depend on the news media for coverage, and the news media depend on candidates to make the news; as a result, both groups behave in ways that depend on the other. These changes may in part explain Trump's victory in 2016 (Cohen et al. 2016). In the sections that follow we will briefly cover recent influential changes to the presidential nomination process and conventions, before characterizing media coverage and the role of such coverage in the 2016 presidential election.

CHANGES IN PRESIDENTIAL NOMINATION CAMPAIGNS AND CONVENTIONS

There was unrest at the 2016 Nevada state Democratic Party convention. Angered by what they perceived to be unfair treatment of their candidate, some supporters of Senator Bernie Sanders booed, rushed the stage, threw chairs, and published contact information of the state party chair and her grandchildren online (Stuart 2016). Amidst the stand-off, a Sanders supporter said, "This should be national news. This needs to be national news" (Hains 2016). They were protesting the disqualification of fifty-eight Sanders delegates to the state convention—because of insufficient credentials—which gave Clinton a narrow majority of delegates at the state convention. While the enforcement of credentialing rules ultimately amounted to just a four-delegate swing among Nevada's forty-three delegates to the national convention (Snyder

2016), the stakes were high. In the United States, both parties require the nominee to win a majority of delegates. The culmination of the nomination process ends in spectacle at the national party convention, where the presidential and vice presidential candidates are anointed the party's nominees.

The scene in Nevada recalled the 1968 Democratic National Convention (DNC) in Chicago, though the latter was much larger in terms of scale and stakes. In 1968, although anti-war candidate Eugene McCarthy won 39 percent of primary votes to Hubert Humphrey's 2 percent, Humphrey secured nearly three times the number of delegates as McCarthy, easily winning the nomination at the convention on the first ballot ("Democrats Nominate Humphrey on First Ballot" 1968). Disgruntled supporters of both candidates took to the streets and despite heavy-handed efforts to suppress protest, violence and riots ensued. The tumultuous convention combined with narrowly losing the subsequent general election led Democratic elites to embrace reform (Center 1974). These events led to the formation of the McGovern-Fraser commission, which recommended the increased use of primaries and caucuses and binding delegates to their results. By just 1976, over 70 percent of delegates for each party were selected by primaries or caucuses (Pomper 1979).

So why, in the post-reform era, were rank-and-file voters in Nevada protesting elite control over the nomination process and lamenting lack of media coverage? The two complaints are intertwined: although rank-and-file voters cast ballots for their party's nominee, coordinating among voters represents a collective action hurdle that can be offset by media coverage. Coalitions are tenuous, and coordinating those interests is a primary function of the primary process (Cohen et al. 2016). Before 1972, the job of coordinating on a presidential nominee was reserved for party elites (Cohen et al. 2008), who ultimately chose a nominee at their party's convention through negotiations. Since then, the news media have played a critical role in the coordination of information among voters, leading to widespread agreement among scholars that the news media play a much greater role in the post-reform nomination process (Polsby 1983; Ansolabehere et al. 1991).

We can better understand the media's role in the nomination process by looking at models predicting primary outcomes. These models tend to include poll results, fundraising, elite support, and media coverage (Steger, Dowdle, & Adkins 2004). Intuitively, previous electoral standings and primary results tend to be the strongest predictors of a candidate's success (Norrander 2000; Dowdle et al. 2009), while amount of media coverage is a close second (Dowdle et al. 2009). Media coverage signals important viability cues to elites and voters alike, increasing the likelihood donors and party loyalists will mobilize (Bartels 1988; Abramson et al. 1992; Mutz 1997).

As the adoption of primaries requires support from the primary electorate, candidates must take their case to the public early and often, via the news media. Changes to information communication technology, namely television, facilitated these sorts of direct appeals. Besides offering a compelling medium, the news media ostensibly influence nomination campaigns most by altering their shape. Nomination reforms changed the process from one focusing on coalition building to one focusing on mobilization. While the pre-reform nomination process resembled a long deliberation among party elites culminating with a convention in which coalitions are fused, the post-reform process more closely resembles a diffuse, episodic, public relations campaign. Covering the nominations process, then, requires news events such as the Iowa caucuses to organize coverage. At the same time, a primary-driven nomination process forces candidates to mobilize voters earlier, making it essential to begin the race with a sufficient base of support. The news media are influential at this stage as they give more coverage to viable candidates, which meets journalistic preference for covering frontrunners (Zaller 1999).

Nomination reforms not only changed dynamics between elites and voters, they changed the dynamics of the information environment. Since voter preferences are influenced by candidates' prior success, the sequential nature of primaries introduces momentum into the process. In the pre-reform era, the decision on who to nominate was effectively left until the convention. In contrast, the sequential nature of state-by-state primaries means that voters must make decisions with less time to gather information. Thus, viability cues are especially important in primaries otherwise characterized by a scarcity of information (Bartels 1988; Abramowitz 1989). While viability cues themselves contain little substantive information, they can influence voter preferences indirectly and directly. Viability can serve as a heuristic threshold for determining which candidates voters seek additional information about (Redlawsk 2004; Utych and Kam 2014). Although Polsby (1983) argued that nomination reforms opened the nomination process up to rank-and-file voters who were less concerned with party cohesion and electability, we know that primary voters prefer candidates who they think can win (Stone and Abramowitz 1983; Abramowitz 1989). The result is a race to the beginning rather than the end, as candidates attempt to demonstrate viability before the first primary during a period known as the invisible primary (Aldrich 1980).

Media coverage has contributed to concerns regarding front-loading and compression of the primary schedule. Because of the way the post-reform system, aided by the media, compounds early success, states have incentives to move their primaries and caucuses earlier in the calendar (Price 1984; Orren 1985) in efforts to garner more influence over the process. States like California and New York previously held enviable positions at the end of the primary season because of the proximity of these dates to the convention;

in the post-reform era these dates have made their primaries less relevant (Wright 2009). In 1984 and 1988, for example, news coverage of the Iowa caucuses and the New Hampshire primary represented roughly a third of all primary coverage for those cycles (Ridout 1991). However, Castle (1991) finds little evidence that front-loading and compression result in benefits to states in terms of news coverage. Although earlier primary dates are significantly associated with greater coverage, that association loses significance when controlling for Iowa and New Hampshire coverage. Nevertheless, there may be marginal benefits to regional primaries: states may increase coverage of specific, important economic issues, provided that those issues are shared by other states in the regional primaries.

Polsby (1983) warned that the democratizing reforms of the 1970s gave outsized power to the media over nominations. While true that the media's role in primaries has expanded since then, it can be difficult to separate the role of early polls, from elite support, from media coverage. Indeed, the endogenous nature of these relationships means it is difficult to isolate the media's effect on the nomination process without considering institutional context (Dowdle et al. 2009). Namely, both the media and voters operate in an information-scarce environment during the invisible primary. Cohen et al. (2008) argue that elites have learned to control the nomination processes through endorsements and fundraising, thus profoundly shaping early informational cues regarding candidates. The result has been that from 1980 to 2004, the candidate with the most elite endorsements before the first primary would go on to win the nomination.

In this way, Sanders's Nevada supporters may have been right to protest elite control while lamenting media absence in the same breath. Given the lack of quality information during the primary season, coverage has the potential to influence perceptions of viability. And while the protest ultimately garnered more critical than sympathetic coverage (Hains 2016; Snyder 2016; Stuart 2016), research suggests such coverage is still strategic. For example, Kam and Zechmeister (2013) found that name recognition alone increases positive perceptions of candidates via perceptions of viability.

Furthermore, while the media do take cues from endorsements, polls, and fundraising regarding which candidates to cover, the potential for media momentum to lift dark horse candidates still exists. The effects of media momentum can be difficult to parse during invisible primaries, when elites engage in efforts to shape the information environment. Yet, the news media retain a degree of agency in dictating coverage through its own values, norms, and routines. Additionally, technological developments that extend the media's reach have the potential to reshape the dynamics of the nomination process. We discuss some of these characteristics of the news media in the following section.

OFF TO THE RACES:
HOW THE MEDIA CHARACTERIZE PRESIDENTIAL
NOMINATION CAMPAIGNS AND CONVENTIONS

To understand nominations and conventions, one must include the role of the news media. This coverage is shaped by newsroom norms and routines, as well as journalistic training (Schudson 1982); the result is news that is first filtered through news-making processes before it reaches the American voter. For this reason, a complete view of the American primary system is not complete without some understanding of how the media cover elections, and primaries in particular. All of this speaks to the interplay between institutional processes that characterize the media and parties in this country, and the incentives each face to interact strategically. Indeed, this process of campaigning through the media is a focus of work on political communication institutionalism (Cook 1998; Ryfe 2006). Whether these varying incentives produce the sort of news and electoral outcomes the public prefers is an ongoing question, as the Sanders melee discussed above suggests. In fact, this question is increasingly relevant following the 2016 election, in which the Trump campaign appeared to effectively exploit news values to increase their earned media, or media coverage gained through efforts other than paid media advertising. For example, news outlets frequently re-air political ads that are negative, not only resulting in free advertising for campaigns (Ridout and Smith 2008), but potentially distorting the quantity and quality of information voters receive (Darr 2018). Darr (2018) succinctly explains this relationship: "The political information that voters receive before an election is, in a sense, the outcome of a power struggle between politicians and the media" (p. 225). To better understand this interplay, we highlight some of the most important characteristics of news coverage of presidential nomination campaigns.

In the United States, the media are mostly privately owned, which means they have incentives to appeal to audience demands (Hamilton 2004; Dunaway 2008). When it comes to news coverage of elections in this country, these market incentives create tension between the sort of media coverage communication scholars might prefer, and the sort of media coverage we see. Because the public does not demand policy-driven news coverage, for example, there is little incentive for news outlets to cover the platforms of primary candidates. On the other hand, because the audience does demand horse race news, we see more coverage that focuses on the strategies and tactics of campaigns (Iyengar et al. 2004; Dunaway and Lawrence 2015).

When it comes to coverage of the nominations and conventions, this means that news outlets are more likely to cover these processes in terms of who's ahead and who's behind, using the language of sports and war. For example, this preference for election as sport is on display in coverage of "Super Tuesday," which in 2016 featured twelve states holding a primary or caucus on the same day. Media coverage can often resemble an almost cattle-call of candidate wins and losses. This leads to headlines like this one from the *Los Angeles Times*, "With a Big Super Tuesday, Trump Has the Republican Nomination in His Sights" (Barabak 2016). While electoral outcomes are of great import to the public, schedule constraints and incentives to break the story mean there is little time for journalists to give such coverage context and depth. Some suggest horse race coverage can have normatively desirable consequences, such as increasing cognitive engagement (Utych and Kam 2014). Similarly, studies find that horse race coverage offers information to voters, helping them to narrow the field (Mutz 1997; Haynes et al. 2002) and avoid less optimal means of evaluation (Redlawsk 2004). In contrast, other scholars find that a focus on the horse race decreases trust in institutions and increases cynicism (Cappella and Jamieson 1997; Hitt and Searles 2018).

Covering presidential primaries as a horse race satisfies audience demands for entertaining news, but it also meets journalistic criterion for newsworthiness, or what are referred to as news values (Gans 1979). Specifically, the horse race satisfies news values that privilege conflict, proximity, timeliness, and power. Moreover, by allowing journalists to focus on strategies rather than substance, the horse race enables journalists to look more objective when reporting on otherwise partisan politics (Crespi 1980; Schudson and Anderson 2009; Toff 2018). It also allows for a veneer of scientism that has increasingly characterized modern journalism since the introduction of scientific public opinion polling (Weaver and McCombs 1980). This approach has challenges, however; particularly, the focus of the horse race on who is winning and losing makes it a less than ideal vehicle for discussing complex institutions like party nominations and conventions. Instead of focusing on process and the policy implications that result, reporters are more likely to report on election tracking polls, focusing on polls that show close or dramatic results (Searles et al. 2016). They are also likely to focus on news events like the Iowa Caucus, which despite being unrepresentative of most American voters and the primary process, is characterized by candidate appearances and related fanfare, all of which makes for great television.

This focus on some elements of presidential nominations over others is part of the selection process called gatekeeping (Shoemaker and Reese 1996; Shoemaker and Vos 2009; Soroka 2012), in which, from an infinite stream of possible stories, reporters and editors opt to cover some stories and not others. This selection process is functional, as there is not infinite space nor resources to allocate to every possible story, and professional, as reporters are trained and then socialized in newsrooms where they are likely to share similar news values (Breed 1955). Indeed, as gatekeepers, the news media have the power to ensure the public knows—or does not know—about certain topics. For example, when both parties have a crowded field of potential nominees, the news media cannot give depth of coverage to each candidate. Moreover, given increasing newsroom cuts, reporters and editors are likely to pick and choose candidates likely to do well and invest time and resources accordingly (Donovan and Hunsaker 2009). In this way, gatekeeping is likely to result in a selection process biased toward frontrunners (Patterson 1980).

This preference interacts with the nomination process, which imbues added importance to early primaries and caucuses in a way that provides incentives for campaigns to appeal to the public through the media (Norrander 1996). Candidates can do this in a couple of ways. First, they can raise the most money early on. Fundraising signals to news media that candidates are viable. Second, candidates can engage in newsworthy behaviors, either through planned appearances (which are less amenable to an increasingly interpretivist style of journalism) or controversy or by granting media access. Third, candidates can foster a sense of momentum. Campaigns often engage in expectations management in which party elites or campaign advisers will spin wins, losses, and margins to convey momentum without also suggesting dominance (Haynes et al. 2002; Ridout et al. 2009). In this way, campaigns can ensure their candidates look just viable enough to warrant the attention of the party elites and potential donors, without intimating to the same people that victory is assured.

Reforms shifted power from elites to the primary electorate but also made structural factors like the timing and sequential nature of primaries more influential with regard to media coverage. In particular, the change in the structure of primaries makes momentum a critical factor in deciding party nominees as their sequential nature means the results of one primary affect news coverage, and news coverage affects perceptions of viability, and such perceptions may affect the result of future primaries (Bartels 1988; Castle 1991; Ridout 1991; Gurian 1993). In other words, news media coverage compounds the effects of the sequential nature of presidential nominations in the United States because horse race coverage emphasizes early wins and losses. Simply, news media prefer a horse race, and this coverage intensifies the effect of momentum in primaries as candidates that do well receive more media coverage, which in turn generates more support for those candidates in the polls.

Moreover, the news media play a vital role in informing the public with regards to party politics, candidate positions, and candidate viability. While voters cast a ballot for the nominee, they are electing delegates in statewide contests. Complicating things further, these contests are spread out over the primary calendar, and delegate apportionment varies by states and party. This complex and indirect nature of the presidential primaries makes nominations difficult for the public to fully understand. Voters offload this burden onto the media, who in turn bears the news gathering responsibility. In general elections, partisan affiliation is an important cue, but as primaries are held within parties, endorsements become an important cue (Jamieson and Hardy 2009). Indeed, while primary reforms are often seen as an effort to democratize the selection of nominees, and as a result, weaken the party's power, several scholars argue that elites have regained a measure of control over the process and outcome of primaries by influencing the "invisible primary," or the pre-primary phase in which candidates attempt to amass resources like money, endorsements, and news coverage. This informal prelude to the primaries is a period where candidates must gain support through fundraising and establish popularity via poll numbers or other appeals to the public. Indeed, to the extent that party elites have regained a measure of control over the process, endorsements—and media coverage of endorsements—are critical components of how they communicate with each other and how they influence rank-and-file voters. Recent work supports this idea of endorsements as cues: Jamieson and Hardy (2009) found that people who have knowledge of an endorsement and know the ideological orientation of the sponsor use this information to ascertain the candidate's orientation and issue positions.

Again the media play an important role as coverage is the primary way the public learns of endorsements during this prelude to the primaries. Still, research is mixed on whether endorsements affect the public's attitudes towards candidates. Some find that endorsements are positively associated with increased public support (Jamieson and Hardy 2009), increased media coverage, and fundraising; however, other studies contest the causality of those factors (Dowdle et al. 2016). Regardless, media coverage of endorsements is one way the public learns about candidates in the lead-up to the nominating convention.

EARNING THE TRUMP CARD: MEDIA COVERAGE OF THE PRIMARY AND CONVENTION DURING THE 2016 ELECTION

Did the 2016 cycle reveal anything new about the media's role in the candidate selection process? Trump's nomination was extraordinary, and the media coverage of his candidacy unprecedented, suggesting a closer look at the media's role in the nomination process is warranted. Indeed, critics and scholars alike suggested that the volume of earned media coverage Trump received was influential (Sides 2015; Silver 2016). This relationship is made more unique in its contrast to conventional wisdom. It is often a strategy of trailing candidates to use earned media to garner donor attention and elite support in absence of rich campaign coffers (Norrander 2000). And while Trump had little-to-no elite support, an important component of the invisible primary (Cohen et al. 2016; Noel 2016), he also eschewed fundraising and ad buys (Clark 2016). In this way the campaign's strategy was atypical and yet, highly successful at securing free media attention. In contrast, the nomination of Clinton—a front-runner with more pre-primary endorsements than any candidate going back to 1984 and formidable fundraising—was as typical as Trump's was anomalous ("The 2016 Endorsement Primary" 2018).

Given the two disparate campaigning approaches, what drove Trump's media coverage during the presidential nomination campaign? As noted above, journalists prefer to cover front-runners or candidates with perceived momentum (Zaller 1999). Momentum is often gauged based on cues like endorsements, fundraising, and poll numbers (Steger 2007). However, during the 2016 presidential nomination campaign, Trump ranked tenth in endorsements and ninth in fundraising out of a field of ten candidates (Francia 2018). In 2015, Trump earned the equivalent of $55 million in free media coverage on a sample of national news outlets including CBS, Fox, the *Los Angeles Times*, the *New York Times*, *USA Today*, and the *Wall Street Journal* (Patterson 2016c). The sheer volume of this media attention is made clear when compared to media coverage of Trump's closest competitor, Jeb Bush, which amounted to $36 million during the same time period. Using a broader range of media outlets and measuring earned media coverage until the race was no longer competitive in March, the media analytics firm MediaQuant found that Trump had earned nearly $2 billion in free coverage compared to $313 million for his then-closest competitor Cruz. In contrast, the same report found that Clinton had earned just $746 million and Sanders just $321 million of earned media coverage (Confessore and Yourish 2016).

What, then, accounts for Trump's advantage in earned media coverage during the primary? As we discussed previously, we know that journalists use a selection process known as gatekeeping to filter information according to a set of professional norms, routines, and news values. News values in particular shape decisions about which stories to cover by helping journalists gauge the newsworthiness of a story. For example, journalists look at whether a story meets news values like human interest, proximity, timeliness, controversy, or scandal (Harcup and O'Neill 2016), and if it does, they are more likely to cover it over other stories. Patterson (2016c) suggests that such a reliance on news values, particularly novelty and celebrity, explains the outsized coverage of Trump during the presidential nomination process (Gans 1979; Graber 2011).

Some may argue that the media's watchdog role explains, in part, why Trump received so much coverage in the lead-up to the general election. Patterson dismisses this notion, suggesting that instead, primary coverage of Trump was slightly more positive on balance (2016a). This can be linked to the media's tendency to cover elections as a horse race. Throughout the course of the primary season, 89 percent of stories among both parties focused on campaign strategies and tactics, as is typical of horse race coverage (Patterson 2016a). Of course, research shows (Farnsworth and Lichter 2003) that the tone of horse-race coverage significantly affects candidate evaluations and can also exacerbate the effect of momentum (Bartels 1985, 1988). Since Trump commanded an early lead to start the primary season, a focus on the horse race—including poll numbers—explains much of Trump's positive primary coverage (Patterson 2016a). In addition, journalists also factor in expectations when determining how to cover candidates; front-runners who win but perform below expectations are penalized while runners-up who exceed expectations are rewarded (Patterson 1980; Ridout 1991). This relationship explains why Clinton's coverage was slightly negative on balance and why Sanders received the most positive coverage of any candidate, Democrat or Republican (Patterson 2016a).

But why did Trump's coverage seem immune to this front-runner tax? It may be that, with the exception of a second-place finish in Iowa, he won a string of early contests until the race was no longer competitive. Of course, it is also possible that Trump's novelty as a candidate gave him the flexibility to "beat expectations" even when he led the field in the polls. Meanwhile, Cruz and Kasich enjoyed positive coverage when they won primaries, while Clinton's coverage was negative despite several victories. It was not until after Super Tuesday, when Clinton moved ahead in the delegate count, that her coverage was more positive on balance.

The tone of coverage for both Clinton and Trump became more negative during the convention stage of the nomination process (Patterson 2016b), during which time coverage is typically characterized by the fanfare of this pseudo-news event (Dayan and Katz 1991). Coverage for both candidates shifted from the horse race to character. While character issues received heightened focus during this period, they only accounted for 8 percent of Trump's coverage. Still, for Trump, that shift was sharp, as negative news accounted for 75 percent of his total coverage. The negative coverage can in part be attributed to Trump's public feud with Khizr Khan, the father of a soldier killed in Iraq, during which time 91 percent of Trump's coverage was negative (Patterson 2016b). For Clinton, coverage of her email scandal was the greatest source of negative news. The 2016 coverage of the conventions marked a sharp departure from the conventional wisdom that conventions are nothing more than free infomercials for the two major parties. Patterson points out that coverage patterns from 2016 suggest that the media has increasingly taken on an interpretive role of nominating conventions, devoting less air time to candidates and speakers and more time to journalists and analysts (Patterson 2016b).

Overall, these patterns of primary coverage in 2016 suggest the media play an influential role in how the public perceives party nominees. News media owe their influence in part to structural changes in the nomination process which elevate the importance of appeals to the public. This influence ultimately means that news media incentives and news values shape what the public knows and does not know about party nominees including their policies and fitness for office. As the media are incentivized by profit more than democratic concerns, this means that the public does not necessarily receive the sort of information required for them to make informed votes. Moreover, if campaigns are successful at taking advantage of this incentive structure in a way that exploits the media's weakness for celebrity and scandal, as work by Darr (2018) suggests, then the sort of information the public does receive is also likely to be distorted.

Looking to 2020, it seems likely that strategic campaigns may employ similar tactics, emphasizing celebrity and conflict over substance and in so doing, capitalizing on the baser instincts of news media. Indeed, the Trump campaign effectively demonstrated that today's 24-hour news cycle means that there is little consequence for disinformation, but much to be gained from making outlandish claims. It is hard to imagine a world in which single-minded campaign consultants have not taken notice of such tactics. If anything, given campaign contexts in which the entertainment value outweighs substance, it is likely that news media will exercise agency by relying even more on game frames. Such an approach permits news media to cover campaigns substantively by focusing on strategies and tactics, without sacrificing the value of celebrity. Moreover, work on media coverage of the 2016 general election found that reliance on horse race coverage was in part related to the strategic environments in which journalists operate, increasingly characterized by a scarcity of resources (Searles and Banda, 2019). One may speculate that, particularly given what promises to be a large field of Democratic candidates for the next nomination contest, lack of resources will play a key role in shaping news coverage as news outlets must pick and choose which candidates receive journalistic attention and by proxy, institutional support. Ultimately, this is yet another example of how characteristics of media coverage have the potential to influence candidate viability and shape the contours of public discourse around campaigns.

Taken together, this discussion of 2016 and 2020 specifically and media coverage of presidential nomination processes broadly, illustrates why Patterson has characterized the news media as the "miscast institution" (Patterson 1980, 2016c) in which, despite being charged with upholding democratic ideals, news media are ultimately motivated by their own values. That these values are often at odds with democratic ideals for an informed citizenry presents a dilemma.

REFERENCES

"The 2016 Endorsement Primary." 2018. FiveThirtyEight. Accessed October 11, 2018. https://projects.fivethirtyeight.com/2016-endorsement-primary/.

Abramowitz, Alan I. 1989. "Viability, Electability, and Candidate Choice in a Presidential Primary Election: A Test of Competing Models." *Journal of Politics* 51: 977–92.

Abramson, Paul R., John H. Aldrich, Phil Paolino, and David W. Rhode. 1992. "Sophisticated Voting in the 1988 Presidential Primaries." *American Political Science Review* 86 (1): 55–69.

Aldrich, John H. 1980. "A Dynamic Model of Presidential Nomination Campaigns." *American Political Science Review* 74 (3): 651–69.

Althaus, S. L., and D. Tewksbury. 2000. "Patterns of Internet and Traditional News Media Use in a Networked Community." *Political Communication* 17 (1): 21–45.

Althaus, S. L. and D. Tewksbury. (2002). "Agenda Setting and the 'New' News: Patterns of Issue Importance among Readers of the Paper and Online Versions of the *New York Times*. *Communication Research* 29: 180–207.

Ansolabehere, Stephen, Roy Behr, and Shanto Iyengar. 1991. "Mass Media and Elections: An Overview." *American Politics Quarterly* 19 (1): 109–39.

Barabak, Mark. 2016. "With a Big Super Tuesday, Trump Has the Republican Nomination in His Sights." *Los Angeles Times*, March 2, 2016. https://www.latimes.com/nation/la-na-gop-super-tuesday-20160301-story.html.

Bartels, Larry M. 1985. "Expectations and Preferences in Presidential Nominating Campaigns." *American Political Science Review* 79 (3): 804–15.

Bartels, Larry M. 1988. *Presidential Primaries and the Dynamics of Public Choice*. Princeton: Princeton University Press.

Breed, Warren. 1955. "Social Control in the Newsroom: A Functional Analysis." *Social Forces* 33 (4): 326–35.

Cappella, Joseph N., and Kathleen Hall Jamieson. 1997. *Spiral of Cynicism: The Press and the Public Good*. Oxford: Oxford University Press.

Castle, David S. 1991. "Media Coverage of Presidential Primaries." *American Politics Quarterly* 19 (1): 33–42.

Center, Judith A. 1974. "1972 Democratic Convention Reforms and Party Democracy." *Political Science Quarterly* 89 (2): 325–50. https://doi.org/10.2307/2149263.

Clark, Dan. 2016. "Trump Was Outspent by His Closest Primary Opponents." *Politifact*. July 1, 2016. https://www.politifact.com/new-york/statements/2016/jul/01/michael-caputo/trump-was-outspent-his-closest-primary-opponents/.

Cohen, Marty, David Karol, Hans Noel, and John Zaller. 2008. *The Party Decides: Presidential Nominations Before and After Reform*. Chicago: University of Chicago Press.

Cohen, Marty, David Karol, Hans Noel, and John Zaller. 2016. "Party Versus Faction in the Reformed Presidential Nominating System." *PS: Political Science & Politics* 49 (4): 701–8.

Coleman, Kevin J. 2015. *The Presidential Nominating Process and the National Party Conventions, 2016: Frequently Asked Questions*. CRS Report No. R 42533. Washington, DC: Congressional Research Service. https://fas.org/sgp/crs/misc/R42533.pdf.

Confessore, Nicholas, and Karen Yourish. 2016. "$2 Billion Worth of Free Media for Donald Trump." *The New York Times*, March 16, 2016. https://www.nytimes.com/2016/03/16/upshot/measuring-donald-trumps-mammoth-advantage-in-free-media.html.

Cook, T. E. 1998. *Governing with the News: The News Media as a Political Institution*. Chicago: University of Chicago Press.

Crespi, Irving. 1980. "Polls as Journalism." *Public Opinion Quarterly* 44, no. 4 (Winter): 462–76.

Darr, Joshua P. 2018. "Reports from the Field: Earned Local Media in Presidential Campaigns." *Presidential Studies Quarterly* 48 (2): 225–47.

Dayan, Daniel, and Elihu Katz. 1991. *Media Events*. Cambridge: Harvard University Press.

"Democrats Nominate Humphrey on First Ballot." 1968. In *CQ Almanac 1968*, 24th ed., 19–1015. Washington, DC: Congressional Quarterly. http://library.cqpress.com/cqalmanac/cqal68-1282681.

Donovan, Todd, and Rob Hunsaker. 2009. "Beyond Expectations: Effects of Early Elections in U.S. Presidential Nomination Contests." *PS: Political Science & Politics* 42 (1): 45–52.

Dowdle, Andrew J., Randall E. Adkins, and Wayne P. Steger. 2009. "The Viability Primary: Modeling Candidate Support Before the Primaries." *Political Research Quarterly* 62 (1): 77–91.

Dowdle, Andrew J., Randall E. Adkins, Karen Sebold, and Jarred Cuellar. 2016. "Forecasting Presidential Nominations in 2016: #WePredictedClintonANDTrump." *PS: Political Science & Politics* 49 (04): 691–95.

Downs, Anthony. 1957. *An Economic Theory of Democracy*. New York: Harper and Row.

Dunaway, Johanna. 2008. "Markets, Ownership, and the Quality of Campaign News Coverage." *The Journal of Politics* 70 (4): 1193–1202.

Dunaway, Johanna, and Regina G. Lawrence. 2015. "What Predicts the Game Frame? Media Ownership, Electoral Context, and Campaign News." *Political Communication* 32 (1): 43–60.

Farnsworth, Stephen J., and S. Robert Lichter. 2003. "The 2000 New Hampshire Democratic Primary and Network News." *American Behavioral Scientist* 46 (5): 588–99.

Fine, Terri Susan. 2003. "Presidential Nominating Conventions in a Democracy." *Perspectives on Political Science* 32 (1): 32–39.

Francia, Peter L. 2018. "Free Media and Twitter in the 2016 Presidential Election: The Unconventional Campaign of Donald Trump." *Social Science Computer Review* 36 (4): 440–55.

Gans, Herbert J. 1979. *Deciding What's News: A Study of CBS Evening News, NBC Nightly News, Newsweek, and Time.* Evanston, IL: Northwestern University Press.

Gautney, Heather. 2018. "Dear Democratic Party: It's Time to Stop Rigging the Primaries." *The Guardian*, June 11, 2018. https://www.theguardian.com/commen tisfree/2018/jun/11/democrat-primary-elections-need-reform.

Gerber, A. S., and D. P. Green. 2000. "The Effects of Canvassing, Telephone Calls, and Direct Mail on Voter Turnout: A Field Experiment." *American Political Science Review* 94 (3): 653–63.

Gold, Hadas. 2016. "The *Huffington Post* Ending Editor's Note That Called Donald Trump 'Racist.'" *Politico.* November 9. https://www.politico.com/blogs/ on-media/2016/11/the-huffington-post-ending-its-editors-note-about-donald -trump-231044.

Graber, Doris A. 2011. *On Media: Making Sense of Politics.* Boulder, CO: Paradigm.

Graber, Doris A., and Johanna Dunaway. 2017. *Mass Media and American Politics.* Thousand Oaks, CA: CQ Press.

Grim, Ryan, and Danny Shea. 2015. "A Note about Our Coverage of Donald Trump's 'Campaign.'" *Huffington Post.* July 15, 2015. https://www.huff ingtonpost.com/entry/a-note-about-our-coverage-of-donald-trumps-campaign_ us_55a8fc9ce4b0896514d0fd66.

Gurian, Paul-Henri. 1993. "Candidate Behavior in Presidential Nomination Campaigns: A Dynamic Model." *The Journal of Politics* 55 (1): 115–39.

Hains, Tim. 2016. "Chaos at Nevada Democratic Convention; State Party Chair Flees Building as Sanders Supporters Demand Recount." *RealClearPolitics.* May 15, 2016. https://www.realclearpolitics.com/video/2016/05/15/chaos_at_nevada_dem ocratic_convention_dnc_leaders_flee_building_as_sanders_supporters_demand_ recount.html.

Hamilton, James. 2004. *All the News That's Fit to Sell: How the Market Transforms Information into News.* Princeton: Princeton University Press.

Harcup, Tony, and Deirdre O'Neill. 2016. "What Is News? News Values Revisited (Again)." *Journalism Studies* 18 (12): 1470–88.

Haynes, Audrey A., Julianne F. Flowers, and Paul-Henri Gurian. 2002. "Getting the Message Out: Candidate Communication Strategy During the Invisible Primary." *Political Research Quarterly* 55 (3): 633–52.

Hitt, Matthew P., and Kathleen Searles. 2018. "Media Coverage and Public Approval of the U.S. Supreme Court." *Political Communication* (2018): 1–21.

Iyengar, Shanto, Helmut Norpoth, and Kyu S. Hahn. 2004. "Consumer Demand for Election News: The Horserace Sells." *Journal of Politics* 66 (1): 157–75.

Jamieson, Kathleen Hall, and Bruce W. Hardy. 2009. "Media, Endorsements, and the 2008 Primaries." In *Reforming the Presidential Nomination Process*, edited by Steven S. Smith and Melanie J. Springer, 64–84. Washington, DC: Brookings Institution Press.

Kam, Cindy D., and Elizabeth J. Zechmeister. 2013. "Name Recognition and Candidate Support." *American Journal of Political Science* 57, no. 4: 971–86.

Mutz, Diana C. 1997. "Mechanisms of Momentum: Does Thinking Make It So?" *The Journal of Politics* 59 (1): 104–25.

Noel, Hans. 2016. "Opinion | Why Can't the G.O.P. Stop Trump?" *The New York Times*, March 1, 2016, sec. Opinion. https://www.nytimes.com/2016/03/01/opinion/campaign-stops/why-cant-the-gop-stop-trump.html.

Norrander, Barbara. 1996. "Presidential Nomination Politics in the Post-Reform Era." *Political Research Quarterly* 49 (4): 875–915.

Norrander, Barbara. 2000. "The End Game in Post-Reform Presidential Nominations." *The Journal of Politics* 62 (4): 999–1013.

Orren, G. 1985. "The Nomination Process: Vicissitudes of Candidate Selection." In *The Elections of 1984*, edited by M. Nelson. Washington, DC: Congressional Quarterly Press.

Patterson, Thomas E. 1980. *The Mass Media Election: How Americans Choose Their President*. New York: Praeger.

Patterson, Thomas E. 2016a. "News Coverage of the 2016 National Conventions: Negative News, Lacking Context." *SSRN Electronic Journal*.

———. 2016b. "Pre-Primary News Coverage of the 2016 Presidential Race: Trump's Rise, Sanders' Emergence, Clinton's Struggle." Cambridge: Harvard Kennedy School of Government.

———. 2016c. "Pre-Primary News Coverage of the 2016 Presidential Race: Trump's Rise, Sanders' Emergence, Clinton's Struggle." *Harvard Kennedy School Shorenstein Center on Media, Politics, and Public Policy*. Retrieved from https://shorensteincenter.org/news-coverage-2016-presidential-primaries.

Polsby, Nelson W. 1983. *Consequences of Party Reform*. Oxford: Oxford University Press.

Polsby, Nelson W., and Aaron B. Wildavsky. 1976. *Presidential Elections: Strategies of American Electoral Politics*. Lanham, MD: Rowman & Littlefield.

"Polls: 2016 Republican Presidential Nomination." 2016. *RealClearPolitics*. https://www.realclearpolitics.com/epolls/2016/president/us/2016_republican_presidential_nomination-3823.html.

Pomper, Gerald M. 1979. "New Rules and New Games in Presidential Nominations." *The Journal of Politics* 41 (3): 784–805.

Price, David. 1984. *Bringing Back the Parties.* Washington, DC: Congressional Quarterly Press.

Prior, M. 2007. *Post-Broadcast Democracy: How Media Choice Increases Inequality in Political Involvement and Polarizes Elections*. Cambridge: Cambridge University Press.

Redlawsk, David P. 2004. "What Voters Do: Information Search during Election Campaigns." *Political Psychology* 25 (4): 595–610.

Ridout, Christine F. 1991. "The Role of Media Coverage of Iowa and New Hampshire in the 1988 Democratic Nomination." *American Politics Quarterly* 19 (1): 43–58.

Ridout, Travis N., and Glen R. Smith. 2008. "Free Advertising: How the Media Amplify Campaign Messages." *Political Research Quarterly* 61 (4): 598–608.

Ridout, Travis N., Brandon Rottinghaus, and Nathan Hosey. 2009. "Following the Rules? Candidate Strategy in Presidential Primaries." *Social Science Quarterly* 90 (4): 777–95.

Ryfe, D. M. 2006. "The Nature of News Rules." *Political Communication* 23 (2): 203–14.

Schudson, Michael. 1982. "The Politics of Narrative Form: The Emergence of News Conventions in Print and Television." *Daedalus* 111 (4): 97–112.

Schudson, Michael, and Chris Anderson. 2009. "Objectivity, Professionalism, and Truth Seeking in Journalism." In *The Handbook of Journalism Studies*, edited by Karin Wahl-Jorgensen and Thomas Hanitzsch, 108–21. New York: Routledge.

Searles, Kathleen, and Kevin Banda. 2019. "But Her Emails! How Journalistic Preferences Shaped Election Coverage in 2016." *Journalism*, May 9, 2019. https://journals.sagepub.com/doi/abs/10.1177/1464884919845459.

Searles, Kathleen, Martha Humphries Ginn, and Jonathan Nickens. 2016. "For Whom the Poll Airs: Comparing Poll Results to Television Poll Coverage." *Public Opinion Quarterly* 80 (4): 943–63.

Shoemaker, P. J., and S. D. Reese. 1996. *Mediating the Message: Theories of Influences on Mass Media Content*. New York: Longman.

Shoemaker, Pamela J., and Timothy P. Vos. 2009. *Gatekeeping Theory*. New York: Routledge.

Sides, John L. 2015. "Why Is Trump Surging? Blame the Media." *Washington Post*. Accessed October 11, 2018. https://www.washingtonpost.com/news/monkey-cage/wp/2015/07/20/why-is-trump-surging-blame-the-media/.

Silver, Nate. 2016. "How Trump Hacked the Media," *FiveThirtyEight*. March 30, 2016. http://tinyurl. com/hdopz66.

Snyder, Riley. 2016. "Allegations of Fraud and Misconduct at Nevada Democratic Convention Unfounded. PolitiFact Nevada." May 18, 2016. Accessed October 12, 2018. https://www.politifact.com/nevada/statements/2016/may/18/jeff-weaver/allegations-fraud-and-misconduct-nevada-democratic/.

Soroka, Stuart N. 2012. "The Gatekeeping Function: Distributions of Information in Media and the Real World." *The Journal of Politics* 74 (2): 514–28.

Steger, Wayne P. 2007. "Who Wins Nominations and Why?: An Updated Forecast of the Presidential Primary Vote." *Political Research Quarterly* 60 (1): 91–99.

Steger, Wayne P., Andrew J. Dowdle, and Randall E. Adkins. 2004. "The New Hampshire Effect in Presidential Nominations." *Political Research Quarterly* 57, no. 3: 375–90.

Stone, W. J., and A. I. Abramowitz. 1983. "Winning May Not Be Everything, But It's More Than We Thought: Presidential Party Activists in 1980." *American Political Science Review* 77 (4): 945–56.

Stuart, Tessa. 2016. "WTF Happened at the Nevada Democratic State Convention?" *Rolling Stone* (blog). May 17, 2016. https://www.rollingstone.com/politics/politics-news/wtf-happened-at-the-nevada-democratic-state-convention-202352/.

Tewksbury, D., and S. L. Althaus. 2000. "Differences in Knowledge Acquisition among Readers of the Paper and Online Versions of a National Newspaper." *Journalism & Mass Communication Quarterly* 77 (3): 457–79.

Toff, Benjamin. 2018. "Rethinking the Debate over Recent Polling Failures." *Political Communication* 35 (2): 327–32.

Utych, Stephen M., and Cindy D. Kam. 2014. "Viability, Information Seeking, and Vote Choice." *The Journal of Politics* 76 (1): 152–66.

Weaver, David H., and Maxwell E. McCombs. 1980. "Journalism and Social Science: A New Relationship?" *Public Opinion Quarterly* 44 (4): 477–94.

Wemple, Erik. 2016. "*Huffington Post* Adding Readers' Notes Calling Trump 'Serial Liar,' 'Racist,' 'Rampant Xenophobe,' among Other Things." *The Washington Post*. January 28. https://www.washingtonpost.com/blogs/erik-wemple/wp/2016/01/28/huffington-post-adding-readers-notes-calling-trump-serial-liar-racist-rampant-xenophobe-among-other-things/?utm_term=.2829f1ec69e3.

Wright, Gerald C. 2009. "Rules and the Ideological Character of Primary Electorates." In *Reforming the Presidential Nomination Process*, edited by Steven S. Smith and Melanie J. Springer, 23–43. Washington, DC: Brookings Institution Press.

Zaller, J. 1999. *A Theory of Media Politics: How the Interests of Politicians, Journalists, and Citizens Shapes the News*. University of California, Los Angeles. Typescript.

Chapter Four

Voter Choice in Presidential Primaries

John Sides, Michael Tesler, and Lynn Vavreck

Presidential primaries often present a challenge for voters. There can be a large number of candidates—seventeen at one point during the 2016 Republican primary—and many are unfamiliar to voters. And because the candidates are seeking one party's nomination, voters cannot rely as much on their own partisan loyalties to choose among them. Contrast this with the presidential general election, in which there are only two major-party candidates and most voters reliably choose the one nominated by their party.

And yet voting behavior in presidential primaries is not random or unpredictable. Indeed, primary voting illustrates a maxim from public opinion research: "Every opinion is a marriage of information and predisposition" (Zaller 1992, 6). What voters think about candidates depends, first, on the messages they receive from candidates, the news media, and other political actors (Vavreck 2009), and second on the durable values, beliefs, and identities that "predispose" them to evaluate that information in particular ways and thus ultimately to form certain opinions.

In campaigns, this is a dynamic process that unfolds over time. Campaigns supply information that helps voters better use their beliefs and identities to choose a candidate. In general elections, the campaign usually rallies partisans to support their party's candidate. In competitive primaries, the campaign also helps voters make choices in line with their predispositions, even if party loyalty is less central. In 2016, this process happened in both the Democratic and Republican primaries, despite the differences between them.[1]

In this chapter, we describe how these two factors—the "information environment" and voters' predispositions—shape how voters view the candidates and thus which candidate ultimately wins the nomination. We draw especially on findings from the 2016 presidential primary, mindful that although these findings illustrate general features of primary voting behavior, their specifics may be unique to 2016. The upshot is that primary voters make choices for readily discernible reasons, even if it is difficult to predict which candidate will benefit from the aggregation of those choices across multiple primaries and caucuses.

THE INFORMATION ENVIRONMENT

American presidential primaries last a long time—typically more than a year between when the first candidate enters the race and one candidate secures the nomination, and arguably longer than that if you factor in candidates' exploration of whether to run in the first place. During these many months, the information environment around voters will strongly influence their opinions of the presidential candidates, as well as whether they have opinions in the first place. That information environment is shaped by three types of actors: the political parties, the news media, and the candidates themselves. Each of these has its own incentives and thus makes a distinctive contribution to the information voters may receive.

Political Parties

Political parties are extended networks of elected officeholders, formal organizations, and allied interest groups and media outlets that have different goals and views of political issues (Bawn et al. 2012). The central challenge for a political party is to coordinate on a presidential nominee who is at least satisfactory to many in this network and has a good chance of winning the general election. But different factions in the party may disagree on which candidate best meets these criteria, creating centrifugal forces within the party that make coordination harder.

In modern presidential primaries, the nomination depends on voters: the better candidates do in state primaries and caucuses, the more delegates they receive at the party conventions that formally nominate the party's presidential candidate. Thus, political party networks attempt to coordinate before any votes are cast. This "invisible primary" unfolds mostly in the year before the presidential election year. The moniker refers to the fact that the conversations and debates within the party are often private and not entirely visible to outside observers or voters.

Nevertheless, the invisible primary does produce visible consequences that shape the information environment for voters: politicians, interest groups, and others publicly endorse presidential candidates (Cohen et al. 2008). These endorsements do not simply reflect which candidate has raised the most money or gotten the most media coverage to date. They reflect judgments about the candidate's record, political beliefs, and electability. Endorsements serve as signals to other party leaders, donors, the media, and, ultimately, to voters. When a party effectively coordinates on a candidate during the invisible primary, that candidate often goes on to win the nomination.

But there is no guarantee that parties will coordinate successfully or that the support of party leaders will readily smooth the path to nomination. The 2016 election illustrates both points. The Republican party struggled to coordinate. Very few party leaders endorsed any candidate, even with seventeen to choose from. For example, among sitting Republican governors, U.S. House members, and U.S. senators, only 35 percent endorsed a presidential candidate before the Iowa caucus took place in February 2016. Moreover, those that did endorse were divided (figure 4.1). The candidate with the most endorsements, Jeb Bush, received only 9 percent of the possible endorsements from these officeholders. This lack of coordination had its roots in years of factionalism within the GOP, especially between its more moderate or "establishment" faction and its more conservative or "insurgent" factions.

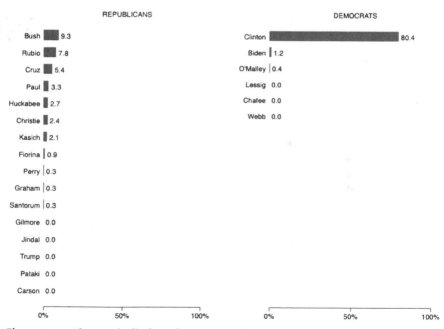

Figure 4.1.   The graph displays the percent of each party's governors, U.S. senators, and U.S. House members endorsing a presidential candidate in that party before the 2016 Iowa caucus.
Source: FiveThirtyEight and the authors' own collection.

It also arose because even within these factions there was no clear frontrunner. For example, in 2016, candidates like Bush, Florida senator Marco Rubio, New Jersey governor Chris Christie, and Ohio governor John Kasich were all seen as "establishment" candidates. Notably, Donald Trump received exactly zero endorsements.

The situation in the Democratic party was entirely different. The vast majority (80 percent) of Democratic governors, U.S. House members, and senators endorsed a candidate before the Iowa caucus and nearly every single one endorsed Hillary Clinton—201 in total (figure 4.1). Her main competitor, Senator Bernie Sanders of Vermont, an independent, received only two of the endorsements from these leaders. This was arguably the most effective coordination by a political party during a modern invisible primary, and it was certainly more effective than in Clinton's first presidential primary campaign in 2008, when only 16 percent of the same types of Democratic officeholders endorsed her. Clinton's strength in 2016 not only marginalized several other Democratic candidates, like Maryland governor Martin O'Malley, but arguably kept other potential candidates from even getting into the race—especially Vice President Joe Biden. However, Clinton's path to the nomination still encountered a significant challenge from Sanders. Throughout the primaries and caucuses, Clinton always led in the delegate count, but Sanders still managed to amass 43 percent of the votes cast. Clinton was less dominant than her support from party leaders implied.

The News Media

News coverage of presidential primaries also affects what voters read, hear, and see about the political candidates. The importance of news coverage is magnified in primaries precisely because voters know little about many candidates. In a classic paper, Paul Lazarsfeld and Robert Merton (1948, 101) described how the media can "confer status" on individuals: "The mass media bestow prestige and enhance the authority of individuals and groups by legitimizing their status. Recognition by the press or radio or magazines or newsreels testifies that one has arrived, that one is important enough to have been singled out from the large anonymous masses, that one's behavior and opinions are significant enough to require public notice." In a presidential primary, the candidates often approximate a "large anonymous mass" and thus the media's ability to "single out" particular candidates sends crucial information to voters.

So which candidates to single out? In part, this is determined by the same factors that affect political parties, such as the judgments of editors and reporters about who is in fact a credible or electable candidate. But the news media rely on other criteria and especially "newsworthiness." Newsworthy coverage often includes fresh evidence of which candidates are winning and losing; this type of campaign coverage is called "horserace journalism" (e.g., Brady and Johnston 1987). Thus, the news media pick up on the signals sent by political party networks and donors, including public endorsements and fundraising, as well as on public opinion polls. Newsworthy events often involve controversy or conflict, such as arguments among the candidates. Unsurprisingly, these are the features that make news interesting to consumers as well, making newsworthiness intrinsically connected to the audiences that news organizations need to be profitable.

During presidential primaries, news coverage can therefore shift sharply, and with it the fortunes and poll numbers of candidates. For many candidates, coverage follows a predictable cycle of "discovery, scrutiny, and decline" (Sides and Vavreck 2013). Discovery occurs when a candidate first does something deemed newsworthy and receives an initial round of news coverage. The newsworthy event can be as simple as entering the race. In the 2012 presidential primary, for example, Texas governor Rick Perry received a spike in news coverage upon entering the race in August 2011, with his polling numbers increasing soon thereafter. Discovery can also occur when a candidate is judged to have performed well in a debate. In the 2016 presidential primary, this happened to former Hewlett Packard CEO Carly Fiorina after a September 2015 debate in which she coolly responded to an insulting remark that Trump earlier made about her physical appearance. The discovery phase demonstrates how new information changes the views of voters, whose attention is drawn to the candidate being "singled out."

But discovery is soon followed by scrutiny, as the news media investigate this candidate more thoroughly. The mostly positive coverage of the discovery phase then gives way to more negative coverage, as the news media report on a candidate's past scandals, mistakes, controversial statements, and the like. For Rick Perry, the coverage reported on topics like his controversial statements about Social Security (he called it a "Ponzi scheme" and a "monstrous lie"). For Carly Fiorina, the coverage reported on her rocky tenure at Hewlett Packard and unpaid bills from her earlier California Senate campaign.

Media scrutiny affects voters, whose support for the scrutinized candidate typically wanes—and in many cases permanently, thereby constituting the third "decline" phase. That decline can also be hastened by the discovery of another candidate. For Perry, this other candidate was businessman Herman Cain, who won a nonbinding and ultimately meaningless straw poll among Florida Republicans that news outlets judged as an "upset" of Perry.

Not every candidate experiences discovery, scrutiny, and decline. Some are never "discovered" because few consider them viable contenders. Others never do anything judged newsworthy. Other candidates are so familiar that they do not need to be discovered. Indeed, sometimes this includes the eventual nominees themselves—such as Mitt Romney in 2012 or Hillary Clinton in 2016, neither of whom experienced the sharp initial spike in news coverage that is associated with discovery. And although some scrutiny is inevitable for most candidates, the volume and nature of that scrutiny varies and does not necessarily produce a decline. Indeed, that was what happened to Donald Trump and Bernie Sanders in the 2016 primary—and why news coverage was so vital for their campaigns.

Sanders initially attracted coverage of well-attended rallies organized in part through his campaign's social media presence (figure 4.2). News coverage of these rallies was framed explicitly in terms of the horserace. For example, an early rally with an overflow crowd of three hundred in rural Iowa was framed as a story of Sanders's "gaining momentum" and possibly

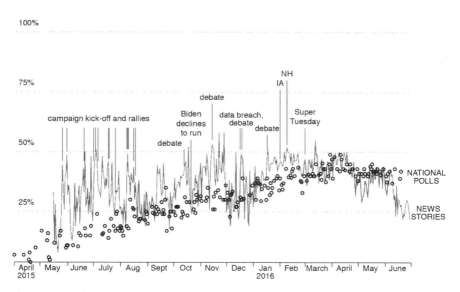

Figure 4.2. The graph displays the percent of stories in 24 top media outlets mentioning Bernie Sanders and the percent of Democratic primary voters supporting him in national polls. The media outlets include broadcast television networks (CBS, NBC, ABC, and PBS), cable news networks (CNN, Fox, and MSNBC), radio (National Public Radio and the Hugh Hewitt Show), websites (Huffington Post, Politico, and Breitbart), and 12 of the country's largest newspapers. Sanders's share of news coverage is calculated as a fraction of all stories in these outlets that both mentioned at least one Democratic candidate's name and used the phrase "presidential campaign."
Source: Huffington Post's Pollster (polling) and Crimson Hexagon (media).

mounting a "credible challenge" (Gabriel and Healy 2015). As the campaign continued, media coverage of Sanders was typically more positive than negative; it was telling the story of an underdog candidate doing unexpectedly well by horserace metrics except party endorsements. And coverage of Sanders was certainly more positive than coverage of Clinton, with its ongoing scrutiny of her use of a private email server as secretary of state in the Obama administration (Patterson 2016).

It is no wonder, then, that Sanders's standing in the polls increased steadily from April 2015 to April 2016 (figure 4.2), while Clinton's declined at certain points. Even Clinton supporters came to have a more favorable view of Sanders, although they did not vote for him. Of course, better polling numbers for Sanders helped generate more and more positive news coverage, illustrating the symbiotic relationship between polls and news that helped power his candidacy. The correlation between Sanders's poll numbers and news coverage in figure 4.2 is 0.49 (and even higher, 0.69, if day-to-day noise in both time series is smoothed out).

Trump's success also depended on the media. Indeed, without any clear signal coming from Republican party leaders about a preferred frontrunner, information from the news media was even more important to Republican primary voters. For Trump, this started with a typical period of discovery. After he announced his candidacy at Trump Tower on June 15, 2015, he received a sharp spike in news coverage (figure 4.3). This spike was larger than other candidates had received when they entered the race, perhaps because Trump's speech that day included controversial comments, such as the notion that "rapists" were coming across the border from Mexico. Trump continued to dominate coverage except at two moments: when neurosurgeon Ben Carson was "discovered" in late October (which led to the subsequent scrutiny and decline of Carson) and after Trump's underwhelming performance in the Iowa caucus (which he quickly overcame with a victory in the New Hampshire primary). Trump's dominance of the news left the other candidates starved for media attention, which they desperately needed to break out of the pack.

It might seem surprising that Trump never experienced the full cycle of media scrutiny and decline, especially given his "rapists" comment and many other controversies. But systematic analysis of news coverage showed that the scrutiny of Trump was episodic and often outweighed by more positive horserace coverage, which focused on his increasing poll numbers (Patterson 2016; Silver 2016). This helps explain why Trump's poll numbers not only shot up in the wake of his announcement but also never declined sharply: news coverage buoyed Trump's poll numbers, and good poll numbers justified further news coverage. The correlation between Trump's poll numbers and news coverage in figure 4.3 was 0.77.

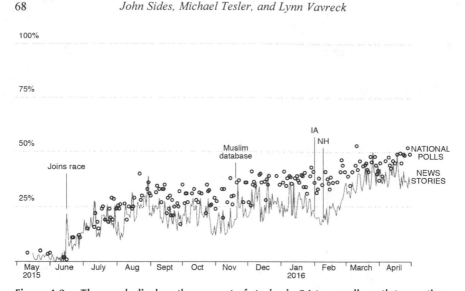

Figure 4.3. The graph displays the percent of stories in 24 top media outlets mentioning Donald Trump and the percent of Republican primary voters supporting him in national polls. The media outlets include broadcast television networks (CBS, NBC, ABC, and PBS), cable news networks (CNN, Fox, and MSNBC), radio (National Public Radio and the Hugh Hewitt Show), websites (Huffington Post, Politico, and Breitbart), and 12 of the country's largest newspapers. Trump's share of news coverage is calculated as a fraction of all stories in these outlets that both mentioned at least one Republican candidate's name and used the phrase "presidential campaign."
Source: Huffington Post's Pollster (polling) and Crimson Hexagon (media).

Of course, Trump's dominance of the news caused no end of consternation among Trump's rivals, who thought that Trump got far too much attention. Jeb Bush told reporters that Trump was playing them "like a fine Stradivarius violin" (Parker 2015). Certainly Trump got more coverage that one would expect, given the number of candidates in the race, its competitiveness, and his own modest poll numbers. But at the same time, Trump's coverage was entirely explicable in terms of newsworthiness. Trump was a compelling personality who delivered controversy and conflict seemingly every day, if not several times a day. This allowed him, as Fox News anchor Bret Baier put it, to "contort the day's media stories" (Grynbaum 2016). His controversial comments, such as his suggestion that there should be a database of Muslims living in the United States, frequently produced spikes in news coverage (figure 4.3). In turn, the interest Trump generated meant large audiences and profits for news organizations. The head of the CBS network, Les Moonves, summed up the Trump phenomenon thusly: "It may not be good for America, but it's damn good for CBS" (Bond 2016).

Candidates

The candidates themselves also shape the information environment. Their decisions help affect how much coverage they and therefore other candidates receive and also what specific messages reach voters. These messages determine what the primary election is "about," and which predispositions voters rely on when choosing among the candidates.

One central messaging decision that the candidates make is whether and how often to attack their opponents. In 2016, these decisions had important consequences. In the Democratic primary, Clinton and Sanders had their testy exchanges, but, remarkably, neither candidate ran a televised ad criticizing the other. This decision may have reflected Clinton's sense that she would win without "going negative" as well as Sanders's sense that his positive message was more persuasive than attacks on Clinton herself.

On the Republican side, Trump's opponents waited very late to attack Trump. Even though Trump had many opponents not only among the primary candidates but in the broader Republican party network, there was no coordinated effort to attack him and perhaps knock him from the top of the polls. This lack of coordination was illustrated by the GOP strategist Mike Murphy, who led a well-funded super PAC supporting Jeb Bush. At the end of 2015, after Trump had been leading the polls for months, Murphy said that Trump was "other people's problem." Indeed, the GOP candidates did not begin airing televised attack ads against Trump until he had won the New Hampshire and South Carolina primaries. By then, it was arguably too late. The unwillingness of Republican candidates to attack Trump mitigated the scrutiny that could have come from the news media because journalists often rely on candidate attacks to serve as fodder for stories and further investigation.

Another messaging decision involves the ideas and issues that the candidates promote. Here, the important question is whether the candidates agree or disagree among themselves. If the candidates agree or take similar positions, then voters' own views on those issues will not help them choose among the candidates. But if the candidates disagree, and if those differences are broadcast widely, then voters will divide along similar lines.

In 2016, many commentators believed that the Democratic primary was an ideological battle royale between the more liberal Sanders and the more centrist Clinton. But the differences between the candidates were often matters of degree—not so much whether, for example, the government should do more to provide health care or education, but exactly how much. Moreover, on many other issues, such as civil rights and immigration, Sanders and Clinton largely agreed. The differences between them had more to do with, first, their stance toward the Democratic Party itself and also Barack Obama. Clinton was a lifelong Democratic politician (as both first lady and senator) and Obama's secretary of state. Sanders was an independent long critical of the Democratic party and Obama. Sanders and Clinton also differed in their rhetorical style, even if their policy positions were not miles apart. Sanders called for a revolution that would fundamentally change politics, while Clinton ran as a pragmatic incrementalist—"a progressive who likes to get things done," she said, implying that Sanders's revolution was an unlikely event at best.

In the Republican primary, Trump and his opponents did agree on a few points: all were critics of Obama, of course, and argued that the country was headed in the wrong direction. But on many other issues, Trump—who had never been a loyal Republican to begin with—took heterodox positions compared to the rest of the party. Trump's positions and especially his rhetoric on immigration were harsher even than those of Republicans who viewed policies like a pathway to citizenship for undocumented immigrants as an unwanted "amnesty." Thus, when Trump suggested that there should be a database of Muslims in the United States, he was widely criticized by prominent Republicans.

Trump was even more heterodox on other issues. On foreign policy, he criticized U.S. alliances, free trade agreements, and the Iraq War. On economic issues, he appeared to oppose the GOP's enduring goal of entitlement reform, promising instead to protect Social Security, Medicare, and Medicaid benefits. He advocated raising taxes on the wealthy, including himself. He supported government spending on infrastructure. These apostasies earned him more opposition within the party. The editors of the conservative *National Review* (2016) called him "a philosophically unmoored political opportunist who would trash the broad conservative ideological consensus within the GOP in favor of a free-floating populism with strong-man overtones." Trump therefore seemed a poor fit for stereotypically conservative Republican primary voters. But in fact, Trump was better matched to these voters than many in the party believed.

PREDISPOSITIONS AND CHOOSING A CANDIDATE

The earliest research on Americans elections found that durable predispositions such as group identities and political beliefs guided voters' choices and that campaigns helped voters make choices in line with those predispositions (Lazarsfeld et al. 1948; Campbell et al. 1960). This is apparent both in presidential general election campaigns and presidential primaries. Although some voters may come to support a primary candidate just because of the pure buzz of media coverage, durable momentum usually requires that candidates appeal to specific identities or beliefs. As Larry Bartels (1988, 83) puts it, "Through the din of horse race coverage, the hoopla of rallies, and the frantic chasing after 'Big Mo,' the enduring political identities of candidates and citizens gradually shape the perceptions and evaluations on which primary votes are based."

Earlier primary campaigns provide many examples. In 1984, Colorado senator Gary Hart's support in the Democratic primary was concentrated among better-educated, white progressives who liked Hart's message of "new ideas" more than Walter Mondale's traditional New Deal policies (Bartels 1988). In the 1987 invisible primary, revelations about Hart's extramarital affair with Donna Rice led Democrats with traditional family values to oppose Hart (Stoker 1993). In 2008, Barack Obama's support came from people with liberal views on racial issues, who were unsurprisingly the most likely to vote for an African-American candidate (Tesler and Sears 2010). In the 2012 Republican primary, the social conservative Rick Santorum garnered votes from social conservatives who agreed with his positions on abortion and same-sex marriage (Tesler 2012).

These examples show how the predispositions that help voters choose primary candidates can vary from election to election and even within a single primary campaign. The relevant predispositions depend on the candidates and their messages, as well as which candidates rise to the fore because of news coverage or other factors. A primary campaign can reproduce existing divisions within parties, introduce new divisions, and/or tamp down old divisions—depending on the identities and messages of the candidates.

The 2016 Democratic Primary

The 2016 Democratic primary both reproduced and rearranged divisions within the party. Two divisions that were reproduced involved age and loyalty to the Democratic party. As in previous primaries, such as in 1984, the candidate with the more dramatic message of change—in 1984, Gary Hart, and in 2016, Sanders—had more appeal to younger voters than older voters, while the opposite was true for Clinton. By the end of the campaign, about two thirds of voters over forty-five supported Clinton, compared to one third of voters under thirty. Similarly, the candidate with fewer ties to the party— again, Sanders—received more support from independent-leaning primary voters, while Clinton received more from those loyal to the Democratic Party.

Two divisions that were muted concerned ideology and racial attitudes. It is typical for primaries in both parties to divide moderates and ideologues. But in 2016, Democratic voters were not much divided along ideological lines. To be sure, Democrats believed that Sanders was more liberal than

Clinton, and Sanders supporters were more likely to describe themselves as "liberal," but on specific policy questions there were few differences between Clinton and Sanders supporters. For example, in the January 2016 American National Election Pilot Study, Sanders supporters were only slightly more likely than Clinton supporters to favor increasing government spending for health insurance (83 percent of Sanders supporters vs. 81 percent of Clinton supporters) and for child care (76 percent vs. 68 percent) and to favor raising the minimum wage (83 percent vs. 77 percent). Thus, policy views on economic issues were weakly associated with Democratic primary voting in 2016.

The muting of the divisions based on racial attitudes becomes clear when comparing 2016 to 2008. In 2008, the primary battle between Clinton and Barack Obama divided white Democratic primary voters based on their views of race (Tesler and Sears 2010). More racially conservative voters—those who tended to attribute racial inequality to blacks' lack of effort—gravitated to Clinton; while racially liberal voters—those who tended to attribute racial inequality to discrimination against blacks—gravitated to Obama (figure 4.4). This was the consequence of having an African-American candidate in the race. But in 2016, without any such candidate and with Clinton and Sanders taking similarly liberal positions on civil rights issues, racial attitudes had little relationship to Democratic primary voting (figure 4.4).

The differences between the candidates in 2008 and the candidates in 2016 also inverted a division in the party: race. In 2008, black Democratic primary voters unsurprisingly gravitated to Obama after his initial victory in Iowa established him as a viable candidate. According to state exit polls, among blacks who voted for either Obama or Clinton, 84 percent voted for Obama and 16 percent for Clinton. Meanwhile, Clinton did much better among whites, winning 59 percent (and an even higher fraction among racially conservative whites). But in 2016, this divide was reversed: Clinton did better with black voters than white voters: she won 77 percent of blacks but 51 percent of whites (figure 4.4B). This can be attributed not only to Obama's absence as a candidate but to Clinton's historical ties to the African-American community and a warm relationship with Obama himself. As a frequent critic of Obama, Sanders struggled to build support among African Americans.

On balance, the factors that did and did not explain Democratic primary voting help explain why Clinton was able to win, despite the extensive and positive news coverage of Sanders. Two of Sanders's key constituencies— young people and independents—were not that numerous among Democratic primary voters. For example, voters under thirty comprised only 12 percent of the Democratic primary electorate in Texas. Similarly, exit polls showed that independents were less than a third of the primary electorate in most states.

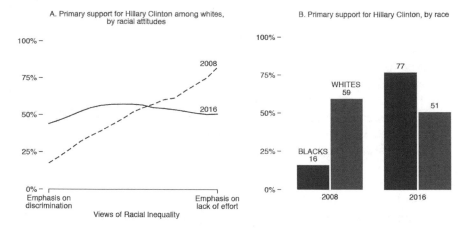

Figure 4.4. Views of racial inequality is a scale based on agreement or disagreement with these statements: "Over the past few years, blacks have gotten less than they deserve"; "Irish, Italian, Jewish, and many other minorities overcame prejudice and worked their way up. Blacks should do the same without any special favors"; "It's really a matter of some people not trying hard enough. If blacks would only try harder they could be just as well off as whites"; and "Generations of slavery and discrimination have created conditions that make it difficult for blacks to work their way out of the lower class." The righthand panel presents Hillary Clinton's average support among whites and blacks in 20 state exit polls. Clinton's support is calculated as her share of the vote for her and Obama in 2008 and her and Sanders in 2016. The averages are weighted by the number of primary votes for her and Obama or her and Sanders. The states included are: Alabama, Arkansas, Connecticut, Florida, Georgia, Illinois, Indiana, Maryland, Michigan, Mississippi, Missouri, New York, North Carolina, Ohio, Pennsylvania, South Carolina, Tennessee, Texas, Virginia, and Wisconsin. The lefthand panel is based on the 2008 and 2016 American National Election Studies Time Series.

Clinton's strong support among African Americans also helped give her an early victory in the South Carolina primary and then in a series of Southern states that held their primaries on Super Tuesday. In the modern Democratic Party, 40 percent of whose voters are non-white, it is difficult to build a winning coalition based primarily on white voters.

The 2016 Republican Primary

On the Republican side, one important intraparty division was replicated: ideology. It has been commonplace for Republican primaries to feature candidates who are relatively moderate or conservative. In 2016, Trump's positions on issues like entitlements and taxes put him squarely at odds with conservative Republicans—and in turn that division was reflected among voters. Voters with more liberal views on economic issues were much more likely to support Trump compared to his prominent opponents (figure 4.5). Conversely, conservative Republicans gravitated to one of the most conservative candidates in the field, Texas senator Ted Cruz. Other data showed that Cruz supporters were also more likely than Trump supporters to describe themselves as "very conservative."

But more distinctive in the 2016 Republican primary was the role of attitudes about racial issues, immigration, Islam, and a politicized white identity. These issues had long divided Republicans and Democrats, and increasingly so in the years leading up to the 2016 election (Sides, Tesler, and Vavreck 2018). But they had not divided Republicans in recent presidential primaries. In 2016, however, Trump's positions and rhetoric not only put race and immigration in the headlines but also produced sharp contrasts between him and the other candidates, who often rejected that rhetoric. Thus, racial attitudes were a much stronger predictor of support for Trump than they had been for either the 2008 or 2012 nominees, John McCain and Mitt Romney (figure 4.5B). The same was true for attitudes about immigration: whether Republican primary voters supported a pathway to citizenship, for example, became more strongly associated with Trump support than support for McCain or

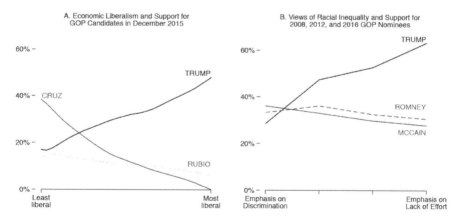

Figure 4.5. Economic liberalism is a scale combining these items: the difference in favorability of labor unions and "big business" (coded so that those with more favorable views of unions than of business are more liberal); and agreement or disagreement with three policies: "the government paying necessary medical costs for every American citizen"; "increasing taxes on individuals who make more than $200,000 a year"; and "raising the federal minimum wage." Views of racial inequality is the same scale as in Figure 4.4. The lefthand panel is based on the December 2015 Presidential Election Panel Study. The righthand panel is based on the 2008 and 2012 Cooperative Campaign Analysis Projects and 2016 YouGov/Economist polls.

Romney. The same was true for views of Muslims, and for whites' own racial grievances as whites' perceptions of discrimination against whites became associated with support for Trump.

Unlike ideology and attitudes about identity-inflected issues, economic anxiety played little role in Trump's support. The 2016 ANES Pilot Study included questions not only about whether the economy was getting better but also about economic mobility: "How much opportunity is there in America today for the average person to get ahead?"; whether it was harder "for you to move up the income ladder"; and " whether people's ability to improve their financial well-being" was better than, worse than, or the same as it was twenty years ago. If anything, the more that anxious Republicans were based on a composite scale of these items, the *less* likely they were to support Trump in the primary, once other factors were taken into account. Instead, economic concerns became politically potent when refracted through the prism of race—a phenomenon we call "racialized economics." As of January 2016, polls showed that Trump support was weakly connected to concerns about losing your job, but it was strongly connected to concerns that whites could not find jobs because employers were hiring minorities.

To many political analysts, a controversial and heterodox candidate like Trump was not well positioned to win over Republican primary voters. But Trump's coalition had been hiding in plain sight for many years. There had always been an important segment of Republicans who identified as conservative but had liberal positions on economic issues (Ellis and Stimson 2012). Among likely Republican primary voters in the December 2015 Presidential Election Panel Study (see figure 4.5), these liberals were not a tiny minority: 30 percent favored the government's paying medical costs, 47 percent supported raising the minimum wage, 51 percent supported increasing taxes on the wealthy, and 25 percent had more favorable views of unions than of big business.

Moreover, the percentage of Republicans with conservative views on identity-inflected issues had been increasing in the years leading up to 2016—in part because of Obama's presidency (Tesler 2016). This is one reason why Trump's controversial statements about issues like a ban on Muslims coming to the United States did not necessarily hurt him. A December 2015 *Washington Post*/ABC News poll found that 59 percent of Republicans supported the ban (Clement 2015). In Republican primary exit polls, support for the ban ranged from a low of 63 percent in Michigan and Virginia to a high of 78 percent in Alabama.

Trump's appeal to Republican voters was certainly limited: he won only 45 percent of all the votes cast in the Republican primary. However, that was enough to win the nomination in a year when a fractured party could not coalesce around any alternative.

CONCLUSION

That primary voting has predictable features does not necessarily make primary election outcomes predictable. Both Sanders's and Trump's successes certainly ran contrary to many predictions. Moreover, their successes raised important questions about how much political parties can effectively coordinate on a candidate and shape the information environment and thus the decisions of primary voters (Cohen et al. 2016). Candidates can break through by raising money outside of traditional party gatekeepers and relying on buzz from the news media's increasing coverage of the invisible primary. Of course, a breakthrough does not mean that a candidate will win, but it can still put the outcome, at least temporarily, in question.

Moreover, that voters' predispositions help them choose a primary candidate does not help us predict which predispositions will matter and thus the shape of the winner's coalition. That depends on the candidates who run and what they communicate to voters. For this reason, there is no way to know whether the central factors in primary voting in 2016 will be important in 2020—especially as the Democratic party's primary shifts from a two-person race between a presumptive favorite and party outsider to a multi-candidate race with no favorite.

The 2020 Democratic primary will thus test the party's ability to coordinate on a frontrunner or at least narrow the field to a smaller number of plausible nominees. The challenge may be more acute if several candidates compete within factions of the party. Rather than have only Bernie Sanders representing the more liberal faction, for example, there could be Sanders himself but also Massachusetts Senator Elizabeth Warren and others. The primary will likely also feature not only multiple women candidates but also multiple candidates from non-white racial or ethnic backgrounds—including former San Antonio mayor Julián Castro, California senator Kamala Harris, and possibly New Jersey senator Cory Booker and others. It may therefore be harder for any one candidate to quickly gain the support of non-white voters, as Clinton did among African Americans in 2016. To be sure, a long and divisive primary is no necessary hindrance to winning a general election; both Barack Obama and Donald Trump are testament to that. But a long 2020 primary would again demonstrate the power of centrifugal forces within the presidential primary process.

NOTE

1. Unless otherwise noted, our discussion of the 2016 presidential primary is based on Sides, Tesler, and Vavreck (2018) and our discussion of the 2012 presidential primary is based on Sides and Vavreck (2013).

REFERENCES

Bartels, Larry M. 1988. *Presidential Primaries.* Princeton: Princeton University Press.

Bawn, Kathleen, Martin Cohen, David Karol, Seth Masket, Hans Noel, and John Zaller. 2012. "A Theory of Political Parties: Groups, Policy Demands and Nominations in American Politics." *Perspectives on Politics* 10, no. 3 (September): 571–97.

Bond Paul. 2016. "Leslie Moonves on Donald Trump: 'It May Not Be Good for America, but It's Damn Good for CBS.'" *Hollywood Reporter*, February 29, 2016. https://www.hollywoodreporter.com/news/leslie-moonves-donald-trump-may-871464.

Brady, Henry E., and Richard Johnston. 1987. "What's the Primary Message: Horse Race or Issue Journalism," In *Media and Momentum*, edited by Gary R. Orren and Nelson W. Polsby, 127–86. Chatham, NJ: Chatham House.

Campbell, Angus, Philip E. Converse, Warren E. Miller, and Donald E. Stokes. 1960. *The American Voter.* New York: John Wiley & Sons.

Clement, Scott. 2015. "Republicans Embrace Trump's Ban on Muslims While Most Others Reject It." *Washington Post*, December 14, 2015. https://www.washingtonpost.com/politics/americans-reject-trumps-muslim-ban-but-republicans-embrace-it/2015/12/14/24f1c1a0-a285-11e5-9c4e-be37f66848bb_story.html?noredirect=on&utm_term=.78174ae89ef7.

Cohen, Marty, David Karol, Hans Noel, and John Zaller. 2008. *The Party Decides: Presidential Nominations Before and After Reform.* Chicago: University of Chicago Press.

Cohen, Marty, David Karol, Hans Noel, and John Zaller. 2016. "Party versus Faction in the Reformed Presidential Nominating System." *PS: Political Science and Politics* 49, no. 4 (December): 701–8.

Ellis, Christopher, and James A. Stimson. 2012. *Ideology in America.* New York: Cambridge University Press.

Gabriel, Trip, and Patrick Healy. 2015. "Challenging Hillary Clinton, Bernie Sanders Gains Momentum in Iowa." *New York Times*, May 31, 2015. https://www.nytimes.com/2015/06/01/us/politics/challenging-hillary-clinton-bernie-sanders-gains-momentum-in-iowa.html.

Grynbaum, Michael M. 2016. "Television Networks Struggle to Provide Equal Airtime in the Era of Trump." *New York Times*, May 30, 2016. https://www.nytimes.com/2016/05/31/business/media/television-networks-struggle-to-provide-equal-airtime-in-the-era-of-trump.html.

Lazarsfeld, Paul, and Robert Merton. 1948. "Mass Communication, Popular Taste, and Organized Social Action." In *The Communication of Ideas*, edited by Lyman Bryson, 95–118. New York: The Institute for Religious and Social Studies.

Lazarsfeld, Paul F., Bernard Berelson, and Hazel Gaudet. 1948. *The People's Choice: How the Voter Makes Up His Mind in a Presidential Campaign.* New York: Columbia University Press.

National Review editors. 2016. "Against Trump." *National Review*, January 21, 2016.

Parker, Ashley. 2015. "Jeb Bush Takes Voter Questions, but Has No Answer for Donald Trump." *New York Times*, December 8, 2015. https://www.nytimes.com/politics/first-draft/2015/12/08/jeb-bush-takes-voter-questions-but-has-no-answer-for-donald-trump/.

Patterson, Thomas. 2016. "Pre-primary News Coverage of the 2016 Presidential Race: Trump's Rise, Sanders' Emergence, Clinton's Struggle." Shorenstein Center on Media, Politics and Public Policy, June 13, 2016. https://shorensteincenter.org/pre-primary-news-coverage-2016-trump-clinton-sanders/.

Sides, John, and Lynn Vavreck. 2013. *The Gamble: Choice and Chance in the 2012 Presidential Election*. Princeton: Princeton University Press.

Sides, John, Michael Tesler, and Lynn Vavreck. 2018. *Identity Crisis: The 2016 Presidential Campaign and the Battle for the Meaning of America*. Princeton: Princeton University Press.

Silver, Nate. 2016. "How Trump Hacked the Media." *FiveThirtyEight*, March 30, 2016. https://fivethirtyeight.com/features/how-donald-trump-hacked-the-media/.

Stoker, Laura. 1993. "Judging Presidential Character: The Demise of Gary Hart," *Political Behavior* 15, no. 2 (April): 193–223.

Tesler, Michael. 2012. "Moral Conservatives Spark the Santorum Surge," YouGov, February 21, 2012. https://today.yougov.com/topics/politics/articles-reports/2012/02/21/moral-conservatives-spark-santorum-surge.

Tesler, Michael. 2016. *Post-Racial or Most-Racial? Race and Politics in the Obama Era*. Chicago: University of Chicago Press.

Tesler, Michael, and David O. Sears. 2010. *Obama's Race: The 2008 Election and the Dream of a Post-Racial America*. Chicago: University of Chicago Press.

Vavreck, Lynn. 2009. *The Message Matters*. Princeton: Princeton University Press.

Zaller, John. 1992. *The Nature and Origins of Mass Opinion*. New York: Cambridge University Press.

Chapter Five

Backward Looking, Future Rule-Making

How 2016 Affected the 2020 Presidential Nomination Rules

Josh Putnam

"The system is rigged, it's crooked. There was no voting. I didn't go out there to make a speech or anything, there's no voting. The people out there are going crazy, in the Denver area and Colorado itself, and they're going absolutely crazy because they weren't given a vote. This was given by politicians—it's a crooked deal."

—Donald J. Trump

(to Fox News following the April 9, 2016, Colorado Republican state convention that selected delegates for the Republican National Convention)

- National parties set the guidelines.
- States and state parties react.
- Candidates and their campaigns adapt to both and construct strategies to maximize their odds of winning.

That is the sequence that has repeated itself every four years since the McGovern-Fraser reforms were instituted by the Democratic National Committee for the 1972 presidential nomination cycle, fundamentally reshaping how presidential candidates are nominated. The sequence does always have more nuance, and more importantly, each iterative cycle of that series is interconnected. In other words, while each actor or group of actors technically follows another in the sequence, all look back through a variety of lenses at the previous cycle for some guidance on how to improve, whether national party, entities at the state level, or the candidates (or prospective candidates) themselves, for the next iteration.

Before the 2016 primaries were even over, for example, the Minnesota state legislature passed legislation that was later signed into law providing a primary option in subsequent cycles (Putnam 2016b). The reason was not because of any change in the national party rules. Rather, the change was made due to overrun caucuses in the "Land of 10,000 Lakes" (Minnesota) during the 2016 nomination process. Similarly, even before the national parties had set their respective sets of rules for the 2020 cycle, legislators in the Golden state passed a bill moving the presidential primary in California from June to the first Tuesday in March, typically the earliest date on which states can schedule delegate selection events without penalty (Putnam 2017b). That, too, came about not because of a change in national party rules, but because state legislators wanted to increase turnout in the California primary and give voters in the state a greater voice.[1]

But while those concurrent state actions add to the patchwork of rules and considerations the national parties undertake in the two years following a presidential election, often their collective gaze is centered on what transpired during the previous stress test on the nomination rules. Although those conditions are unlikely to repeat themselves, national party rules makers often set about to right the wrongs of the previous cycle for the next cycle. It is that type of maneuvering—fighting the last battle with the next one in mind—that frequently leads to unintended consequences (Polsby 1983; Reiter 1985). The post-reform era is littered with examples of these very effects, but the 2016 cycle serves not only as example but as an interconnected backdrop for the changes triggered for the 2020 cycle.

FROM 2012 TO 2016: REPUBLICANS TINKER AND DEMOCRATS REST ON THEIR LAURELS

The Republicans

Following the reelection of Barack Obama in 2012, the Republican Party was again left to wander the desert in search of a path to the White House. That journey often finds national parties considering the presidential nomination rules as part of the equation (Klinkner 1994), as the Republican National Committee (RNC) did after 2012.

For much of the post-1972 period, the party adopted changes at the convention that would dictate the nomination process in the next cycle. That had the effect of leaving the party vulnerable and unable to adapt the rules to any midstream changes at the state level or to other evolving conditions under which the next nomination fight could or would be waged. Coming out of the 2008 St. Paul convention, the RNC broke from that traditional pattern by empowering an external RNC panel, the Temporary Delegate Selection Committee (TDSC), to propose some alterations between conventions.[2]

Between 2012 and 2016, the party considered several streams of information as they revised their delegate selection rules. Republicans left the 2012 Republican National Convention in Tampa with a baseline set of rules, devised by those in the Romney circle running the convention and with a particular goal in mind.[3] Within that group, both Republican rules expert Ben Ginsberg, who raised a number of rules changes, and New Hampshire Governor John H. Sununu, who chaired the convention rules committee, pushed through an initial iteration of the rules for 2016 that would have benefited a hypothetical President Romney seeking renomination then. However, as part of that package, a new rule—Rule 12—was added as a contingency that would allow inter-convention delegate selection rules changes in the event that Romney was not elected president. He was not. And in January 2013, the RNC convened in Charlotte, North Carolina, for its winter meeting and selected the members of the new standing Committee on Rules that would consider rules changes for the 2016 cycle.

Concurrent with that official channel was another but broader self-examination commissioned by the RNC. The Growth and Opportunity Project report, or "the autopsy," as it came to be known, laid out a wider variety of recommended changes from messaging and issue positioning to fundraising and digital campaigning to the rules of the presidential nomination process.[4] The report, issued in March 2013, served as another input into the deliberations of the RNC Rules Committee during the remainder of 2013 and into 2014. Specifically, the autopsy recommended an earlier convention, a revised and more controlled primary debates process, a retention of the four carve-out states at the beginning of the primary calendar, and a regional primary system that would follow in the months between the earliest contests and the national convention.

Together, both provided a baseline set of rules and a series of broad, aspirational nomination system changes that the RNC and the Rules Committee worked toward. The vision that emerged was one with a more managed invisible primary period, especially for debates, and a compressed primary calendar, with a more rigorously enforced buildup on the front end. The vast majority of that vision was built on the perceived shortcomings of the 2012 cycle. Two committees of the Republican National Committee dealt with these issues. The Committee on Arrangements is tasked with the planning and scheduling of the national convention, while the remainder was squarely within the Rules Committee purview.

The Calendar

Maneuvers over the calendar of primaries and caucuses demonstrate the willingness and ability of the national party, but also its limits. Overall, the main goal for Republicans in 2012 was a familiar one that the parties have faced ever since 1972: To have a more orderly progression of primaries and caucuses. That has always been difficult, however, because they share the scheduling process with state governments and state parties, neither of which is necessarily interested in doing what the national party organizations want.

Several issues about the front end of the calendar lingered from the 2012 process. Chief among them was the early process, or the "on ramp," which meant reserving February for the "carve out" states of Iowa, New Hampshire, South Carolina, and Nevada, the four states that both parties have agreed to schedule at the very beginning of the calendar. On that front, the Rules Committee began work on tweaking the guidelines shaping the window of time on the calendar within which state parties were allowed to select their delegates to the national convention. State parties have incentives to leapfrog other states on the calendar, to let their voters have more of a say in shaping the candidate field, and to violate national party rules in other ways (Mayer and Busch 2004; Putnam 2010). To combat state party rule-breaking in 2012, some rules makers in the RNC informally coordinated a basic calendar structure with some of the membership from the Democratic National Committee (DNC): Four carve-out states (Iowa, New Hampshire, South Carolina, and Nevada) would hold February contests and the remaining states were free to schedule their primaries and caucuses in a position of the state parties' and/ or state government's choice in a window ranging from the first Tuesday in March to June. However, as part of that set-up on the Republican side in 2012, there was one exception to that freedom of choice. States that allocated delegates using a winner-take-all method either had to schedule a delegate selection event for April or later or change the method of delegate allocation to a more proportional system. A violation of that rule—holding a winner-take-all contest before April 1—carried a 50 percent reduction in a state's national convention delegation. Yet, as both Florida (with a late January winner-take-all primary) and Arizona (with a late February winner-take-all primary) highlighted, there were two potential violations—calendar timing and allocation method—but only one 50 percent sanction that could only be meted out once in the 2012 rules.

As the Rules Committee deliberated between 2012 and 2014, several issues lingered from the 2012 process. Chief among them was preserving the early status of the four carve-out states and the slower build up of a nomination race in order to reduce the incentives for other states to move into the early calendar territory. And on that front the Rules Committee offered a mixed message in response for the 2016 cycle. First, to avoid the two violations– one penalty trap, a new penalty was added. States that violated the allocation rules—by holding winner-take-all contests too early—would continue to face a 50 percent reduction to the national convention delegation. But those states that violated the timing rules by conducting a primary or caucus prior to the first Tuesday in March would be met with a much stiffer "super" penalty.[5] The more delegate-rich a state was, the greater the penalty would be. The party achieved that by setting a floor number of delegates states in violation would have, post-penalty: twelve for states that had thirty or more delegates and nine for states with fewer than thirty delegates. Applied retrospectively to Florida and Arizona in 2012, that would have equated to a roughly 80 percent to 90 percent delegate reduction.

The RNC also tightened its language for what constituted proportional allocation for 2016 relative to 2012. The goal was to eliminate direct winner-take-all elements in the allocation in early calendar contests. Basically, only a candidate who received greater than majority level support statewide or on the congressional district level could win all the delegates in the jurisdiction. In turn, that was intended to increase early competition through a slower build in the delegate count. However, that cycle-over-cycle alteration was counteracted by a rules-based shrinking of the proportionality window. The area of the calendar between the carve-out states and when states could begin allocating delegates with any winner-take-all elements was cut in half from 2012 to 2016. Rather than the entire month of March serving as a restricted area for winner-take-all contests as was the case in 2012, the proportionality window for 2016 was set as the first *half* of March (through March 14).

The penalties, then, were recalibrated and the proportionality requirements tightened, but the window where winner-take-all rules were restricted shrunk. All were intended to fix problems made apparent in the 2012 cycle and all were intended to fit within the broader vision of a more compressed timeline for 2016.

The Debates

Another issue that arose during the Republican invisible primary period of 2011 was a perceived negative impact of primary debates. While the number of debates did not increase from 2008 to 2012, there were still twenty debates between May 2011 and the end of February 2012. And many of the roughly two debates every month (on average) during that span were perceived as hostile, pitting media partners against the field of Republicans vying for the nomination. Not only were the candidates attacking one another, but certain media partners were viewed as contributing to that as well. The combination of the number of debates and perception of unfriendly media partners, against the backdrop of the surge and decline of candidates from Rick Perry to Michele Bachmann to Herman Cain, seemingly fueled the divisiveness of the nomination race before any votes were cast, and continued in the first two months of primary season in 2012. That and a competitive primary season that stretched into the beginning of April left the eventual nominee, Mitt Romney, bruised heading into the general election. Or at least that's what many Republicans believed.

This was something the RNC sought to correct for in 2016. The party took a two-pronged approach. Initially, during the summer RNC meeting in 2013, the party passed a resolution to not partner with either CNN or MSNBC for primary debates (O'Keefe 2013). But later, at the spring 2014 meeting, the RNC adopted Rule 10(h), creating a standing committee to deal with the debates' scheduling, frequency, formats, media partners, and "best interests of the Republican Party."[6] The committee was also tasked with devising criteria for candidate inclusion in debates, including prohibiting any candidate who participated in an unsanctioned debate from participating in any of the future debates sanctioned by the RNC.

The true innovation was not in the rules themselves but in the fact that the RNC had codified within the rules of the party a structure to deal with the issue, real or perceived. It was an institutional body that could resolve to some degree the two problems left lingering from 2012: controlling the number of debates and selecting the media partners with which the national party would coordinate. However, those moves were surface-level changes that could control neither the candidates' attacks on one another nor the voice they gave to constituencies not perfectly aligned within the party. In other words, media partners were given incentive to not push divisiveness among the candidates, but candidate-initiated divisiveness was left unchecked both in the rules and in the actions of the debates-sanctioning committee within the RNC.

Regional Primaries

While the RNC Rules Committee directly or indirectly addressed the above issues from the Growth and Opportunity Project report, there was no active effort to push from within the national party for a regional primary system. Other, more radical reforms, such as upending the traditional calendar and shifting to a series of regional primaries, had been considered by Republicans in previous cycles, but the party did not seriously consider anything like that after 2012 or 2016.[7]

Unbound Delegates

The RNC also dealt with one additional calendar issue—one not prioritized in the Growth and Opportunity Project report. While Florida was brazen about moving its primary earlier than it was allowed to and having early influence over the 2012 Republican nomination race, a handful of caucus states—

Colorado, Maine, Minnesota, and Washington state—were able to more covertly schedule contests earlier than technically allowed under the rules of the Republican Party, but unlike Florida, without penalty. The reason those caucus states managed to pull that off was that no delegates were allocated based on the preference votes cast at precinct caucuses across a window that extended from late January through early March (but before the first Tuesday in March). Stemming from the maneuvering of those states—both the primary states like Florida that were willing to take the 50 percent reduction in their national delegations and these early caucus states—was a calendar much more spread out than the frontloaded primary calendar of 2008. The on-ramp the Growth and Opportunity Project report described as ideal was much longer in 2012, expanding across the two months before Super Tuesday complete with a three week period of no contests in mid-February.

But the development of the calendar was not exclusively where the impact of these changes were felt. It affected the course of the primary season as well. Although no delegates were allocated early on in those caucus states, the statewide results of preference votes in the precinct caucuses across those states were publicly reported. And the latter had no bearing on the former. Allocation was not tethered in any way to those beauty contest preference votes. As a result, a candidate could claim victory in the statewide preference vote but lose in the delegate selection process in later district caucuses and state conventions. The Ron Paul campaign was particularly adept at winning those battles while losing preference votes. They did so in the aforementioned caucus states but also in Iowa and Nevada, sending a less establishment-friendly group of delegates to the national convention.

In the lead-up to 2016, the Rules Committee sought to deal more directly with the delegates not bound in those early caucus states or not bound at all in some of the others.[8] The result was a new rule to bind delegates to the results of any statewide preference vote. It was a change intended to rein in state activity viewed as outside the norm at best or an attempt at skirting the rules at worst. But another goal was to remedy a slower build of delegates and a later resolution to the nomination process, one that could potentially fuel divisiveness within the process and the party.

The Democrats

As the RNC attempted to work out the kinks in its nomination rules, the Democratic National Committee (DNC) took a different tack. Occupying the White House, the party pursued a path often taken by parties in power: if it ain't broke, don't fix it. The rules changes that were adopted by the Rules and Bylaws Committee and later the DNC in 2010 on the recommendation of the preceding Democratic Change Commission (DCC) made only minor changes for 2012, driven by the heated competition in the previous cycle. At its most basic level, the 2008 nomination process was different from 2012. The former was a far more robust test of the Democratic nomination rules than the latter. The closely fought and extended battle for the 2008 Democratic nomination waged between Barack Obama and Hillary Clinton highlighted a number of issues within the system the DNC sought thereafter to remedy. Changes were made to the delegate incentive structure to attempt to address the crowding at the beginning of the 2008 primary calendar. Superdelegates changes were made as well with the goal of slightly reducing the influence of party leaders and elected officials on the outcome of the nomination process.

The party simplified the timing bonus—additional delegates added to the state delegation to the national convention—that it used as a carrot to encourage states to schedule later primaries and caucuses. But on the recommendation of the DCC, the DNC also added a new clustering bonus to three or more neighboring states that coordinated a regional or subregional primary during the latter half of the primary calendar.

Additionally, add-on delegates, a subgroup of superdelegates—one party leader or elected official added for every four DNC members from a state—were shifted from the unpledged category to pledged for 2012. That helped by some small measure to reduce the ratio of pledged-to-unpledged delegates in the Democratic presidential nomination process. But that move did not have as large an impact on the superdelegate-to-delegate ratio as the decision to change the base number of delegates from 3,000 to 3,700. The additional 700 delegates, roughly as many as the total number of superdelegates, had the effect not only of diluting the potential influence of superdelegates during the renomination bid of President Obama, but also decreased the percentage of superdelegates to the lowest point in the superdelegate era (see figure 5.1). It was a change that was all the easier to push through in the Call for the 2012 Democratic National Convention because it was an uncompetitive and low stakes nomination cycle.[9] Superdelegates were not going to tip the balance under those conditions and it was a way to reward an additional seven hundred activists heading into the general election campaign.

While those were minor changes on the whole to the rules for the 2012 cycle, it was quite a number of changes given that the Democratic Party was defending the presidency and the president was unchallenged.

But after the 2012 cycle, when the nomination process was uncompetitive and more about delegate selection rather than allocation among candidates, the DNC had less to fix. And the process to review the rules for the 2016 cycle reflected that. There was no external commission like the McGovern-Fraser commission or the Democratic Change Commission chartered at the

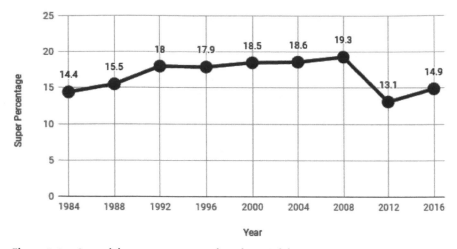

Figure 5.1. **Superdelegate percentage of total DNC delegates (1984-2016). Data come from Appendix B of the Call to the Democratic Convention.**
Source: Data compiled by author.

national convention. Instead, the review process went directly to the Rules and Bylaws Committee (RBC). And the RBC was given little impetus under that scenario to make many changes to a system that did not appear broken.

In fact, other than some technical changes to the language of both the delegate selection rules and the Call for the 2016 Democratic National Convention, there were very few substantive changes made to the overarching series of rules behind the Democratic nomination process.[10] The one change of significance to how candidates are nominated was the decision to decrease the number of base delegates from 3,700 to 3,200. Although the change for 2012 had been intended to lower the ratio of pledged-to-unpledged delegates, the 700 delegate increase placed a logistical burden on the arm of the DNC tasked with planning and conducting the national convention in Charlotte. The 3,700 delegates plus superdelegates plus media covering the event and other dignitaries greatly limited the number of cities and venues that could accommodate the gathering. It was that consideration that prompted the scaling back of base delegates for the 2016 cycle.

Importantly, however, there were no other changes to the 2016 rules. Effectively, the 2012 rules were carried over to 2016. But that one change to the number of base delegates would indirectly affect the later discussion that revolved around the superdelegates in 2016.

THE 2016 STRESS TEST ON DEMOCRATIC
AND REPUBLICAN NOMINATION RULES

The Republicans: 2014 Rules Changes, 2015–2016 Realities

Rules in the Invisible Primary

The party was successful in curtailing the number of debates relative to the 2012 cycle. Twelve sanctioned debates were scheduled, one a month starting in August 2015 and increasing to roughly two per month as calendar year 2016 began. In addition, the party had some success in picking the media outlets with which it wanted to partner for those debates. Where the RNC fell short, however, was in dealing with the flood of candidates who threw their hats in the ring throughout the middle stages of 2015. The debates committee not only had to devise the criteria whereby candidates would qualify, but it had to consider how to best accommodate so many candidates on one (or more) debate stages. More broadly, and perhaps out of the purview of the debates committee, the RNC had another related question with which to deal: how to treat Donald Trump, a candidate who announced a run for the nomination as of mid-June 2015 but had not had the longest history with the party nor the deepest of connections to its orthodoxy.

The answers to those questions would prove to have some impact on the winnowing of the 2016 field of Republican candidates. Trump's rise to the top of the polls in the lead-up to the first debate made the question of whether to include the New York business mogul moot.[11] And the debates committee's solutions to the other matters offered mixed results. On the one hand, the committee outsourced the development of debate qualifying criteria to its media partners. National polling was used and the threshold was set low enough that seventeen candidates qualified for the initial August debate. On the other hand, however, the committee's solution to the number of candidates was to separate them into two groups, a main event debate in primetime for the top ten candidates in the polling average and an undercard debate for the remainder that preceded the main event debate. The cut point between the polling average for the last candidate included in the main debate and the first to qualify for the lower-tier debate could often be arbitrary, but the overall set-up had the effect of providing some momentum to the winnowing process. Mainly, that was a function of how stable the two groups were. Only three candidates ever moved from one category to the other and two of those—Carly Fiorina and Chris Christie—both rose to the main stage and fell to the second-tier event.

While the debates influenced the initial winnowing of the field of Republican candidates, they also helped to solidify Trump as the clear, albeit plurality, frontrunner heading into primary season as the calendar flipped to February. And that was a position not unlike the one Trump's predecessor, Mitt Romney, found himself in heading into the voting phase of the 2012 nomination process.

Rules in Primary Season

There were remarkable similarities between Romney's and Trump's paths to a majority of delegates (see figure 5.2 below). Both Trump and Romney surpassed the 25 percent delegates mark on Super Tuesday (on the first Tuesday in March in both cycles). Both candidates crossed the 50 percent threshold on the day of the first contests after the prohibition on winner-take-all contests ended (April 1 in 2012 and March 15 in 2016). And both candidates clinched the nomination on the last Tuesday in May.

The main difference cycle-over-cycle from 2012 to 2016 was the calendar. The primaries and caucuses were much more spread out in 2012, beginning in early January and ending in late June. In 2016, the Republican calendar began a month later, on February 1, and ended nearly a month earlier than in 2012, on the first Tuesday in June. The rules changes instituted to keep rogue states in check worked. No states opted to take the new super-penalty for violating the timing rules in exchange for earlier influence. Nor did the three caucus states that opted not to hold first-round preference votes at precinct caucuses. Colorado, North Dakota, and Wyoming all held district and/or state conventions to *select* national convention delegates after the beginning of March. Together, that meant that the four carve-out states were able to schedule their primaries or caucuses in February 2016 as intended.

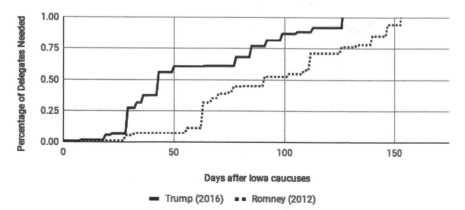

Figure 5.2. Time to Secure Enough Delegates to Clinch Republican Nomination, 2012–16. Delegate counts based on media accounts and national party's public reports.
Source: Data compiled by author.

Super Tuesday, too, was different in 2016. It remained the date on which the most delegates were at stake, but it was more southern in 2016, adding Alabama, Arkansas, and Texas to a list that had included Georgia, Oklahoma, Tennessee, and Virginia in 2012 as well. That collection of states coordinated what came to be known as the SEC primary after the collegiate Southeastern Conference that had a presence in most states. The RNC may have passed on attempting to craft rules facilitating regional primaries, but one developed nonetheless, although it was a date shared by eight other states and territories from outside the region, and was less encompassing than the 1988 Southern Super Tuesday. Despite the changes, however, and the emphasis on the potential impact of the SEC primary on the progress if not the outcome of the Republican nomination race, the date continued to serve as the point at which the frontrunning candidate surpassed the 25 percent mark in the delegate count.

Additionally, the delegate allocation rules changes the RNC put in place for 2016 were largely a wash in view of the similar delegate allocation trajectories of the two nominees in 2012 and 2016. Given the comparability across cycles, the tightening of the proportionality language appears to have been canceled out by the halving of the proportionality window in 2016 as compared to 2012. But that hinged to a great degree on the calendar and specifically how frontloaded it was. With a different mix of more or fewer states from different regions, the rate of delegate accrual may have been different.

Generally, Trump earned delegates at a rate that largely tracked with the rate at which all delegates were being allocated on the calendar. As the proportionality window closed on March 15, and half of all of the delegates had been allocated after the series of contests on that date, for example, he eclipsed the 50 percent mark in the number of delegates needed to win the nomination. Four years earlier, Romney, on the other hand, ran behind the pace of total delegates allocated. The former Massachusetts governor did not catch up to and surpass the pace of total delegates allocated in his own fraction of delegates needed for the nomination until 75 percent of the total delegates had been allocated.

There were differences. The 2016 calendar was, as intended, more compressed, coming in at forty-eight days shorter than in 2012. What's more, at least part of the impetus for the changes in the Republican binding rules for 2016 was to reduce the prevalence of unbound delegates. That there were so many unbound delegates in 2012 slowed down Romney's march to the nomination.

Competition also mattered (Norrander 2000). Romney began to win delegates at a faster clip and caught up to the overall allocation pace once Rick Santorum withdrew from the race in mid-April. That occurred despite the unbound delegates layered into the process that cycle. Trump, on the other hand, faced viable competition deeper into the calendar than did Romney. Yet, Ted Cruz and John Kasich staying in until after the Indiana primary at the beginning of May did not pull Trump's trajectory off, nor did it allow him to exceed the overall pace with so few contests left on the calendar at that point. Trump's surge to the nomination happened on the last day of primary season where delegate-rich California was scheduled on the calendar alongside several other much smaller states.

In the end, the RNC got a much more orderly calendar in 2016. There was less chaos at the front due to the new stricter penalties, and all fifty-six contests fit into a more compressed window relative to 2012. But the process, despite an unconventional frontrunner, moved through the rules as it typically does. The invisible primary produced a clear frontrunner and primary season elevated that frontrunner to presumptive nominee status by the end of the calendar in many of the same ways that it had in 2012. While the frontrunner may have added an element of chaos to the overall proceedings and invited some resistance within the broader party coalition, the process itself—the rules—did not.

The Democrats: A System Largely Unchanged Goes Under the Microscope in 2015–2016

Rules in the Invisible Primary

The Democratic Party also had an unconventional outsider running in 2016. But Bernie Sanders, a self-described Democratic-Socialist, had a rise to prominence that played out differently in 2015 than Donald Trump's did on the Republican side. Whereas Trump entered the race in June 2015 and nearly immediately shot to the top of the polls in the Republican contest, Sanders did not. Sanders rose more gradually against a prohibitive frontrunner. Whereas Trump entered a contest with some variation on the rules that had existed in 2012 and had to on some level adapt as his competition did, Sanders entered the Democratic race as an outsider operating in a system of rules that had changed little relative to 2012. His campaign had to face the start-up costs of learning those carried-over rules while the Clinton campaign, full of seasoned hands, did not. By contrast there were varying levels of rules-related start-up costs across the Republican field.

The Democrats' rules had not changed from the ones adopted in the summer of 2010 for the 2012 cycle other than the base number of delegates at stake across all fifty-seven primaries and caucuses being reduced by five hundred. Everything else was the same. And that Clinton was such a prohibitive favorite not only froze most of the potentially viable candidates from entering the race, but it also squelched activity on the state level as well. After the midterms of 2010 and 2014, there were not many remaining states with unified Democratic control of state government. And in the seven states with unified Democratic control after 2014, there was little motivation to move around primaries on the calendar in order to position for a nomination race that looked like a foregone conclusion (Putnam 2015a). That was especially true during the first half of 2015 when state legislatures were in session and could make changes, to better position contests and/or help out candidates.

None of the seven unified Democratic states made any changes. State legislators had little reason to suspect, when Sanders announced the formation of an exploratory committee in April 2015, that the candidacy of an outsider would take off. There was no urgency in those states to move a primary to a different date, whether it hypothetically would have been done to positively or negatively affect the Vermont senator. State-level inaction signaled that the conventional wisdom there seemed to be that Clinton was going to win. And if that was the case, then there was little need to push to the front of the queue in order to grab the candidates' attention in a race that looked like it would be over early.

Clinton's advantage also froze the DNC preparations for other elements of the race, namely the primary debates. Given the minor changes to the overall rules of the nomination process, the national party was behaving as if it was laying the groundwork for an incumbent renomination. That extended to preparations for the primary debates as well. The DNC did not announce its slate of debates until August 6, the day that the Republican candidates were to have their first debate in Cleveland. In stark contrast, the RNC had not only created a standing committee to officially sanction debates, but the resulting committee publicly released the schedule in January 2015 (Dann 2015). The DNC, by comparison, appeared flat-footed and less than transparent at a point in the race where Clinton's polling advantage had trailed off some, although it remained a slightly more than 30-point advantage on the date the Democratic debate schedule was released.

While invisible primary inaction was a significant issue in several facets of the process with respect to the rules, there was one clear area of rules-based activity as summer transitioned to fall in 2015. The Clinton campaign had the public backing of more than half of the 712 superdelegates as of mid-November 2015 (Ochlemacher 2015). And that disparity continued (and grew) as the race moved into primary season in 2016. It was an ever-present manifestation of the institutional support the former secretary of state had in the race despite the fact that her advantage in the polls had dipped below 15 percent on the eve of the Iowa caucuses (Cohen et al. 2008). But that superdelegate lead—one built before any votes had been cast—was a point of contention throughout primary season and beyond.

Rules in Primary Season

As primary season kicked off in Iowa, Clinton began to follow the path Obama forged in the early states in 2008. She narrowly won in Iowa, lost in New Hampshire, won in Nevada, and won handily in South Carolina. That served as a springboard to the Super Tuesday series of primaries and caucuses on the heels of the four February carve-out state contests. The SEC primary-heavy Super Tuesday provided a boost to Clinton, increasing a *pledged* delegate lead established after the Nevada caucuses and never relinquished. And that was a lead built on the support of African-American voters not only in the South but elsewhere as well.

Another pattern that emerged over primary season—outside of those regional differences—was the level of success that Clinton and Sanders enjoyed in states based on participation type. Sanders consistently outperformed Clinton in the caucus states after February (see figure 5.3 below). The Clinton caucus wins in Iowa and Nevada came in the early calendar, positions where the Clinton campaign was more organized than it was in later caucus states. Even then, Sanders only narrowly lost both contests. But the enthusiasm of his caucus supporters overran any organization Clinton's team had in those later caucuses. Moreover, the Vermont senator also excelled in states where primaries were open to independents. Clinton, on the other hand, did well in both primaries closed off to all but registered Democrats, and in the (mostly southern) open primary states with no party registration.

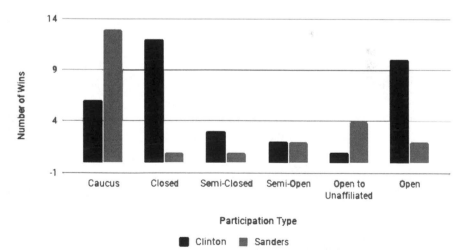

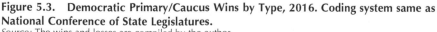

Figure 5.3.   Democratic Primary/Caucus Wins by Type, 2016. Coding system same as National Conference of State Legislatures.
Source: The wins and losses are compiled by the author.

And those trends largely held throughout primary season. The pledged delegate lead Clinton established after Nevada and expanded on Super Tuesday never dissipated. Under the proportional allocation rules mandated by the DNC nomination process, Clinton was never able to break away, while Sanders could not catch up. So long as both candidates continued to win contests—and both did into June—the difference in the delegate count only changed at the margins. And although the superdelegate advantage for Clinton was viewed by the Sanders campaign and their supporters as an unfair institutional bonus for Clinton before any voters participated, their addition to the delegate count was superfluous. Clinton comfortably won in the pledged delegate count. Nonetheless, those early superdelegate endorsements—delegates in Clinton's column—were an important and mostly unified signal of established party support for the former Democratic nomination runner-up.

The marginal rules changes did raise the share of the total number of superdelegates (14.9 percent) to around the average level during the superdelegate era in the Democratic process (14.7 percent). And while the other delegate allocation rules remained unchanged relative to 2012, the split in where Clinton and Sanders did well triggered a discussion about participation focused on impediments to voting layered into the caucus process or in allowing unaffiliated voters to participate (as a means of drawing them into the party). Those points of nomination phase tension all quickly became fodder for discussions of future rules changes starting at the Democratic National Convention in Philadelphia.

FROM 2016 TO 2020: ROLE REVERSAL ON RULES CHANGES

As primary season came to a close at the national conventions, the focus in both parties was squarely on formally nominating either Hillary Clinton or Donald Trump and setting the stage for the 2016 general election. But that was not the only business at either convention. Contentious convention Rules Committee meetings on both sides saw not only the dredging up of the implementation of the rules during the 2016 primaries and caucuses, but extensive discussions over the respective rules packages that would be adopted by the full convention, the precursors to the 2020 rules.

As courses for prospective 2020 rules changes emerged from both national conventions, their trajectories were conditioned by the results of the general election. Both parties' extra-convention bodies were set to examine rules, but one party would be more motivated to make changes—to correct the problems of the 2016 cycle—than the other. Donald Trump's election put

Republicans back in the White House and charted the Democrats on a quest to right the wrongs of the past cycle with an eye toward the next one.

The Republicans: If It Ain't Broke, Don't Fix It . . . and Protect President Trump

In the week leading up to the Republican National Convention in Cleveland, the convention Rules Committee convened to hammer out a rules package that it could collectively send to the floor for consideration by the full convention. In a marathon session that stretched well into the evening, the committee essentially maintained the status quo (Putnam 2016b). The ability of the RNC to make rules changes to the nomination outside of the convention was retained.[12] Both the calendar and allocation rules[13] and the penalties for violation[14] were left untouched, and a temporary committee was created to examine the need for rules changes on either front outside of the convention. The committee also more forcefully defined the binding rules in the face of an effort among a faction of Trump detractors in the group to unbind the delegates on the floor, opening up the nomination. And finally the committee walked back the controversial 2012 convention changes that lowered the threshold to have a candidate's name placed in nomination back to a plurality of delegates in at least five states.[15] Ultimately that package was adopted by the full convention and provided the predicate for the 2020 rules. But the convention Rules Committee also shunted the bulk of the consideration of rules changes for 2020 to the Temporary Committee on Presidential Nominations, placing the decision making on the shoulders of the RNC Rules Committee outside of the national convention.

Once in the White House, the Republican Party in 2017 quietly looked at a set of delegate selection rules that were left largely unchanged at the national convention and had successfully nominated a candidate who went on to win the general election. The urgency, then, behind the considerations of the Temporary Committee on Presidential Nominating Process (TCPNP) was low. Ideally, the task of the TCPNP was similar to that of the Democratic Change Commission in 2009 after Barack Obama had been elected: to carry over the rules that had nominated the new president and make any necessary changes to ensure that the party's president is reelected. Two of the ideas that came out of the TCPNP that the RNC Rules Committee discussed were, first, to incentivize caucus states to transition to primaries, and second, to reconsider the necessity of the debates committee created for the 2016 cycle (Putnam 2018a). The impetus behind the first proposal was President Trump's performance in caucuses in 2016. It was not a format, particularly in the handful of unbound delegation states, where the president's campaign had found any sustained success. And the advantages of eliminating the debates committee were apparent as well. It not only got the RNC out of the business of having to *not* sanction debates if someone were to challenge Trump in 2020, but it also helped the president by not creating debates that would give a platform to any would-be challenger.

The Rules Committee took up both proposals, but never came to any consensus on how to motivate states to shift from caucuses to primaries. However, it did pass on to the full RNC a recommendation for ending the Standing Committee on Presidential Primary Debates, a recommendation that was passed by the RNC (Putnam 2018b). And that became the one change the RNC instituted for the 2020 cycle. With another pass—this time outside of the convention—nothing was touched with respect to the calendar or allocation rules or penalties.

The Democrats: Change Is Going to Come

Following the Republican National Convention, the Democratic Party convened in Philadelphia and went down a similar path. Like the Republicans, the Democrats' convention Rules and Bylaws Committee got bogged down in the real and perceived problems leftover from the Clinton-Sanders battle in the 2016 primaries. Quickly, the pre-convention meeting divided along Clinton-Sanders lines until a compromise was reached, chartering a Unity Reform Commission to examine the 2016 issues with an eye toward remedying them before 2020.[16] The unity amendment created a body with nine Clinton appointees, seven Sanders appointees, and left three additional appointees to be named by the DNC chair elected in 2017. That placed significance on the party chair election because those three appointees could boost Clinton's advantage on the Unity Reform Commission or give Sanders the slightest of edges on the commission. Specifically, the amendment called on the new commission to examine both participation in primaries and caucuses (with an eye toward increasing it) and the role of superdelegates in the Democratic presidential nomination process (with explicit instructions to reduce their number by two thirds). It would be a return to the regular rhythms of a post-convention commission exploring future rules changes after a one-cycle hiatus in the lead-up to 2016.

Consideration of rules changes on the Democratic side following Trump's 2016 win was more active as is to be expected of parties out of the White House. And that process picked up in the first quarter of 2017 where it left off at the national convention the year before. The intended next step in the rules-making sequence laid out in the unity amendment that emerged from

Philadelphia hinged on the election of a new DNC chair. The election battle that ensued became an extension of the Clinton-Sanders divide that developed during 2016. Former labor secretary Tom Perez, who had the backing of President Obama, was the establishment proxy while Representative Keith Ellison was the stand-in for the progressive faction in the DNC. Perez narrowly won and, in a show of unity, named Ellison his vice chair. But Perez also won the ability to name the final three members of the Unity Reform Commission, a group that would be slightly more weighted toward the establishment end with twelve total Perez or Clinton appointments to Sanders's seven.

The DNC formally announced the members of the group in April 2017 and after fact-finding efforts and regional meetings, they met in Washington, DC, in December 2017 to make their final recommendations (Marans 2017). Over the course of the two-day meeting, the Unity Reform Commission (URC), despite its naturally fractious membership, came to consensus on most of what it would recommend to the Rules and Bylaws Committee. Part of the reason for the unanimity on nearly every recommended change was that the group was working from a draft report on which agreement had been forged on most points. Yet both the urgency of completing its task on time and the Clinton-Sanders divisions on the committee drove dissent on at least one item in each of the three rules areas.

On primaries, the group unanimously agreed to encourage the use of primaries in states with a government-run option available[17] and to require states and state parties to tamp down on voter suppression and other onerous registration requirements where possible. However, the URC voted down a proposal offered by Sanders surrogate and former campaign manager Jeff Weaver to additionally require states and state parties to open their primaries to unaffiliated voters under threat of penalty from the national party.[18]

While the URC also had wide-ranging discussions on the superdelegates issue, the unity amendment that chartered the group at the national convention tied the hands of the commission on the matter. The commission had to create a proposal to shift roughly two thirds of the superdelegates—the DNC members—from unpledged to bound. That required a vote to create a third category of delegates—bound delegates—that drew a pair of symbolic votes in dissent. But that was the only break from the unanimity on the superdelegates recommendations. The URC signed off on a couple of proposals for how to accomplish the reduction in the number of superdelegates.

Rules and Bylaws Committee

As the Unity Reform Commission report went before the DNC Rules and Bylaws Committee in early 2018, the tenor of the discussion changed from

Clinton versus Sanders, a dynamic that had colored the URC meetings, to one focused on taking the recommendations from the report and translating them into actual rules (Putnam 2017d). That proved easier for some recommendations than others. Most of the new requirements and encouragements concerning increasing participation in primaries and caucuses were tackled with a series of additions to Rule 2 in the DNC delegate selection rules.[19]

With respect to the superdelegates question, the RBC rejected the two complex formulas raised in the URC report. In their place, the committee tried to thread the needle on reducing the role of superdelegates in the Democratic nomination process with a simpler proposal. Rather than reducing their number by making DNC members bound delegates, the RBC plan kept them unpledged but stripped the superdelegates of voting rights on the first nomination ballot at the national convention unless a presumptive nominee had emerged with a delegate advantage larger than the total number of superdelegates.

THE 2020 INVISIBLE PRIMARY
AND UNINTENDED CONSEQUENCES OF CHANGE

Although there was some dissension at the August 2018 DNC meeting against the superdelegates changes in particular, the full DNC adopted the complete package of changes from the RBC. And while that specific change was labeled "dramatic" in the press, the result is more nuanced than that (Carter and Gonyea 2018). No Democratic convention has gone past the first ballot on the presidential nomination vote in the post-reform era. Under that reasoning, if a presumptive nominee is clear by the time of the 2020 convention, then the superdelegates are likely to participate in the first vote as usual, representing no net change relative to 2016 and other prior cycles.

However, with a larger field of Democratic presidential candidates in 2020 and a more frontloaded calendar because of California leaping from June to March, the potential is there, especially if the field does not winnow fast enough, that the pledged delegate count will be split in ways that could keep the superdelegates out of the first vote at the convention. The rules changes instituted in response to 2016, then, do not necessarily fit with the conditions of 2020, raising the likelihood of unintended consequences (Putnam 2015a). This has been the nature of delegate selection rule changes in the post-reform era.

Nevertheless, that only addresses the reduced part of the role superdelegates typically play. The part that was so controversial in 2016 to Sanders, his allies, and supporters was left untouched by the DNC during its quadrennial tinkering with the rules. While superdelegate voting privileges may have been curbed under certain conditions, their role earlier in the process remained intact. Just as superdelegates lined up behind Hillary Clinton in 2014–2015, they retained the ability to do just that in the 2020 cycle.

The question is, will they continue to exercise that role? If they do, in whole or in part, that traditionally plays some role in how and how quickly the field of candidates narrows over the invisible primary period. But if any elected officials feel any pressure to remain silent, frozen by memories of the 2016 division over the role of superdelegates, then that may hinder the winnowing process. That, in turn, would make the split pledged delegate count scenario more likely and keep superdelegates out of that first convention vote.

While that was the big ticket item in the rules changes adopted by the DNC in 2018, it was not the only rules change of consequence. The progress of the new encouragements for caucus states may have played some small role in nudging some traditionally caucus states toward primaries. As of April 2019, seven states—Colorado,[20] Idaho,[21] Maine,[22] Minnesota,[23] Nebraska,[24] Utah,[25] and Washington state[26]—have all made moves in the direction of conducting primaries in 2020. Most of the seven will have primary options and the early evidence from draft delegate selection plans from state parties in those states is that the new government-run primaries will be utilized for delegate allocation.

Although that overall change is consistent with the DNC encouragement of using primaries where available, the push seems to have been more bottom up from the states than top down and based on the rules changes. Four of the seven states made changes in or before 2017 prior to when the URC report was issued. And another, Idaho, chose the primary option before the DNC adopted the final rules for 2020. In many cases, administrative issues with overrun 2016 caucuses pushed state parties toward primaries.[27] But even in the remaining handful of caucus states, the evidence from early draft delegate selection plans is that the traditional caucus will become a relic of the past. Most of the later caucus states—other than Iowa and Nevada—have moved toward the "firehouse caucus" model of party-run primaries and with early voting that will operate under several variations of ranked choice voting. That is no small change. And again, overall it is consistent with the DNC push to increase participation in the process. But it does come at the expense of Sanders or Sanders-like candidates who can harness the enthusiasm of participants in the higher demand, lower turnout format. That will impact how candidates approach caucus states and may affect the progress of primary season in 2020.

One additional change that was not made and codified through the Democratic rules process as it was on the Republican side for the 2016 cycle concerned primary debates. That matter was handled by the chair but outside of the rules-making process. The rules devised in that area, too, may have an impact on how the 2020 Democratic nomination race progresses. Rather than separating candidates into tiers—a top and a bottom—like the RNC did in 2016, the DNC planned to separate the candidates into two groups of no more than ten candidates each, but to do so randomly. Additionally the qualifications for the initial couple of rounds of debates set a low bar (Putnam 2019a). Candidates were able to qualify by polling at 1 percent or higher in any of three polls approved by the party or by the breadth of a candidate's grassroots fundraising base. The latter is set at 65,000 donors across at least twenty states with no fewer than two hundred donors per state. Those debates may also have an effect on the extent to which the field of Democratic candidates winnows and how quickly. And that is particularly true if the DNC imposes incremental increases in what it takes for candidates to qualify for debates over time.

The invisible primary in 2019 and beyond will be marked by that question about winnowing. More than anything else, the answer about the extent to which the field winnows matters most for how the 2020 Democratic process under a new set of rules will fare. If the field winnows some in the invisible primary and that continues to pick up pace as votes begin to be cast in 2020, then the changes will likely have a minimal impact. However, if that process is slow and multiple candidates hang around deeper into primary season, then that could make the rules changes made with 2016 in mind ill-fitting for a 2020 race waged under far different conditions.

NOTES

1. And that latter state-level change was large enough—a shift of more than four hundred pledged delegates from near the end of the primary calendar in one cycle to near the beginning in the next—that it was raised on more than one occasion as both the Unity Reform Commission and the DNC Rules and Bylaws Committee considered rules changes for the 2020 cycle during 2017–2018.

2. The committee was empowered to examine the delegate selection section of the overall Rules of the Republican Party outside of the convention. Nevertheless, the TDSC could only make recommendations for changes to the rules adopted by the 2008 convention for the 2012 cycle.

3. See the 2012 Rules of the Republican Party at http://www.scribd.com/doc/122649980/2012-Rules-of-the-Republican-Party.

4. See the Growth and Opportunity Project report at https://www.scribd.com/document/131083498/RNC-Growth-and-Opportunity-Project-Report-2013.

5. See the language of the super penalty in Rule 17(a) of the 2012 Rules of the Republican Party and a further discussion of the implications in Putnam, 2015b,

"The 2016 RNC Super Penalty," *Frontloading HQ* at https://frontloading.blogspot.com/2015/01/the-2016-rnc-super-penalty.html.

6. See the language for Rule 10(h) in the 2012 Rules of the Republican Party and a further discussion of the change at Josh Putnam, "RNC Creates New Rule Dealing with Presidential Primary Debates." *Frontloading HQ.* May 12, 2014. https://frontloading.blogspot.com/2014/05/rnc-creates-new-rule-dealing-with.html.

7. The nominating conventions in both 2000 and 2008 bottled up two different regional primary systems: the Delaware plan first and then the Ohio plan. Neither George W. Bush in 2000, John McCain in 2008, nor those in their respective orbits running the conventions saw the need for wholesale changes to a nomination system in which both had been successful one cycle or the other. Additionally, neither campaign wanted to change the status quo enough that it would potentially open the door to a future challenge to either candidate's renomination. The Ohio and Delaware plans were both top-down approaches that never fully addressed the obstacles that state governments (especially but not limited to those controlled by the Democratic Party) and state parties represented fully implementing either plan. Regional primaries, to the extent they have existed in the post-reform era, have come to fruition as a function of efforts on the state level, not from the national level. That was true of the Southern Super Tuesday that was formed by Democratic state actors for the 1988 presidential nomination cycle, but also for a number of subregional primaries like the 1996 Great Lakes primary or the 2008 Potomac primary that been formed since the McGovern-Fraser reforms altered the system.

8. It also reacted by altering the requirements to place a candidate's name on the nomination ballot (Rule 40 of the 2012 Rules of the Republican Party).

9. See 2012 Call for the Democratic National Convention.

10. See 2016 Call for the Democratic National Convention at https://www.scribd.com/document/254593792/2016-Call-for-the-Convention; and 2016 Democratic Party Delegate Selection Rules at https://www.scribd.com/doc/237924369/2016-Democratic-Delegate-Selection-Rules.

11. See Huffington Post Pollster, "2016 National Republican Primary" polling aggregation at https://elections.huffingtonpost.com/pollster/2016-national-gop-primary.

12. Rule 12 of the 2012 Rules of the Republican Party.

13. Rule 16 of the 2012 Rules of the Republican Party.

14. Rule 17 of the 2012 Rules of the Republican Party.

15. Rule 40 of the 2012 Rules of the Republican Party.

16. See "Resolution Establishing the Unity Reform Commission" at https://www.scribd.com/document/319155068/Unity-Reform-Commission-Charter; and "The Democrats' Unity Reform Commission" at https://frontloading.blogspot.com/2016/07/the-democrats-unity-reform-commission.html.

17. There was broad agreement on the need to increase participation in caucuses by requiring caucus state parties to devise some form of absentee voting to parallel the regular caucus process and to transition to a "firehouse caucus" model that would operate more like a party-run primary than a traditional caucus. However, the commission was at odds about whether to presume states with government-run primary options available would use that option rather than a caucus/convention system. In

theory the caucus subgroup liked the idea enough to include in the draft report a proposal to apply that presumption to larger states only. But an amendment from Clinton appointee, David Huynh, to broaden that application to include all states regardless of size derailed the effort entirely. The amendment was tabled, the issue was something to which the commission did not return, and no presumption was included in the eventual recommendations. See Putnam 2017c.

18. The vote divided the commission along Clinton-Sanders lines and was voted down, 11–6.

19. The basis of Rule 2 of the Democratic Party delegate selection rules is to provide guidelines for the demonstrable steps to be taken by state parties on participation. That shift would place a burden on the state parties to prove to the RBC that actions were taken in developing delegate selection plans to increase participation. Under the proposed changes if the efforts were insufficient, then the RBC would reject the plan and require revisions.

20. See Josh Putnam, "A 2020 Presidential Primary in Colorado," *Frontloading HQ*, May 22, 2017, at http://frontloading.blogspot.com/2017/05/a-2020-presidential -primary-in-colorado.html.

21. See Josh Putnam, "Idaho Democrats Announce Shift from 'Unwieldy' Caucuses to State-Funded Presidential Primary for 2020," *Frontloading HQ*, July 9, 2018, at https://frontloading.blogspot.com/2018/07/idaho-democrats-announce-shift -from.html.

22. The 2016 adoption of a primary in Maine expired toward the end of 2018.

23. See Josh Putnam, "Dayton Signs Minnesota Presidential Primary Bill," *Frontloading HQ*, May 23, 2016, at http://frontloading.blogspot.com/2016/05/dayton -signs-minnesota-presidential.html.

24. See Josh Putnam, "Nebraska Democrats Opt to Move Back to Presidential Primary for 2020," *Frontloading HQ*, December 8, 2018, at https://frontloading .blogspot.com/2018/12/nebraska-democrats-opt-to-move-back-to.html.

25. See Josh Putnam, "Utah Democrats Will Use New Presidential Primary Option for 2020," *Frontloading HQ*, April 9, 2019, at https://frontloading.blogspot .com/2019/04/utah-democrats-will-use-new.html.

26. See Josh Putnam, "Washington State Democrats Opt for Presidential Primary Over Caucuses," *Frontloading HQ*, April 8, 2019, https://frontloading.blogspot .com/2019/04/washington-state-democrats-opt-for.html.

27. For a broader discussion of the 2016 logistical problems faced in caucus states see Josh Putnam, "Idaho Democrats Announce Shift from 'Unwieldy' Caucuses to State-Funded Presidential Primary for 2020," *Frontloading HQ*, July 9, 2018, at https://frontloading.blogspot.com/2018/07/idaho-democrats-announce-shift-from .html.

REFERENCES

Carter, Brandon, and Don Gonyea. 2018. "DNC Votes to Largely Strip 'Superdelegates' of Presidential Nominating Power." *Weekend Edition Saturday*, NPR.org.

August 25, 2018. https://www.npr.org/2018/08/25/641725402/dnc-set-to-reduce -role-of-superdelegates-in- presidential-nominating-process.

Cohen, Marty, David Karol, Hans Noel, and John Zaller. 2008. *The Party Decides: Presidential Nominations Before and After Reform*. Chicago: University of Chicago Press.

Dann, Carrie. 2015. "Democrats Announce 2016 Primary Debate Schedule." NBC news.com. August 6, 2015. https://www.nbcnews.com/politics/2016-election/ democrats-announce-2016-primary-debate-schedule-n405161.

Klinkner, Philip A. 1994. *Losing Parties: Out-Party National Committees, 1956– 1993*. New Haven, CT: Yale University Press.

Lavender, Paige. 2015. "2016 GOP Primary Schedule Announced by RNC." Huff Post.com January 16, 2015. https://www.huffpost.com/entry/2016-presidential -debates_n_6488380.

Marans, Daniel. 2017. "DNC Announces Members of Unity Reform Commission." Huffpost.com. April 17, 2017. https://www.huffpost.com/entry/dnc-unity-reform - commission_n_58f50d1fe4b0b9e9848d92eb.

Mayer, William G., and Andrew E. Busch. 2004. *The Front-Loading Problem in Presidential Nominations*. Washington, DC: Brookings Institution Press.

Norrander, Barbara. 2000. "The End Game in Post-Reform Presidential Nominations." *Journal of Politics* 62 (4): 999–1013.

Ochlemacher, Stephen. 2015. "Big Nomination Lead for Clinton: Pocketing 'Super-delegates'" APNews.com. November 13, 2015. https://www.apnews.com/98c6fd8 2b5154d01ae2bc998f69d4f23.

O'Keefe, Ed. 2013. "RNC Votes to Exclude CNN, NBC from 2016 Presidential Primary Debates." *The Washington Post*. August 16, 2013. http://www.wash ingtonpost.com/blogs/post-politics/wp/2013/08/16/rnc-to-consider-excluding-cnn -nbc-from-2016-presidential-debates/.

Polsby, Nelson. 1983. *Consequences of Party Reform*. New York: Oxford University Press.

Putnam, Joshua T. 2010. *The Frontloading of Presidential Primaries and Caucuses from the States' Perspective*. PhD dissertation, University of Georgia.

Putnam, Josh. 2014. "RNC Creates New Rule Dealing with Presidential Primary Debates." *Frontloading HQ*. May 12, 2014. https://frontloading.blogspot .com/2014/05/rnc-creates-new-rule-dealing-with.html.

———. 2015a. "Post-2014 State Government Partisan Control and 2016 Presidential Primary Movement." *Frontloading HQ*. January 15, 2015. https://frontloading .blogspot.com/search?q=Post-2014+State+Government+Partisan+Control+and+2 016+Presidential+Primary+Movement.

———. 2015b. "The 2016 RNC Super Penalty." *Frontloading HQ*. January 29, 2015. https://frontloading.blogspot.com/2015/01/the-2016-rnc-super-penalty.html.

———. 2015c. "Post-2014 State Government Partisan Control and 2016 Presidential Primary Movement." *Frontloading HQ*. January 15, 2015. https://frontloading .blogspot.com/2015/01/post-2014-state-government-partisan.html.

———. 2016a. "Dayton Signs Minnesota Presidential Primary Bill." *Frontloading HQ*. May 23. 2016. http://frontloading.blogspot.com/2016/05/dayton-signs-minne sota-presidential.html.

———. 2016b. "Five Takeaways from the 2016 Convention Rules Committee Meeting." *Frontloading HQ*. July 17, 2016. https://frontloading.blogspot.com/2016/07/five-takeaways-from-2016-convention.html.

———. 2017a. "A 2020 Presidential Primary in Colorado" *Frontloading HQ* May 22, 2017. http://frontloading.blogspot.com/2017/05/a-2020-presidential-primary-in-colorado.html.

———. 2017b. "Brown's Signature Sends California Primary Back to Super Tuesday for 2020." *Frontloading HQ*. September 27, 2017. http://frontloading.blogspot.com/2017/09/browns-signature-sends-california.html.

———. 2017c. "Unity Reform Commission: Caucuses Recommendations." *Frontloading HQ*. December 15, 2017. https://frontloading.blogspot.com/2017/12/unity-reform-commission-caucuses.html.

———. 2017d. "DNC Unity Reform Commission Report." *Frontloading HQ*. December 22, 2017. https://frontloading.blogspot.com/2017/12/dnc-unity-reform-commission-report.html.

———. 2018a. "2020 Republican Rules Changes, Part Two: Early Proposals" Frontloading HQ. March 6, 2018. https://frontloading.blogspot.com/2018/03/2020-republican-rules-changes-part-two.html.

———. 2018b. "Protecting the President? RNC Eliminates Primary Debates Committee." *Frontloading HQ*. May 6, 2018. https://frontloading.blogspot.com/2018/05/protecting-president-rnc-eliminates.html.

———. 2018c. "Idaho Democrats Announce Shift from 'Unwieldy' Caucuses to State-Funded Presidential Primary for 2020." *Frontloading HQ*. July 9, 2018. https://frontloading.blogspot.com/2018/07/idaho-democrats-announce-shift-from.html.

———. 2018d. "Nebraska Democrats Opt to Move Back to Presidential Primary for 2020." *Frontloading HQ*. December 8, 2018. https://frontloading.blogspot.com/2018/12/nebraska-democrats-opt-to-move-back-to.html.

———. 2019a. "#InvisiblePrimary: Visible: The DNC Debate Qualification Rules Are In." *Frontloading HQ*. February 14, 2019. http://frontloading.blogspot.com/2019/02/invisibleprimary-visible-dnc-debate.html.

———. 2019b. "Washington State Democrats Opt for Presidential Primary Over Caucuses" *Frontloading HQ*. April 8, 2019. https://frontloading.blogspot.com/2019/04/washington-state-democrats-opt-for.html.

———. 2019c. "Utah Democrats Will Use New Presidential Primary Option for 2020." *Frontloading HQ*. April 9, 2019. https://frontloading.blogspot.com/2019/04/utah-democrats-will-use-new.html.

Reiter, Howard L. 1985. *Selecting the President: The Nominating Process in Transition*. Philadelphia: University of Pennsylvania Press.

Chapter Six

The Short and Mostly Dismal History of Nomination Straw Polls

William G. Mayer

Throughout the invisible primary—the long period that runs for roughly a year before the first actual delegate selection event—political reporters are constantly on the lookout for ways to handicap the presidential nomination races: to make plausible guesses about how the various candidates are faring, who has the best organization, whose message is catching on with the voters, who has that elusive quality known as momentum. A number of indicators are available: polls of national party members or of potential voters in key early states like Iowa and New Hampshire; fund-raising totals; crowd sizes; elite endorsements. The 1976 election added another item to the list: straw polls.

In the context of the presidential nomination process, a straw poll or straw vote—the two terms are used interchangeably—is a nonbinding preference vote, usually conducted at some kind of party conclave or a meeting of an allied interest group.[1] In particular, the results of straw polls have no direct effect on the selection of national convention delegates. (If they do, then they should not be labeled straw polls.)

Though they are both called "polls," straw polls are very different from the public opinion polls or sample surveys that are also a ubiquitous feature of the contemporary nomination process. Whatever the details, the essence of all sample surveys is to contact and interview a small group of people who can be considered representative of some larger population, such as American adults, national party identifiers, or likely primary voters. Straw polls, by contrast, are not obviously representative of anybody. Unlike sample surveys, the participants in straw polls are self-selected. In a properly conducted survey, as opposed to the "call-in polls" that were once commonly conducted by radio and television stations, a person cannot get included in a survey just because he or she would like to take part in it.[2] But that is precisely the way one becomes a participant in a straw poll. This has sometimes led commentators to claim that straw polls are at least representative of highly motivated political activists, who clearly do play an important role in nomination contests, even if their support alone is not enough to win a nomination. As we will see, however, even this inference is quite problematic.

Though they have sometimes received extensive media coverage and had clear effects on some candidates and campaigns, there is, so far as I can determine, virtually no academic writing on the role of straw polls in the contemporary nomination process.[3] This chapter is an attempt to fill the void.

IDENTIFYING STRAW POLLS

Having defined what a straw poll is, the next step presumably is to locate actual straw polls, so we can start formulating some descriptive propositions about how many there are, when and where they are held, who wins them, and with what effect. As it turns out, however, this is difficult to do in any kind of systematic way. Unlike primaries, delegates, or primary votes, there is no official or semi-official agency that monitors straw polls. In the absence of such data, my next thought was to look for any straw polls that were mentioned in a major national news outlet such as the *New York Times*. But this approach also has its problems. Particularly during the 1976 election cycle, there were, so far as I can determine, no clear criteria that news organizations used to decide what was or was not labeled a straw poll. For example, on August 24, 1975, a short article in the *New York Times* said that Senator Birch Bayh of Indiana led all other candidates in a "straw poll" taken at a convention of the Young Democrats of America. Three months later, a survey taken at the National Democratic Issues Convention found that former vice president Hubert Humphrey was the leading choice of the delegates. For reasons that are not clear, this latter test of candidate preferences was called an "informal survey" rather than a straw poll.[4] Both of these articles were taken from the United Press International wire service, but there is no evidence that the *Times* itself used the term more rigorously. On November 17, 1975, a front-page story written by a *Times* reporter described a "county-by-county roll call" taken at a Florida Democratic state convention that was won by Jimmy Carter. But the same episode was called a "straw vote" in a *Washington Post* column published several days later, as well as in a May 1979 *Times* article that recounted the important role that vote had played in helping "lift Jimmy Carter from political obscurity" (Apple 1975; Evans and Novak 1975b; Raines 1979).

Whatever the terminology, there is good reason to believe that the straw polls mentioned in the *Times* and other major media are only the tip of the iceberg. The most dramatic evidence on this point comes from the 2012 Republican nomination contest. Between January 1, 2011, and January 2, 2012 (the day before that year's Iowa caucuses), the *New York Times* mentioned nine different straw polls. (Many of these straw polls, especially the Iowa Straw Poll of August 13, 2011, were referred to in numerous articles, but only nine distinct polls received at least one mention.)[5] In sharp contrast, a Wikipedia article titled "Straw Polls for the 2012 Republican Party Presidential Primaries" listed *fifty-six* such polls held between the same dates.[6] Unfortunately, Wikipedia compiled such an exhaustive list only for the 2012 race.

In the end, for most of the nomination races discussed here, I have used the following procedure for identifying straw polls. First, I have restricted my search to the invisible primary, which I define, for the purposes of this article, as the period between January 1 of the year before the election and the day before the start of the actual delegate selection season (meaning, in most years, the day before the Iowa caucuses).[7] Straw polls are sometimes held two years before the actual election, but they are rarely regarded as anything more than curiosities; many of the people who do well in such polls later decide not to become active candidates for their party's presidential nomination. Straw polls are also sometimes held after the Iowa caucuses, but by then political reporters and commentators are more concerned with the results of real, meaningful primaries and caucuses than with the unofficial, nonbinding straw polls.

Second, I have looked for any event labeled a "straw poll" or a "straw vote" in at least one of three major national publications: the *New York Times*, the *Washington Post*, and *Congressional Quarterly Weekly Report*.[8] In addition, for the 1976 and 1980 nomination races, I have included any event mentioned in the *New York Times Index* that seemed to have all the attributes of a straw poll, even if it was not explicitly described as such. Though this method is an attempt to cast the net more widely then if I relied on information from a single news organization, I have no illusions that I have found every straw poll conducted during these years. A better way to describe the data presented below is that they (hopefully) include every nomination-related straw poll that was deemed significant enough to be mentioned in one of the most thoroughgoing and highly regarded news organizations in the United States.

THE RISE OF STRAW POLLS: 1976–1984

1976. After a diligent search, I have been able to locate seven straw polls or straw-poll-like events that were held between January 1, 1975, and January 18, 1976. All were conducted by the Democrats. Details are shown in table 6.1.

In historical accounts of the 1976 presidential election, however, the only straw poll that is likely to be mentioned is the one that took place in Ames, Iowa, on October 25, 1975 (Witcover 1977; Schram 1977; Arterton 1978; Winebrenner and Goldford 2010). The Jefferson-Jackson Day Dinner was the major fund-raising event of the year for Iowa Democrats, and with the caucuses coming just three months later, seven presidential candidates showed up to give ten-minute speeches and schmooze with their fellow partisans, accompanied by a sizable gaggle of national political reporters. Though the paid dinner attendees were not obviously representative of Iowa Democrats

Table 6.1. Presidential Nomination Straw Polls Held during the 1976 Invisible Primary: Democrats

Event at Which the Straw Poll Was Conducted	Date	Number of Votes	Winner and Percentage	Second-Place Finisher and Percentage
Young Democrats of America National Convention	Aug. 23, 1975	611	Bayh 23	Carter 14
Iowa "Off Year" Caucuses	Sept. 22, 1975	5,762	Carter 10	Shriver 9
Iowa Jefferson-Jackson Day Dinner	Oct. 25, 1975	1,094	Carter 23	Humphrey 12
Florida Democratic Convention	Nov. 16, 1975	1,049	Carter 66	Shapp 6
National Democratic Issues Convention	Nov. 23, 1975	984	Humphrey 17	Bayh 17
Waterloo, Iowa, Fundraiser	Nov. 23, 1975	944	Bayh 29	Harris 20
Sioux City, Iowa, Fundraiser	Jan. 11, 1976	865*	Bayh 36	Carter 29

Source: Compiled by the author from straw polls or straw votes mentioned in the *New York Times*, the *Washington Post*, and *Congressional Quarterly Weekly Report*. Also includes similar events mentioned in the *New York Times Index*.
* indicates that the number of votes is an estimate.

or likely caucus-goers—tickets cost $50 a couple—the *Des Moines Register* decided to conduct a straw poll of their presidential preferences. By all accounts, Jimmy Carter's was the only campaign that made a serious effort to mobilize its supporters and thus try to influence the poll's outcome. (It was also probably the only campaign that had the capacity to do so.) The upshot was a clear victory for Carter. Though Carter won the support of just 23 percent of the poll participants, he ran far ahead of everybody else. Second place actually went to declared non-candidate Hubert Humphrey with 12 percent (all write-in votes), followed by Birch Bayh with 10 percent.[9]

Though few voters were paying close attention to the Democratic nomination race at this point, much less to an obscure Iowa fund-raising dinner, the political press did take notice—in a major way. Two days later, R. W. "Johnny" Apple, Jr., the influential national political correspondent for the *New York Times*, wrote an article that began, "Former Gov. Jimmy Carter of Georgia appears to have taken a surprising but solid lead in the contest for Iowa's 47 delegates to the Democratic National Convention. . . . [Carter] has made dramatic progress while attention was focused on the scramble for liberal primacy."[10] It took the *Washington Post* a bit longer to interpret the tea leaves, but one day after Apple's article, Jules Witcover declared that Carter, "by demonstrating surprising early strength in Iowa, appears well along in his strategy to win recognition as the 'sleeper' Democratic candidate" of the 1976 race (Witcover 1975).

As a result of the press coverage it received, the Jefferson-Jackson Day straw poll had two important effects on the Democratic race. First, it transformed Jimmy Carter from an inconspicuous also-ran into someone who seemed like he had a real chance of winning the Democratic nomination—and therefore had to be taken more seriously by the media. The Apple story in particular, *New Yorker* political correspondent Elizabeth Drew would later note, "was itself a political event, prompting other newspaper stories that Carter was doing well in Iowa, and then more news magazine and television coverage for Carter than might otherwise have been his share." Said another national reporter, "When Jonny [*sic*] Apple writes a story on the front page of the *New York Times* out of the blue, ordaining a new phenomenon, that . . . was the most important single event in the relationship between the media and Jimmy Carter."[11]

Second, the straw poll and the stories it generated also convinced the media to devote more attention to the Iowa caucuses—which, in turn, affected the strategies of the other candidates. Prior to the October straw poll, Mo Udall had largely ignored Iowa in order to focus his energies on the New Hamp-

shire primary. Now he decided to shift ten precious days of personal campaign time to Iowa, where it proved too late to have much effect.[12] In the end,
Udall finished a weak fourth in Iowa but came in second in New Hampshire,
just a few percentage points behind Carter.

To return to table 6.1, of the seven straw polls shown there, Carter finished
first in three of them, second in two others. In addition to his widely heralded
success in Iowa, he also received a burst of favorable attention when he won
two thirds of the votes in a poll held at a Florida Democratic convention in
November, thereby establishing himself as essentially the only alternative to
George Wallace in that state's primary.[13]

But Carter was not the only candidate to show strength in such polls. As
table 6.1 indicates, Indiana senator Birch Bayh also won three straw polls,
including two in Iowa, and came in a close second to Hubert Humphrey in
a fourth poll. Bayh's straw poll victories received less press coverage than
Carter's, but shortly after one of his wins Evans and Novak wrote a syndi-
cated column in which they opined that Bayh had "suddenly emerged as the
liberal with the best chance of winning the Democratic presidential nomination in the primaries" (Evans and Novak 1975a). In Bayh's case, however,
the straw polls turned out to be quite misleading. Bayh was the second best
performing candidate in the Iowa caucuses, but his support in that event was
less than half of Jimmy Carter's. (Though it was widely ignored by the media, the real winner of the 1976 Iowa caucuses was "uncommitted." Where
Carter won 27 percent of the delegates to the next round of the Iowa delegate-
selection process, 37 percent were uncommitted.) Bayh then finished a weak
third in the New Hampshire primary and ran seventh in the Massachusetts
primary. Two days after Massachusetts, Bayh withdrew from the race
entirely.

The predictive record of the 1976 straw polls, in short, was actually rather
mixed. These polls did provide the first solid evidence about the appeal of
Jimmy Carter and the striking effectiveness of his campaign, at a time when
70 percent of the Americans questioned in a mass sample survey said they
didn't know who he was.[14] But straw polls significantly overestimated the
vote-getting prowess of Birch Bayh.

1980. Like generals, political reporters are prone to refight the last war.
Whatever their actual track record, the takeaway from 1976—the thing most
reporters remembered—was that straw polls had been an early sign of the po-
tency of the Carter campaign, a far better indicator, in retrospect, than elite endorsements, early public opinion polls (state or national), or fund-raising totals.

The result was that straw polls played a much more prominent part in the
1980 nomination races than they had in 1976. Table 6.2 shows two simple
measures of the difference. For both the *New York Times* and the *Washington
Post*, I have counted (a) the number of articles during each election cycle's

Table 6.2. Press Coverage of Straw Polls during the 1976 and 1980 Invisible Primaries

	1976	1980
New York Times		
No. of Articles That Mention a Straw Poll	13	80
No. of *Times* Articles in Which Straw Polls were the Principal Subject	4	26
Washington Post		
No. of Articles That Mention a Straw Poll	12	67
No. of *Post* Articles in Which Straw Polls Were the Principal Subject	2	24

Note: The invisible primary is defined as period between January 1 of the year before the election and the day before the Iowa Caucuses. Thus, the 1976 invisible primary runs from January 1, 1975 to January 18, 1976. The 1980 invisible primary runs from January 1, 1979 to January 20, 1980.
Source: Compiled by the author.

invisible primary period that included at least *one mention* of a straw poll or straw vote; and (b) the number of articles in which one or more straw polls was the *principal subject*.[15] The difference is striking. Of all the articles on the presidential campaign that the *New York Times* ran during 1975 and the first eighteen days of 1976, just thirteen included even the most fleeting mention of a straw poll, and in only four of those articles was a straw poll the principal subject.[16] (Three of these four articles were very short and buried well inside the paper, the famous Apple article being the lone exception.) During the comparable period in 1979 and 1980, the *New York Times* published eighty stories that mentioned at least one straw poll and in twenty-six cases it was the main topic of the story. The *Washington Post* data show a similar trend.

Whether as cause or as effect of the media's behavior, the presidential candidates and their campaigns also paid a lot more attention to straw polls during the 1980 race. During the 1976 invisible primary period, the exertions of the Carter campaign at the Jefferson-Jackson Day Dinner is the only instance I can find where a campaign made a notable effort to affect the outcome of a straw poll. By contrast, several straw polls held in 1979 were the scene of major, all-out battles between rival campaigns.

In the Battle for Early Attention: Straw Poll Edition, the state of Florida was the clear winner. On the weekend of November 17 and 18, the Florida Democratic and Republican parties each decided to hold a state convention, the sole apparent purpose of which was to conduct a nonbinding poll of the delegates' presidential preferences. The campaign of former Texas governor John Connally, determined to show that its candidate was the only person who could compete with Ronald Reagan in the South, decided to make the Florida straw poll the first demonstration of its vote-getting prowess. Connally accordingly spent an estimated $300,000 (more than $1 million in 2018 dollars) on a campaign that included television commercials, direct mail, numerous trips to the Sunshine State by the candidate and his family, and personal phone calls to many delegates. Though the Reagan campaign's strategy at that point was to keep its candidate "above the fray" and not engage with the other candidates, the prospect of losing to Connally and thus ending its aura of inevitability compelled the Reaganites to wage a counter-campaign that reportedly cost $250,000 (Broder 1979a, 1979b; Clymer 1979a, 1979b).

In an analogous way, the Florida Democratic convention emerged as the first major test of strength between Jimmy Carter's reelection campaign and what was, in the beginning, the Draft Kennedy movement.[17] To avoid the perception that the president was vulnerable even in his home region, the Carter campaign used all the considerable resources of the presidency to ensure a victory in the Florida straw poll: awarding and expediting federal grants to the state; appointing Floridians to executive branch positions; inviting Florida political leaders to the White House for special briefings; and sending a small army of administration officials and Carter family members to campaign on the president's behalf (Barbash 1979; Tolchin 1979).

Did all this campaigning and press coverage reveal anything useful about the state of the 1980 nomination races? At least on the Republican side, I believe it did. Straw polls provided the first indication that George H. W. Bush, like Jimmy Carter in 1976, was running an energetic campaign with a strong organization and had thereby gotten a jump on his rivals. In May 1979, when sample surveys showed him with the support of just 2 percent of the nation's Republicans, Bush won a solid victory in a straw poll taken at an Iowa fundraising dinner. Bush also won a string of five Iowa straw polls held in the fall of 1979, though only one of these, the first of the Ames straw polls, was covered in any detail (Kneeland 1979; Peterson 1979). Bush's most impressive straw poll victory may have been the one that occurred in Maine in early November. Senate Majority Leader Howard Baker, who had just announced his candidacy, was widely expected to win that poll, largely because he had the support of Maine senator William Cohen. So Baker dragged a considerable contingent of national political reporters up to the Maine Republican convention to witness his triumph—only to have Bush win the straw poll and thereby earn front-page coverage in both the *New York Times* and the *Washington Post* (Clymer 1979a; Lyons 1979). In mid-November, as noted earlier, a straw poll in Florida was generally portrayed as the first showdown between Reagan and Connally. Reagan handily beat Connally, but another major story line from this event was the "surprisingly strong" third-place showing of George Bush.[18] Of course, there was one crucial difference between Jimmy Carter's experience in 1976 and George Bush's record in 1980: Carter actually won his party's nomination; Bush fell short. But Bush did succeed in

Table 6.3. Presidential Nomination Straw Polls Held during the 1980 Invisible Primary

Party	Event at Which the Straw Poll Was Conducted	Date	Number of Votes	Winner and Percentage	Second-Place Finisher and Percentage
Democrats	Democratic National Committee Spring Meeting	May 25, 1979	170	Carter 69	Kennedy 26
	Virginia State Federation of Labor	Aug. 11, 1979	N/A	Kennedy 71	Carter 19
	Iowa Jefferson-Jackson Day Dinner	Nov. 3, 1979	2,224	Carter 71	Kennedy 26
	Democratic National Committee Fall Meeting	Nov. 9, 1979	157	Carter 64	Kennedy 28
	Florida Democratic Convention	Nov. 18, 1979	1,502	Carter 74	Kennedy 23
	Tennessee Democratic Fundraising Dinners	Dec. 8, 1979	1,685	Carter 85	Kennedy 14
	Los Angeles County Democratic Central Committee	Mid Dec. 1979	184	Carter 47	Kennedy 46
	California Democratic Platform Convention	Jan. 20, 1980	1,471	Kennedy 42	Carter 40
Republicans	Midwest Republican Leadership Conference	March 10, 1979	300*	Connally 29	Reagan 21
	Fundraising Dinner in Ames, Iowa	May 21, 1979	1,288	Bush 40	Reagan 26
	California Republican Convention	Sept. 16, 1979	728*	Reagan 72	Connally 18
	Ames, Iowa Straw poll	Oct. 13, 1979	1,454	Bush 36	Connally 15
	New England Republican Caucus	Oct. 27, 1979	327	Crane 50	Reagan 11
	Maine Republican Convention	Nov. 3, 1979	1,340	Bush 35	Baker 33
	Florida Republican Convention	Nov. 17, 1979	1,326	Reagan 36	Connally 27

* indicates that the number of votes is an estimate; N/A means that data on the number of voters are not available.
Source: Compiled by the author from contemporary news accounts, especially the *New York Times* and the *Washington Post.*

establishing himself as Reagan's principal competitor and thereby laid claim to the Republican vice presidential nomination.

It is more difficult to say just what, if anything, the straw polls said about the campaign of Ronald Reagan. For a consensus frontrunner, well ahead in all the national and state polls, Reagan's performance in the straw polls was hardly very impressive. Besides his victory in Florida, his only other triumph came in his home state of California. On the other hand, Florida excepted, there is little indication that the Reagan campaign put much effort into such matters. George Bush's numerous wins in Iowa straw polls might have alerted the Reagan high command that their lead in the low-turnout Iowa caucuses was not very secure, and that their strategy of keeping Reagan "above the fray" and refusing to engage with the other candidates was a complete misreading of the nature of contemporary nomination campaigns. But mass sample surveys and simple common sense should have told them the same thing.

The Democratic straw polls were less revealing. Carter prevailed in most of them. Not only was he the incumbent president and thus a heavy favorite among the sorts of party leaders and elected officials who often take part in straw polls, but the Carter campaign also had a huge organizational advantage. Though Carter did not formally announce his candidacy until December 4, 1979, he had filed his statement of candidacy with the Federal Election Commission (FEC) on March 16, and he and his advisors had clearly been planning his reelection drive well before that. Kennedy did not make his first FEC filing until October 29, and then had to create a national campaign from the ground up.[19] In the battle for delegates to the Florida convention, the Carter campaign was thus pitted not against a well-oiled Kennedy machine but a group of Draft Kennedy volunteers.

1984. To no one's surprise, straw polls also played a major role in the 1984 Democratic nomination race. In part, this was because of their purported predictive value. Equally important, there were two Democratic candidates who made the straw polls a central element in their pre-Iowa strategy.

As the frontrunner, former Vice President Walter Mondale would always have been under some pressure to perform well in such events. But the Mondale campaign also made a decision to "set a fast and vigorous pace" throughout the invisible primary period and thus actively contest most of the major Democratic straw polls. As one Mondale aide explained their strategy, "Competitors would be forced to travel extensively and enter numerous straw polls and thus exhaust their resources early" (Weinraub 1984). And in some cases, it worked. When Florida Democrats decided to hold a straw poll at their state convention in October 1983, the Mondale campaign refused to concede the poll to former Florida Governor Reubin Askew, thus forcing the Askew campaign to spend money it could ill afford to divert from its campaign in Iowa and New Hampshire. According to Askew's campaign manager, the effect was devastating:

> Our undoing was the Florida straw poll, which we could not avoid. . . . While we won the straw poll, Mondale was able to hurt our finances terribly, and this in the end proved to be our undoing because we didn't have the money for media in Iowa and New Hampshire (Bacchus 1986).

The other candidate who invested heavily in the straw polls was California senator Alan Cranston. From early in the 1984 race, it was clear that the two leading candidates—in the polls and in fund-raising—were Walter Mondale and John Glenn. They thus also received the lion's share of media coverage. The other five candidates were consigned to a second tier where they received scant press coverage and little support from major contributors and were thus denied the resources that might have enabled them to improve their poll standings. For candidates in this position, the key strategic imperative was to find some way to break out of the pack of also-rans and propel themselves into the ranks of the frontline contenders. The Cranston campaign decided that straw polls were the way to do this. By giving special emphasis to the nuclear freeze issue, Cranston hoped to attract disproportionate support from anti-nuclear activists, who were just the type of highly motivated people who were likely to show up at straw polls. As the *New York Times* noted,

> [Senator Cranston] has used the straw polls to try to project himself as a candidate who can compete, at least organizationally, with Mr. Mondale. "Without straw polls," said John Russonello, a Cranston campaign aide, "there would have been no way for a Cranston to distinguish himself from the others" (Gailey 1983).

The result, as table 6.4 shows, was that the 1983–1984 straw polls were dominated by Mondale and Cranston. Of the ten straw polls listed there, Mondale won four and finished second in three others. Cranston won three and finished second twice.[20] As for the straw polls that weren't won by either Cranston or Mondale, almost all can be accounted for by one simple principle: it pays to show up. Straw poll attendees, it is clear, love attention. When only one candidate shows up and asks for their support, that candidate almost invariably finishes first. This explains Glenn's victory in the New Jersey straw poll as well as Askew's lopsided victory at the Manchester Democratic picnic (Sawyer 1983; Sullivan 1983).

Table 6.4. Presidential Nomination Straw Polls Held during the 1984 Invisible Primary: Democrats

Event at Which the Straw Poll Was Conducted	Date	Number of Votes	Winner and Percentage	Second-Place Finisher and Percentage
California Democratic Convention	Jan. 15, 1983	1,322	Cranston 59	Mondale 23
Massachusetts Democratic Convention	April 9, 1983	3,453	Mondale 29	"Jobs" 26
Wisconsin Democratic Convention	June 11, 1983	2,035	Cranston 39	Mondale 36
Alabama Young Democrats	June 18, 1983	124	Cranston 52	Hollings 15
Manchester, NH Democratic Committee Picnic	July 17, 1983	1,143	Askew 93	Glenn 3
New Jersey Democratic Convention	Sept. 13, 1983	1,125	Glenn 38	Mondale 28
Maine Democratic Convention	Oct 1. 1983	1,849	Mondale 51	Cranston 29
Iowa Jefferson-Jackson Day Dinner	Oct. 8, 1983	4,143	Mondale 47	Cranston 37
Florida Democratic Convention	Oct. 23, 1983	2,325	Askew 45	Mondale 35
Virginia Young Democrats	Jan. 6, 1984	108	Mondale 41	Glenn 23

Source: Compiled by the author from contemporary news accounts, especially the *New York Times* and the *Washington Post.*

Just as in 1976, however, the 1984 straw polls had a mixed predictive record. The resources of organization, money, and elite endorsements that helped Walter Mondale do so well in straw polls eventually brought him his party's nomination. But Cranston's success in the straw polls failed to transfer to the caucuses and primaries. The California senator finished fifth in the Iowa caucuses, behind Mondale, Hart, McGovern, and Uncommitted. He then ran seventh in the New Hampshire primary, receiving just 2 percent of the vote. One day after New Hampshire, he ended his campaign.

If the straw polls significantly overestimated Cranston's appeal, they failed entirely to forecast the success of Gary Hart. Of the ten straw polls in table 6.4, Hart never finished better than third in any of them. Press coverage of these polls often suggested that Cranston and Hart were competing to be the "liberal alternative" to Mondale—and that Cranston was consistently winning that battle (Raines 1983a, 1983b; Safire 1983). Primary voters had something else in mind.

UNCERTAIN MESSAGES: 1988–2000

In retrospect, 1984 was probably the high point of candidate and media attention to straw polls in the presidential nomination process. Never again would they play quite so prominent a role.

<u>1988</u>. The first blow against straw polls was struck by the Democrats. At a number of points during the 1984 nomination race, Democratic National Committee (DNC) chairman Charles Manatt had criticized the straw poll mania that gripped his party. Straw polls, he said, were "divisive, non-useful, expensive and extraordinarily irritating." "I think they are bogus," he complained to reporters on another occasion. "They are a waste of time. They drain our candidates' time and attention. They are unrepresentative" (Dickenson and Fishman 1983; Sawyer 1983). In March 1986, the Democratic National Committee showed that they shared this opinion, adopting a resolution that condemned straw polls as "premature and false barometers" that "undermine the party's efforts" to shorten the nomination process. The DNC accordingly urged state parties not to "sponsor, condone, support or lend credence" to any straw poll (Gailey 1986; Taylor 1986).

Though the DNC has often had problems controlling the behavior of its state party affiliates, its resolution on straw polls was notably successful.[21] In the lead-up to the 1988 primary and caucus season, so far as I can determine from contemporary press coverage, not one Democratic state or local party group sponsored a straw poll of any kind. The Democratic race wasn't entirely free of straw polls. A number of union locals held straw polls among their members, and the candidate who prevailed in such soundings would sometimes send out a press release announcing his victory.[22] The only Democratic straw poll that received a modicum of attention was conducted at the national convention of the League of United Latin American Citizens in June 1987. Though there was some question about the completeness of the reported results, both the *New York Times* and the *Washington Post* noted that Bruce Babbitt and Michael Dukakis had each received 24 percent of the vote, followed by Jesse Jackson with 17 percent (Applebome 1987; Walsh 1987). Deprived of straw polls, some pundits lamented that they found the 1988 Democratic race unusually difficult to handicap. One political consultant was actually quoted as saying, "I crave a straw poll"—but I doubt many voters shared this sentiment.[23]

The Republicans, on the other hand, held a goodly number of straw polls in 1987 and early 1988; these are listed in table 6.5. Just as in the 1984 Democratic race, the 1988 Republican straw polls were dominated by two candidates: George Bush and Pat Robertson. And in another parallel with the 1984 Democrats, one of these candidates went on to win his party's nomination—while the other flamed out badly in the delegate selection season. Properly interpreted, Robertson's success in the Republican straw polls did say something valid about the strengths of his candidacy. Though representative sample surveys invariably showed that most Americans disliked the man and wanted him nowhere near the White House, he did have a small but very zealous following—not enough to win any primaries, much less a general election, but definitely a force to be reckoned with in low-turnout straw polls and caucuses. In an earlier article, I have calculated that during the contested phase of the 1988 nomination race (the period before Dole and Robertson withdrew), Robertson won, on average, just 12 percent of the vote in Repub-

Table 6.5. Presidential Nomination Straw Polls Held during the 1988 Invisible Primary: Republicans

Event at Which the Straw Poll Was Conducted	Date	Number of Votes	Winner and Percentage	Second-Place Finisher and Percentage
Conservative Political Action Conference	Feb. 20, 1987	287	Kemp 68	Buchanan 9
Cedar Rapids Republican Meeting	April 26, 1987	90	Bush 34	Dole 30
Wisconsin Republican Convention	June 7, 1987	636	Bush 36	Dole 30
Iowans for Life Annual Meeting	Sept. 12, 1987	N/A	Kemp 37	Robertson 31
Ames, Iowa Straw Poll	Sept. 12, 1987	3,843	Robertson 34	Dole 25
Minnesota Republican Convention	Sept. 26, 1987	716	Kemp 35	Dole 30
Maryland Republican Convention	Oct. 24, 1987	929	Bush 69	Dole 18
Florida Republican Convention	Nov. 14, 1987	2,313	Bush 57	Robertson 37
Virginia Republican Conference	Dec. 5, 1987	1,325*	Robertson 83	Bush 8
Texas Conservative Leadership Conference	Jan. 9, 1988	N/A	Robertson 46	Kemp 28

* indicates that the number of votes is an estimate; N/A means that data on the number of voters are not available.
Source: Compiled by the author from contemporary news accounts, especially the *New York Times* and the *Washington Post*.

lican presidential primaries, as compared to 30 percent in the caucuses, a difference that holds up after controlling for a variety of other variables (Mayer 1996, table 4.12).

1992. The 1992 election may be disposed of very quickly. In all the sources I have examined, there was exactly one presidential straw poll that received any mention. In December 1991, the Florida Democratic Party decided to defy the resolution that the DNC had adopted in 1986 and hold a straw poll in conjunction with its state convention. As was widely expected, fellow southerner Bill Clinton was the clear winner, with 54 percent of the vote (Berke 1991; Cook 1991; Edsall 1991).

The Republicans apparently held no straw polls during the 1992 election cycle—certainly no well-publicized polls. For the first six months of 1991, it appeared that George Bush would win renomination with no opposition—hence, no need to hold a straw poll. As the economy and Bush's approval ratings declined, Republican state and local organizations probably believed that a straw poll would only show that even many Republicans were dissatisfied with the president's performance.

1996. In 1996, by contrast, there was once again an abundance of straw polls. Without an incumbent president to shield from a pesky opponent, many Republican state and local parties decided that a contested presidential nomination race was a perfect occasion to hold a nonbinding vote among their members, especially if they could charge the participants a small fee and thus use the poll as a fund-raising device. In the end, twelve Republican straw polls were deemed significant enough to be reported by either the *New York Times* or the *Washington Post*, though several of the Virginia polls probably received mention only because they took place close to the *Post*'s home turf. And as shown in table 6.6, the dominant figure in these polls was unquestionably Texas senator Phil Gramm, who won eight of them outright, tied for first in a ninth, and finished second in one other.

Unfortunately for Gramm—and for the straw polls' predictive record—he fared much less well in contests where the votes actually mattered. The first major encounter in the 1996 Republican race took place in Louisiana, which had somehow managed to hold its caucuses six days ahead of Iowa's. Though most of the Republican candidates had agreed not to campaign in Louisiana, both Gramm and Pat Buchanan mounted a serious effort there, thus making the Bayou State caucuses what Gramm himself called "a sort of semifinal to determine who is the real conservative candidate" (Berke 1996). In spite of Gramm's overwhelming victory in the Louisiana straw poll a year earlier, it was Buchanan who narrowly won the more meaningful caucus vote. Six days later, Gramm finished a weak fifth in the Iowa caucuses, despite having tied Bob Dole in the Ames straw poll. Gramm ended his campaign two

Table 6.6.   Presidential Nomination Straw Polls Held during the 1996 Invisible Primary: Republicans

Event at Which the Straw Poll Was Conducted	Date	Number of Votes	Winner and Percentage	Second-Place Finisher and Percentage
Louisiana Republican Convention	Jan. 7, 1995	1,247	Gramm 72	Buchanan 12
Arizona Republican Convention	Jan. 28, 1995	852	Gramm 54	Buchanan 13
Conservative Political Action Conference	Feb. 12, 1995	421	Gramm 40	Dole 12
California Republican Convention	Feb. 25, 1995	515	Gramm 56	Wilson 14
Fundraiser in Columbia, SC	March 3, 1995	1,213*	Gramm 34	Alexander 26
Virginia Young Republicans	May 13, 1995	N/A	Buchanan 58	Dole 11
Fundraiser in Tysons Corner, VA	June 17, 1995	1,083	Buchanan 59	Keyes 11
Ames, Iowa Straw Poll	Aug. 20, 1995	10,598	Tie: Gramm and Dole 24	
National Federation of Republican Women Convention	Sept. 17, 1995	1,198*	Gramm 35	Alexander 17
Maine Republican Convention	Nov. 4, 1995	1,418	Gramm 42	Lugar 21
Florida Republican Convention	Nov. 18, 1995	3,325	Dole 33	Gramm 26
Maryland Republican Central Meeting	Dec. 2, 1996	149	Gramm 51	Dole 26

* indicates that the number of votes is an estimate; "N/A" means that data on the number of voters are not available.

Source: Compiled by the author from contemporary news accounts, especially the *New York Times* and the *Washington Post.*

days later. All his victories in the straw polls, in short, had apparently done nothing to bolster his campaign or increase his popularity with rank-and-file Republicans. Meanwhile, Dole, whose performance in the straw polls was wholly uninspiring, made a few early stumbles, then won thirty-eight straight primaries and coasted to an easy first-ballot nomination.

2000. With Republicans still out of the White House, one might have expected another large batch of straw polls in the lead-up to the 2000 Iowa caucuses. In fact, there were relatively few. George W. Bush was so far ahead in the polls, had such a fund-raising juggernaut, and was supported by so many party leaders that he was, in many ways, the functional equivalent of an incumbent. A key element in the early Bush campaign strategy was to cultivate an image that their candidate was the inevitable, unstoppable nominee and thus compel/persuade most of his opponents to exit the race before any of the actual delegates were selected. That image might have been endangered if Bush had had to compete in a series of high-profile straw polls. So Bush agreed to participate in only one: the by-now traditional Ames, Iowa Straw Poll, which he probably could have ducked only at the risk of antagonizing many of the voters who would later take part in the caucuses. (According to one report, however, Bush campaign manager Karl Rove tried to convince the Iowa Republican Party to cancel the Ames straw poll; Novak 1999). In other states, Bush supporters obliged their candidate by deciding not to hold straw polls. In 1979, 1987, and 1995, the straw poll that had been conducted at the Florida Republican state convention had been a major event, that had attracted a lot of attention—and consumed a lot of time and money—from the major candidates. It had also, in every instance, correctly predicted the eventual nominee. This time, however, the governor of Florida was Jeb Bush, the presidential candidate's brother, who made sure that the 1999 convention did not hold a straw poll (Ayres 1999b; Novak 1999).

Table 6.7 provides details about the four Republican straw polls that were mentioned in either the *New York Times* or the *Washington Post*. As a guide to the way the topic was treated in the media, however, table 6.7 is quite misleading. Of the four polls mentioned there, three received only passing notice. The Ames straw poll, by contrast, generated a torrent of coverage, including front-page stories in both papers on both the day before and the day after it occurred.

Table 6.7. Presidential Nomination Straw Polls Held during the 2000 Invisible Primary: Republicans

Event at Which the Straw Poll Was Conducted	Date	Number of Votes	Winner and Percentage	Second-Place Finisher and Percentage
Conservative Political Action Conference	Jan. 23, 1999	1,010	Bauer 28	Bush 24
Ames, Iowa Straw Poll	Aug. 14, 1999	23,685	Bush 31	Forbes 21
Alabama Republican Convention	Aug. 28, 1999	1,287	Keyes 39	Hatch 36
Maryland Republican Convention	Nov. 20, 1999	170	Bush 74	McCain 19

Source: Compiled by the author from contemporary news accounts, especially the *New York Times* and the *Washington Post*.

As many in the media conceded, it was by no means clear that the Ames straw poll deserved such attention. The 1988 and 1996 nomination races had shown that the Ames result was not an especially good predictor of how the Iowa caucuses would turn out, much less who would win the Republican nomination. In May 1999, a news analysis piece in the *New York Times* had declared, "Straw polls are, in truth, little more than straws in the wind. Many national party leaders say they should be outlawed because they are unscientific, subject to mischievous manipulation by candidates and, ultimately, misleading and even harmful" (Ayres 1999a). In June, however, Bush unexpectedly announced, "We not only ought to compete, I think we ought to go win the Ames straw poll" (Broder 1999). Suddenly, the Ames poll was a big deal: the only contest before the primary and caucus season that just might, possibly, maybe, show how potent the Bush machine really was and who, if anyone, had a chance of derailing it. The *New York Times* reporter who one month earlier had dismissed straw polls as "little more than straws in the wind" now said that the Ames straw poll "is beginning to loom as the first real make-or-break test" in the 2000 nomination race. "The poll could well take on the winnowing role of the caucuses and cut the dozen-candidate field to three or four true contenders" (Ayres 1999a).

In the end, Bush won the Ames straw poll, after spending a reported $750,000; millionaire publisher Steve Forbes finished second, at a cost of $2 million (Balz and Broder 1999). Yet, for all the hoopla, there is little reason to think the Ames result had any substantial effect on the subsequent nomination race. Lamar Alexander ended his presidential campaign just two days after the Ames poll, leading some commentators to claim that he exited the race *because* of his sixth-place finish there. But this is a misdiagnosis: it was really a lack of financial resources that drove Alexander from the field. Desperately short of funds, having already laid off some of his top staff, Alexander held on to one last hope: that a strong showing at Ames would improve his fundraising prospects (Firestone 1999). When that sort of showing failed to materialize, Alexander had no choice but to withdraw. In sum, the most one could say about the impact of the Ames straw poll was that it failed to resuscitate a campaign that was dying of other causes. By way of comparison, Elizabeth Dole finished third in the straw poll, a result that received generally favorable commentary and was supposed to give a major boost to her campaign (Dao 1999). Yet, just two months later, she too ended her campaign because of her inability to raise sufficient funds. In an end-of-the-year column on the Republican nomination race, E. J. Dionne suggested that the real winner of the Ames straw poll was Arizona senator John McCain, who had called the whole thing a "sham" and chose not to participate in it at all. Yet, by late December, McCain was running second in the national polls and was especially well positioned to win the critical New Hampshire primary (Dionne 2000).

As for the Democrats, once again a single state party decided to ignore the national committee and hold a straw poll at its state convention. This time it was Massachusetts doing the honors. Vice President Al Gore beat former senator Bill Bradley by a three-to-one margin, though the result was little noted nor long remembered (Goldberg 1999; MacQuarrie 1999).

MORE OF THE SAME: STRAW POLLS IN THE TWENTY-FIRST CENTURY

Most of what follows is anticlimactic: variations on themes and patterns that closely resemble those from earlier elections.

2004. There were no straw polls in 2004, at least none that were deemed worth mentioning by the *New York Times* or the *Washington Post*. At one point, Florida Democrats threatened to hold a straw poll at their state convention, but eventually decided against it (Archibold 2003a, 2003b).

2008. For a stark example of just how little straw polls can mean in the long run, it is hard to top the 2008 Republican race. Three straw polls in 2007 attracted particular attention: the poll conducted at the Conservative Political Action Conference (CPAC) in March; the Ames, Iowa Straw Poll in August; and the Values Voter Summit poll in October. Former Massachusetts governor Mitt Romney won all three. Romney's victories were the product of a deliberate strategy. To gain greater visibility in a crowded field of candidates and to show that he had support among hardcore conservatives, Romney's campaign actively recruited participants for all three events and helped pay their expenses, including transportation and ticket prices (Kirkpatrick 2007; Luo 2007; Nagourney and Zeleny 2007). And in the short run, it seemed to work. By the end of summer, voter surveys showed Romney leading the pack in both Iowa and New Hampshire. In contrast, John McCain's record in the straw polls could hardly have been worse. After coming in a distant fifth in the CPAC poll, he ran tenth of eleven candidates in the Ames poll and ninth of nine Republicans at the Values Voter Summit.[24]

But things looked very different when the primary and caucus season began in January 2008. Romney lost the Iowa caucuses to Mike Huckabee, then lost New Hampshire to McCain. Romney won the Michigan primary and Nevada caucuses, but McCain was the victor in two primaries that were more hotly contested and therefore received much more extensive media coverage: South Carolina and Florida. On February 5, the 2008 edition of Super Tuesday, McCain, now riding high in the national polls, won all the big prizes,

Table 6.8.   Presidential Nomination Straw Polls Held during the 2008 Invisible Primary: Republicans

Event at Which the Straw Poll Was Conducted	Date	Number of Votes	Winner and Percentage	Second-Place Finisher and Percentage
Conservative Political Action Conference	March 3, 2007	1,705	Romney 21	Giuliani 17
Virginia Federation of Republican Women	April 22, 2007	N/A	F. Thompson 22	Giuliani 19
Ames, Iowa Straw Poll	Aug. 11, 2007	14,302	Romney 32	Huckabee 18
Texas Republican Straw Poll	Sept. 1, 2007	1,300	Hunter 41	F. Thompson 21
Values Voter Summit	Oct. 20, 2007	5,775	Romney 28	Huckabee 27
Virginia Republican Party Advance	Dec. 1, 2007	N/A	Paul 38	F. Thompson 23

Source: Compiled by the author from contemporary news accounts, especially the *New York Times* and the *Washington Post.*

including the New York, New Jersey, Illinois, and California primaries. Two days later, Romney announced that he was ending his campaign, as McCain coasted to a comfortable first-ballot nomination.

<u>2012.</u> Though I have elsewhere criticized the management of the 2012 Romney presidential campaign (Mayer 2012), they do seem to have learned one useful lesson from 2008: winning straw polls isn't worth the effort involved. So in his second run for the Republican nomination, Romney declined to participate actively in any of the straw polls, including the Ames Straw Poll that he had won so decisively in 2007. With the Romney campaign making no effort to contest the straw polls, and no other campaign having the resources to do so, the 2012 straw polls were fertile ground for whichever candidate(s) had the kinds of zealous supporters who were likely to show up at such events without much prompting.

As mentioned in the first section of this chapter, for the 2012 election cycle we have, from Wikipedia, an unusually comprehensive list of fifty-six Republican straw polls that were held between January 1, 2011, and January 2, 2012. The first- and second-place finishers in these polls are tallied in table 6.9. More than 70 percent of them were won by two candidates, Ron Paul and Herman Cain, neither of whom was an important factor in the primary and caucus season. In Cain's case, it can at least be said that he was actually leading in some national polls of likely Republican primary voters before accusations of sexual harassment forced him from the race in early December 2011.[25] But the only primary Ron Paul won in 2012 was held in the Virgin Islands. Notably less successful in the 2011 straw polls were not only even-

Table 6.9. Winners and Second-Place Finishers in 2012 Republican Straw Polls

Candidate	Number of Victories	Number of Second-Place Finishes
Ron Paul	23	10
Herman Cain	17	7
Mitt Romney	4	13
Newt Gingrich	3	8
Rick Perry	2	8
Michele Bachmann	2	4
Rick Santorum	2	2
Other	4	3

Source: Compiled by the author from data reported in "Straw polls for the 2012 Republican Party presidential primaries," at https://en.wikipedia.org/ wiki/Straw_polls_for_the_2012_Republican_Party_presidential_primaries (accessed January 30, 2019).
Note: Cain and Gingrich tied for the lead in one straw poll. Both are counted here as the winners of that poll.

tual nominee Mitt Romney but the two men who turned out to be his strongest competitors, Rick Santorum and Newt Gingrich. Even if we restrict our attention to the more high-profile straw polls, the results are no more revealing about the outcome of the Republican nomination race. Of all the straw polls held in 2011, three received more than cursory coverage in the contemporary press: the CPAC poll in February, the Ames Straw Poll in August, and the Florida "Presidency 5" poll in September. They were won by, respectively, Ron Paul, Michele Bachmann, and Herman Cain.

2016. Three different Websites—Wikipedia, Ballotpedia, and The Green Papers—have compiled lists of the Republican straw polls held during the 2016 invisible primary.[26] While the three lists include somewhat different sets of straw polls, they agree that literally all of the Republican straw polls were won by one of four candidates: Ben Carson, Rand Paul, Scott Walker, and Ted Cruz. Of the four, Cruz proved to be Donald Trump's toughest opponent; but Walker dropped out of the race well before the Iowa caucuses and neither Carson nor Paul finished better than fourth in any primary or caucus. As for the eventual nominee, Trump won not a single straw poll. He did finish second on two occasions, but generally lagged well behind the leaders.

THE AMES STRAW POLL

Though many reporters now express considerable skepticism toward straw polls in general, up until 2015 one such poll continued to receive a remarkable amount of coverage in the major media: the Ames Straw Poll, held by the Iowa Republican Party. Though straw polls are a poor indicator of a candidate's general popularity, many commentators argued, they are a valid indicator of the state of a candidate's campaign organization.[27] And since organization is also a key to doing well in caucuses, the Ames affair may at least tell us something valuable about the state of the race in Iowa.

Several features of the Ames Straw Poll, however, sharply distinguish it from the caucuses that come about a half year later. To begin with, not until 1999 was the Ames poll restricted to Iowa residents.[28] Before that time, it was possible for candidates like Pat Robertson and Phil Gramm to fly or bus in supporters from other states, who could then cast votes in what purported to be an *Iowa* straw poll. Second, the Ames Straw Poll was also (some would say principally) a fund-raising device for the Iowa Republican Party—which meant that all attendees had to buy a ticket, or have some candidate's organization buy a ticket for them, in order to be allowed to vote. As shown in table 6.10, ticket prices ranged from $25 to $50.

Table 6.10 also shows the six winners of the Ames Straw Poll and whether they went on to win either the Iowa caucuses or the Republican nomination. In three of six cases, the straw poll winner won the Iowa caucuses. In only two of the six cases did the poll winner become the Republican presidential nominee. There are, however, other ways of measuring the predictive accuracy of the straw poll than seeing what happened to the winner. A more inclusive test, since it takes all the Republican presidential candidates into account, is to calculate the correlation between the results of the straw poll and the results of the Iowa caucuses. These numbers are also shown in table 6.10. By this criterion, the straw poll results bore a close relationship to the caucus results in 1980, 1988, and 2000. The correlation was much weaker in 1996 and 2008 and actually negative in 2012.

The worst embarrassment for the Ames Straw Poll undoubtedly took place in 2011. The winner that year was Minnesota representative Michele Bachmann—but that was almost her only good moment in the entire campaign. She finished a distant sixth in the Iowa caucuses, receiving just 5 percent of the vote. One day later, she suspended her campaign. In 2015, faced with mounting opposition from the candidates and a sense that maintaining the straw poll might endanger Iowa's first-in-the-nation caucuses, the Iowa Republican Central Committee voted to cancel the Ames poll. One anonymous committee member, however, insisted, "We're not saying that there's never going to be a straw poll ever, ever, ever again. But the politics of it were not going to work this year" (Cheney 2015). Since Donald Trump will likely face only weak opposition in his quest for renomination, Iowa Republicans will probably not bring it back in 2019.

Table 6.10. The Ames Straw Poll as a Predictor of the Iowa Caucuses and the Republican Presidential Nomination

Date	Ticket Price (in dollars)	Winner of the Ames Straw Poll	Winner of the Iowa Caucuses	Correlation between Straw Poll and Caucus Results	Winner of Republican Nomination
Oct. 13, 1979	50	George H. W. Bush	George H. W. Bush	0.96	Ronald Reagan
Sept. 12, 1987	25	Pat Robertson	Bob Dole	0.75	George H. W. Bush
Aug. 20, 1995	25	Bob Dole–Phil Gramm tie	Bob Dole	0.51	Bob Dole
Aug. 14, 1999	25	George W. Bush	George W. Bush	0.84	George W. Bush
Aug. 11, 2007	35	Mitt Romney	Mike Huckabee	0.45	John McCain
Aug. 13, 2011	30	Michele Bachmann	Rick Santorum	−0.11	Mitt Romney
Number Correctly Predicted			3 of 6		2 of 6

Source: Compiled by the author.

CONCLUSION: THE ROLE OF STRAW POLLS
IN THE CONTEMPORARY NOMINATION PROCESS

Their (partial) predictive accuracy in 1976 and 1980 notwithstanding, straw polls have not had a very good record in predicting the outcome of contested presidential nomination races. On the one hand, it is possible to do very well in the straw polls and then fail rather miserably in the primaries and caucuses. Alan Cranston in 1984, Phil Gramm in 1996, Ron Paul and Herman Cain in 2012, and Ben Carson in 2016 all learned this lesson. On the other hand, performing poorly in the straw polls doesn't preclude a candidate from running a quite competitive race when real delegates are at stake. Examples include Ronald Reagan in 1980, Gary Hart in 1984, John McCain in both 2000 and 2008, Mitt Romney in 2012, and Donald Trump in 2016. The other indicators that reporters and scholars have used to assess presidential nomination races—national and state voter surveys, fund-raising reports (available since 1976), and elite endorsements—don't have a perfect predictive record either, but they have been, in general, far more accurate than straw polls.[29]

By 2000, most commentators had concluded that straw polls were a poor guide as to a candidate's general popularity. For that purpose, regular old public opinion polls were a far better vehicle. Still, some pundits maintained, straw polls were at least a valid indicator of the quality of a candidate's campaign organization. But even this was unclear. Some candidates did well in straw polls not because their own campaign had a good field organization, but because they had a special appeal to certain kinds of highly motivated activists: nuclear freeze supporters in Cranston's case, conservative Christians in Pat Robertson's. Straw polls are also plainly affected by which candidates show up for them and how much effort they put in. Based on his record in 2007, Mitt Romney almost certainly could have run much better in the 2011 straw polls if he had simply made the effort to do so.

Do straw polls affect candidate behavior? In particular, do they play an important role in "winnowing" the field by getting many candidates to drop out of the race before the delegate selection season begins? Here, too, the straw polls' record is not terribly impressive. There are three instances I have found in which a presidential candidate ended his campaign shortly after a poor showing in the Ames Straw Poll, with subsequent press coverage frequently drawing a link between the two events. I have already noted the case of Lamar Alexander in 1999, where it was fund-raising difficulties more than straw poll results that really brought his candidacy to an end. The second case involves former Wisconsin governor Tommy Thompson, who announced before the 2007 Ames poll that he would end his campaign if he finished lower than second. He actually came in sixth, with just 7 percent of the vote, and one day later kept his promise.[30] Thompson's campaign, however, had been in trouble well before the showdown in Ames. According to mid-summer public opinion polls, only 1 percent of the nation's Republicans wanted Thompson to be their party's next presidential nominee.[31] Since commencing his campaign in April, Thompson had raised a mere $992,000, and was $167,000 in debt.[32] In short, the Ames Straw Poll merely administered the coup de grace to a campaign that was already on life support.

The third case, that of former Minnesota governor Tim Pawlenty in 2011, seems significantly different. Pawlenty had raised $5.5 million during the first nine months of the year, though his national poll numbers were not substantially better than Thompson's had been.[33] Coming from a state that bordered on Iowa, Pawlenty decided to make an all-out effort for the Ames Straw Poll. He actually finished third in the poll, with 14 percent of the vote, but one of the candidates who beat him was Rep. Michele Bachmann, who also came from Minnesota. One day later, Pawlenty dropped out of the race (Shear 2011; Zeleny 2011; Zeleny and Shear 2011). As table 6.10 indicates, the results of the 2011 Ames poll bore no relationship to the results of the 2012 Iowa caucuses. The top two finishers in the straw poll, Bachmann and Ron Paul, ran sixth and third, respectively, in the caucuses. The caucus winner, Rick Santorum, had finished fourth in the straw poll, substantially behind Pawlenty. Second place in the caucuses went to Mitt Romney, who finished seventh in the straw poll. In sum, it is hard not to conclude that Pawlenty ascribed too much importance to the Ames Straw Poll and ended his campaign much earlier than he needed to.

If straw polls are not as meaningful as some of their sponsors might wish, neither are they as harmful as some of their critics have contended. Contrary to the hopes of the Democratic National Committee, eliminating or at least radically reducing the number of straw polls did not make contested nomination races appreciably shorter. The Democratic contests in 1988, 2000, 2004, 2008, and 2016 were about as long as the race in 1984.[34] Not having to participate in straw polls, presidential candidates found lots of other ways to occupy their time during the year before the delegates were selected: raising money, recruiting consultants and volunteers, taking part in candidate forums and televised debates, campaigning in Iowa and New Hampshire. Nor do straw polls seem particularly divisive. In the lead-up to an important straw poll, the rival candidates may sometimes attack one another, but the charges and accusations don't really start to fly fast and furious until actual delegates are at stake.

Straw polls do consume time and money that some campaigns can ill afford to expend—but only if a campaign decides to contest them. Over time, however, most campaigns appear to have recognized that participation in straw polls is optional. When a straw poll is held in a candidate's home state, as was the case for both Alan Cranston and Reubin Askew in 1984, he may be forced to compete in it. In all other cases, a candidate can probably skip a straw poll—even the vaunted Ames Straw Poll—with no long-term damage to his or her campaign.

As for the 2020 election cycle, straw polls rarely play a prominent role in races where an incumbent president is seeking renomination (the 1980 Democratic race is the lone exception), so Republican state parties are un-likely to hold any in the coming months. A few conservative groups may conduct them in conjunction with their meetings, but unless significant op-position to Trump's renomination develops, the results are unlikely to receive much attention. At the 2019 Conservative Political Action Conference in late February and early March, a straw poll found 80 percent of the participants supporting Trump, 6 percent hoping Mitt Romney would be the Republican nominee, and 1 percent favoring former Massachusetts governor William Weld. But the only news source I can find that reported the results was the *Washington Times*, which cosponsored the poll (Sherfinski and Dinan 2019).

On the Democratic side, the action will probably all be on the Internet. In January 2019, the Daily Kos, a popular left-wing website, began conducting straw polls of its members every two weeks. MoveOn.org and Democracy for America have also held straw polls (Hagen 2019). And regardless of straw polls' past record, most political reporters are probably monitoring the re-sults, wondering if this year the straw polls just might yield important insights about who will be the next Democratic presidential nominee.

NOTES

The author would like to thank Emmett Buell, David Shribman, Dan Balz, Casey Dominguez, and Jonathan Bernstein for their help with this chapter.

1. For comparable definitions, see Hill and Hill (1994), p. 263; and Safire (1993), pp. 764–65.

2. So-called Internet surveys are a mixed bag. In some cases, the group conducting the survey contacts a random sample of people and asks them to fill out one or more surveys. Given certain assumptions about the people likely to participate in such an arrangement, these can be valid surveys, that permit inferences to be made about the opinions and characteristics of some larger population. The more common type of Internet survey, where visitors to a website are invited to register their opinion on one or more issues, are no more meaningful than the old call-in polls.

3. The only exception I can find is Emmett H. Buell, Jr., "The Invisible Primary," in *In Pursuit of the White House: How We Choose Our Presidential Nominees*, edited by William G. Mayer (Chatham, NJ: Chatham House, 1996), 20–24. There is also a

small historical literature on the straw polls that were a prominent part of elections in the nineteenth and early twentieth centuries, before they were replaced by modern sample surveys. See, in particular, Susan Herbst, "Partisan Politics and the Symbolic Use of Straw Polls." chap. 4 in *Numbered Voices: How Opinion Polling Has Shaped American Politics* (Chicago: University of Chicago Press, 1993), 69–87; and Tom W. Smith, "The First Straw: A Study of the Origins of Election Polls." *Public Opinion Quarterly* 54 (Spring 1990): 21–36.

4. The two articles referred to are "Bayh Leads '76 Straw Poll as Young Democrats Meet," *New York Times*, August 24, 1975, p. 40; and "Convention Poll," *New York Times*, November 24, 1975, p. 26.

5. Based on a search of all *New York Times* articles in the ProQuest Historical Newspapers data base that contained the words "straw poll" or "straw vote."

6. See https://en.wikipedia.org/wiki/Straw_polls_for_the_2012_Republican_Party_presidential_primaries (accessed January 30, 2019). Since many academics question the reliability of Wikipedia, I should point out that most of the straw polls listed in this article are linked to articles from reputable news organizations.

7. In 1988, the Republican delegate selection season began with the selection of state convention delegates in Hawaii on February 4. In 1996, the first event was the Alaska caucuses on January 29.

8. I have omitted a small number of straw polls that are referred to briefly in one of these sources if it proved impossible to get relevant details on such matters as when and where the poll was held, the number of participants, and the exact results.

Though *Congressional Quarterly Weekly Report* (now called *CQ Weekly*) no longer devotes much attention to the presidential nomination races, it was once an essential source of information about primary and caucus rules, delegate counts, and party reform commissions, almost entirely due to the superb reporting of Rhodes Cook.

9. As noted in table 6.1, Carter also finished first, with just 10 percent of the vote, in a straw poll that was conducted on September 22, 1975, in conjunction with the Iowa Democrats' "off year" caucuses. See Winebrenner and Goldford (2010), *Iowa Precinct Caucuses*, p. 60; and Witcover (1977), *Marathon*, pp. 199–200. But that event was only noticed by the national media after Carter's victory at the Jefferson-Jackson Day Dinner.

10. R. W. Apple, Jr., "Carter Appears to Hold a Solid Lead in Iowa as the Campaign's First Test Approaches," *New York Times*, October 27, 1975, p. 17, https://www.nytimes.com/1975/10/27/archives/carter-appears-to-hold-a-solid-lead-in-iowa-as-the-campaigns-first.html. For a good account of Apple's standing among national political reporters, see Timothy Crouse, *The Boys on the Bus* (New York: Ballantine Books, 1974), pp. 73–90. There was some variation in the placement of Apple's article. In the microfilm version of the *New York Times*, which is based on the late city edition, and which I have relied upon in the writing of this chapter, Apple's piece appears on page 17. That is also the way it is listed in the *New York Times Index*. But the New Jersey edition (and perhaps some other editions as well) had the article on page 1.

11. Elizabeth Drew and Dick Duncan, both quoted in Arterton, "Media Politics of Presidential Campaigns," p. 39.

12. The debate within the Udall campaign about the relative priority of Iowa and New Hampshire is chronicled in Witcover, *Marathon*, 203–5.

13. See, in particular, Apple (1975), "Reagan Is Termed Florida Favorite"; and Evans and Novak (1975b), "Jimmy Carter's Challenge to Wallace."

14. In an October 31–November 3, 1975, Gallup Poll, respondents were asked to rate Jimmy Carter on a scale ranging from positive 5 to negative 5. Fully 70 percent of the respondents said they didn't know who Carter was.

15. In case it isn't clear, the first category includes the second. For those interested in replicating my results, several points are worth noting. First, my analysis is based on the articles contained in the ProQuest Historical Newspapers data base. Second, the terms "straw vote" and "straw poll" are sometimes used in circumstances that have nothing to do with the presidential nomination process. In 1975, for example, the *New York Times* published two articles that mentioned a straw vote designed to see how much support there was for reelecting Bowie Kuhn as commissioner of baseball; there were also several handbag ads that included the words "straw poll." All such articles were, of course, not included in the figures shown in table 6.2. During this period, the *New York Times* regularly published a "Table of Contents" or "News Summary" that sometimes referred to articles that included the words "straw poll" or "straw vote" in the title. While the articles were included in my counts, the mention in the table of contents was not.

16. Both of these counts include the small number of events I have identified that were not explicitly called straw polls but had all the attributes of one.

17. The county caucuses that picked most of the delegates to the Florida Democratic state convention took place on October 13, before Kennedy had announced his intention to become an active presidential candidate. After Carter's victory in the caucuses, the Draft Kennedy forces "disbanded and conceded the straw vote to Carter. The [official] Kennedy for President Committee made no effort to revive the campaign for the Florida convention vote." See Rhodes Cook, "Carter, Reagan Win Florida Convention Tests." *Congressional Quarterly Weekly Report*, November 24, 1979, 2662.

18. Bush received prominent mention in both Broder, "Reagan Defeats Connally," 1979; and Clymer, "Reagan Wins a Poll," 1979c. Bush's showing is described as "surprisingly strong" in the latter article.

19. Announcement and FEC filing dates for the 1980 presidential candidates can be found in Silverleib and Mayer 2012, 203–8.

20. Cranston was also the second highest candidate in the Massachusetts straw poll, though he ran behind "Jobs."

21. The frequently contentious relationship between the national and state parties is examined in William G. Mayer and Andrew E. Busch, *The Front-Loading Problem in Presidential Nominations*, 140–46.

22. For one of the few such straw polls that did get covered, albeit very briefly, see "On Straw Polls," *New York Times*, September 7, 1987, 20.

23. Bob Squier, as quoted in Robin Toner, "Presidential Race Puzzles the Pundits," *New York Times*, December 11, 1987, A32, https://www.nytimes.com/1987/12/11/us/politics-political-memo-presidential-race-puzzles-the-pundits.html.

24. The Values Voter straw poll is one of the few that allows participants to vote for either Democratic or Republican candidates. Since attendees are generally affiliated with conservative Christian groups, however, all of the Democratic candidates usually finish behind all of the Republican candidates. Thus, in 2007, there were some Democratic candidates who received fewer votes than McCain.

25. See, for example, CBS News/*New York Times* poll of October 19–24, 2011; Fox News Poll of October 23–25, 2011; Quinnipiac University poll of October 25–31, 2011; and Politico/George Washington University poll of November 6–9, 2011.

26. See "Straw Polls for the 2016 Republican Party Presidential Primaries" at https://en.wikipedia.org/wiki/Straw_polls_for_the_2016_Republican_Party_presidential_primaries (accessed January 30, 2019); "Presidential Election, 2016/Straw Polls," https://ballotpedia.org/Presidential-election,_2016/Straw_polls (accessed January 30, 2019); and "Presidential Election 2016 Straw Polls," https://www.thegreen papers/com/P16/StrawPolls.phtml (accessed January 30, 2019).

27. See, for example, Ayres, "Iowa Straw Poll" (1999); and Broder (1999), "GOP Rivals Accept Bush's Dare."

28. Ayres, "Iowa Straw Poll."

29. On the predictive value of national pre-primary polls and fund-raising totals, see William G. Mayer, "The Basic Dynamics of the Contemporary Nomination Process: An Expanded View," in *The Making of the Presidential Candidates 2004*, edited by William G. Mayer (Lanham, MD: Rowman & Littlefield, 2004), 83–132. The significance of elite endorsements is defended in Marty Cohen, David Karol, Hans Noel, and John Zaller, *The Party Decides: Presidential Nominations Before and After Reform* (Chicago: University of Chicago Press), 2008.

30. See Nagourney and Zeleny (2007), "Romney Wins Iowa Straw Poll"; and "Ex-Governor Ends Bid." *New York Times*, August 13, 2007, A16, https://www.nytimes .com/1995/08/08/nyregion/ex-governor-ends-bid-for-education-post.html.

31. See, for example, the Gallup Polls of July 6–8, 2007; July 12–15, 2007; and August 3–5, 2007.

32. Based on the October 2007 filing of the Tommy Thompson for President Committee, available at http://fec.gov.

33. Fund-raising numbers are taken from the October 2011 filing of the Pawlenty for President Committee, available at http://fec.gov. A June 2011 national survey found 6 percent of the nation's Republican identifiers supporting Pawlenty for the 2012 nomination, but two later surveys showed him with just 2 and 3 percent support. See Gallup Polls of June 8–11, 2011; July 20–24, 2011; and August 4–7, 2011.

34. For the announcement and first FEC filing dates of Democratic presidential candidates from 1988 through 2008, see Silverleib and Mayer (2012), "By the Numbers," 205–6. The 1992 Democratic nomination contest was significantly shorter, but only because most Democrats apparently decided that it was inappropriate to launch their campaigns while the Gulf War was in progress.

REFERENCES

Apple, R. W., Jr. 1975. "Reagan Is Termed Florida Favorite." *New York Times*, November 17, 1975, A1. https://www.nytimes.com/1975/11/17/archives/reagan -is-termed-florida-favorite-manager-sees-2to1-victory-over.html.

Applebome, Peter. 1987. "Democrats Vying for Hispanic Votes." *New York Times*, June 29, 1987, B7. https://www.nytimes.com/1987/06/29/us/democrats-vying-for -hispanic-votes.html.

Archibold, Randal C. 2003a. "Florida Democrats, Seeking Edge, Consider Early Straw Poll." *New York Times*, October 26, 2003, N26. https://www.nytimes .com/2003/10/26/us/florida-democrats-seeking-edge-consider-early-straw-poll .html.

———. 2003b. "Democrats in Florida Drop Poll Plan." *New York Times*, November 17, 2003, A15. https://www.nytimes.com/2003/11/17/us/democrats-in-florida -drop-poll-plan.html.

Arterton, F. Christopher. 1978. "The Media Politics of Presidential Campaigns: A Study of the Carter Nomination Drive." In *Race for the Presidency: The Media and the Nominating Process*, edited by J. D. Barber, 39–40. Englewood Cliffs, NJ: Prentice-Hall.

Ayres, B. Drummond. 1999a. "The Preview in Iowa Is Drawing a Crowd." *New York Times*, June 25, 1999, A21. http://www.nytimes.com/1999/06/25/us/political -briefing-the-preview-in-iowa-is-drawing-a-crowd.html.

———. 1999b. "A Change of Heart about Straw Polls." *New York Times*, August 1, 1999, p. 23. https://www.nytimes.com/1999/08/01/us/political-briefing-a-change -of-heart-about-straw-polls.html.

Bacchus, James T. 1986. *Campaign for President: The Managers Look at '84*, edited by Jonathan Moore, 15. Dover, MA: Auburn House.

Balz, Dan, and David S. Broder, 1999. "Bush Wins Iowa Poll; Forbes 2nd." *Washington Post*, August 15, 1999, A6. http://www.washingtonpost.com/wp-srv/politics/ campaigns/wh2000/stories/iowa081599.htm?noredirect=on.

Barbash, Fred. 1979. "Senator's Own Signal Set Off Draft-Kennedy Drive." *Washington Post*, September 16, 1979, A1. https://www.washingtonpost.com/archive/ politics/1979/09/16/senators-own-signal-set-off-draft-kennedy-drive/7cbc1470 -03c9-4618-94fb-a5e2da474fc0/.

Berke, Richard L. 1991. "Clinton Claims Solid, if Symbolic, Victory in Florida Democrats' Straw Poll." *New York Times*, December 16, 1991, B1. https://www .nytimes.com/1991/12/16/us/clinton-claims-solid-if-symbolic-victory-in-florida -democrats-straw-poll.html.

———. 1996. "Ever So Quietly, G.O.P. Is Beginning to Choose." *New York Times*, February 6, 1996, A18. https://www.nytimes.com/1996/02/06/us/politics-the -caucuses-ever-so-quietly-gop-is-beginning-to-choose.html.

Broder, David S. 1979a. "Connally vs. Reagan in Florida Straw Vote Today," *Washington Post*, November 17, 1979, A2.

———. 1979b. "Reagan Defeats Connally in Florida Test." *Washington Post*, November 18, 1979, A1. https://www.washingtonpost.com/archive/poli

tics/1979/11/18/reagan-defeats-connally-in-florida-test/c0524af5-a860-4f56-99ce
-1d800c288cdb/?utm_term=.a2759e38794d.
———. 1999. "GOP Rivals Accept Bush's Dare." *Washington Post*, June 15, 1999,
A4. http://www.washingtonpost.com/wp-srv/politics/campaigns/wh2000/stories/
gop061599.htm.
Buell, Jr., Emmett H. 1996. "The Invisible Primary." In *In Pursuit of the White
House: How We Choose Our Presidential Nominees*, edited by William G. Mayer,
20–24. Chatham, NJ: Chatham House.
Cheney, Kyle. 2015. "Iowa Straw Poll Pronounced Dead at 36." *Politico*, June 12,
2015. https://www.politico.com/story/2015/06/iowa-gop-kills-straw-poll-118930
(accessed January 27, 2019).
Clymer, Adam. 1979a. "Maine Republicans, in Informal Ballot, Give Bush a Victory."
New York Times, November 4, 1979, p. 1. https://www.nytimes.com/1979/11/04/
archives/maine-republicans-in-informal-ballot-give-bush-a-victory-upset-for.html.
———. 1979b. "Connally Is Seeking Victory in Florida." *New York Times*, November 17, 1979, p. 12. https://www.nytimes.com/1979/11/17/archives/connally-is
-seeking-victory-in-florida-outspends-reagan-in-effort.html.
———. 1979c. "Reagan Wins a Poll of G.O.P. in Florida." *New York Times*, November 18, 1979, p. 1. https://www.nytimes.com/1979/11/18/archives/reagan-wins-a
-poll-of-gop-in-florida-he-turns-back-a-strong-effort.html.
Cohen, Marty, David Karol, Hans Noel, and John Zaller. 2008. *The Party Decides:
Presidential Nominations Before and After Reform*. Chicago: University of Chicago Press.
Cook, Rhodes. 1979. "Carter, Reagan Win Florida Convention Tests." *Congressional
Quarterly Weekly Report*, November 24, 1979, p. 2662.
———. 1991. "Cuomo Says 'No' to Candidacy at Last Possible Moment." *Congres-
sional Quarterly Weekly Report*, December 21, 1991, 3735–36.
Crouse, Timothy. 1974. *The Boys on the Bus*, 73–90. New York: Ballantine Books.
Dao, James. 1999. "In Straw Poll, Dole Got Help from Her 'Sisters,'" *New York
Times*, August 17, 1999, A14. https://www.nytimes.com/1999/08/17/us/in-straw
-poll-dole-got-help-from-her-sisters.html.
Dickenson, James R., and Charles Fishman, 1983. "Anti-Abortionist Group, Israeli
Backers Target Percy Campaign." *Washington Post*, July 7, 1983, A11.
Dionne, E. J., Jr., 2000. "Into Backstretch 2000." *Washington Post*, January 4,
2000, A15. http://www.washingtonpost.com/archive/opinions/2000/01/04/into
-backstretch-2000/6d7b9067-93dc-4be7-9b59-e5a37101a482/.
Edsall, Thomas B. 1991. "Clinton Wins Straw Poll at Florida Convention." *Washington Post*, December 11, 1991, A14. http://www.washingtonpost.com/archive/
politics/1991/12/16/clinton-wins-straw-poll-at-florida-convention/e0b71ae8-73eb
-4c8f-9287-9400f1064935/.
Evans, Rowland, and Robert Novak. 1975a. "The Advent of Birch Bayh." *Washington Post*, September 13, 1975, A15.
———. 1975b. "Jimmy Carter's Challenge to Wallace in Florida." *Washington Post*,
November 20, 1975, A19.

Firestone, David. 1999. "Alexander Cuts Staff and Travel." *New York Times*, June 4, A24. https://www.nytimes.com/1999/06/04/us/alexander-cuts-staff-and-travel .html.

Gailey, Phil. 1983. "Five Democrats Fight to Shed the Also-Ran Title." *New York Times*, October 21, 1983, A20. https://www.nytimes.com/1983/10/21/us/politics -five-democrats-fight-to-shed-the-also-ran-title.html.

———. 1986. "Democrats, with Little Dissent, Approve New Nominating Rules." *New York Times*, March 9, 1986, p. 28. https://www.nytimes.com/1986/03/09/us/ democrats-with-little-dissent-approve-new-nominating-rules.html.

Goldberg, Carey. 1999. "Gore Beats Bradley in Party's First Straw Poll." *New York Times,* May 16, 1999, p. 24. https://www.nytimes.com/1999/05/16/us/gore-beats -bradley-in-party-s-first-straw-poll.html.

Hagen, Lisa. 2019. "Warren Leads First Daily Kos 2020 Straw Poll." *The Hill*, January 8, 2019. https://thehill.com/homenews/campaign/424359-warren-leads-first -daily-kos-2020-straw-poll (accessed March 11, 2019).

Herbst, Susan. 1993. "Partisan Politics and the Symbolic Use of Straw Polls." *Numbered Voices: How Opinion Polling Has Shaped American Politics*, 69–87. Chicago: University of Chicago Press, 1993.

Hill, Kathleen Thompson, and Gerald N. Hill. 1994. *Real Life Dictionary of American Politics: What They're Saying and What It Really Means*. Los Angeles: General Publishing Group.

Kirkpatrick, David D. 2007. "Romney Campaign Focuses on Conservative Straw Poll." *New York Times*, March 1, 2007, A16. https://www.nytimes.com/2007/03/01/ us/politics/01candidates.html.

Kneeland, Douglas E. 1979. "Bush Easily Wins Iowa Straw Vote for Republican Presidential Choice." *New York Times*, October 16, 1979, B10. https://www.ny times.com/1979/10/16/archives/bush-easily-wins-iowa-straw-vote-for-republican -presidential-choice.html.

Luo, Michael. 2007. "Romney Works to Put Skeptics' Doubts to Rest." *New York Times*, May 11, 2007, A1. https://www.nytimes.com/2007/05/11/us/ politics/11romney.html.

Lyons, Richard L. 1979. "Bush's Victory Surprises Baker in Maine Voting." *Washington Post*, November 4, 1979. A1. https://www.washingtonpost.com/archive/ politics/1979/11/04/bushs-victory-surprises-baker-in-maine-voting/f580b483 -1e24-471a-a495-9214d01fb8b2/.

Macquarrie, Brian. 1999. "Gore Trumps Bradley in Straw Poll." *Boston Globe*, May 16, 1999, B1. http://cache.boston.com/news/politics/campaign2000/news/ Gore_trumps_Bradley_in_straw_poll.shtml.

Mayer, William G. 1996. "Caucuses: How They Work, What Difference They Make." In *In Pursuit of the White House: How We Choose Our Presidential Nominees*, edited by William G. Mayer, table 4.12, p. 144. Chatham, NJ: Chatham House.

———. 2004. "The Basic Dynamics of the Contemporary Nomination Process: An Expanded View." In *The Making of the Presidential Candidates 2004*, edited by William G. Mayer, 83–132. Lanham, MD: Rowman & Littlefield.

———. 2012. "How the Romney Campaign Blew It." *The Forum* 10, no. 4 (December): 40–50.

Mayer, William G., and Andrew E. Busch, 2004. *The Front-Loading Problem in Presidential Nominations*, 140–46. Washington, DC: Brookings Institution Press.

Nagourney, Brian, and Jeff Zeleny. 2007. "Romney Wins Iowa Straw Poll by a Sizable Margin." *New York Times*, August 12, 2007, p. 18. https://www.nytimes.com/2007/08/12/us/politics/12straw.html.

Novak, Robert. 1999. "Bumps in Bush's Campaign Trail." *Washington Post*, May 3, 1999, A25. http://www.washingtonpost.com/archive/opinions/1999/05/03/bumps-in-bushs-campaign-trail/9356cbb7-53ca-406f-9589-96a41e97654d/.

Peterson, Bill. 1979. "Republican Hopefuls Grasp at Straws in Iowa Wind." *Washington Post*, October 15, 1979, A5. http://www.washingtonpost.com/archive/politics/1979/10/15/republican-hopefuls-grasp-at-straws-in-iowa-wind/d305ca64-a6af-4933-8bfa-a4f427bb3b63/.

Raines, Howell. 1979. "Pro-Kennedy Bloc in Florida Seeks to Humiliate Carter in Straw Vote." *New York Times*, May 25, 1979, p. 14. https://www.nytimes.com/1979/05/25/archives/prokennedy-bloc-in-florida-seeks-to-humiliate-carter-in-straw-vote.html.

Raines, Howell. 1983a. "Mondale Wins Massachusetts Ballot Despite Labor's Neutral Votes." *New York Times*, April 10, 1983, p. 24. https://www.nytimes.com/1983/04/10/us/mondale-wins-massachusetts-ballot-despite-labor-s-neutral-votes.html.

———. 1983b. "Cranston Beats Mondale in Wisconsin Democratic Straw Poll." *NewYork Times*, June 12, 1983, p. 22. https://www.nytimes.com/1983/06/12/us/cranston-beats-mondale-in-wisconsin-democratic-straw-poll.html.

Safire, William 1983. "The Psychoprimaries." *New York Times*, June 13, 1983, A15. https://www.nytimes.com/1983/06/13/opinion/essay-the-psychoprimaries.html.

Safire, William. 1993. *Safire's New Political Dictionary: The Definitive Guide to the New Language of Politics*, 764–65. New York: Random House.

Sawyer, Kathy. 1983. "Democrats' Straw Polls Are Called Divisive." *Washington Post*, July 19, 1983, A1.

Schram Martin. 1977. *Running for President 1976: The Carter Campaign*, 16–17. New York: Stein and Day.

Shear, Michael D. 2011. "Pawlenty Seeks Out Religious Voters in Iowa." *New York Times*, August 10, 2011, A15. http://query.nytimes.com/gst/fullpage.html?res=9900E6D71F31F933A2575BC0A9679D8B63.

Sherfinski, David, and Stephen Dinan. 2019. "CPAC Straw Poll: Biden Biggest Threat to Trump." *Washington Times*, March 2, 2019. https://www.washingtontimes.com/news/2019/mar/2/cpac-straw-poll-biden-biggest-threat-to-trump/ (accessed March 11, 2019).

Silverleib, Alan, and William G. Mayer. 2012. "By the Numbers: A Statistical Guide to the Presidential Nomination Process." In *The Making of the Presidential Candidates 2012*, edited by William G. Mayer and Jonathan Bernstein, 203–8. Lanham, MD: Rowman & Littlefield.

Smith, Tom W. 1990. "The First Straw: A Study of the Origins of Election Polls." *Public Opinion Quarterly* 54 (Spring): 21–36.

Sullivan, Joseph F. 1983. "Glenn Outpolls Mondale at Jersey Party Meeting." *New York Times*, September 14, 1983, B2. https://www.nytimes.com/1983/09/14/nyre gion/glenn-outpolls-mondale-at-jersey-party-meeting.html.

Taylor, Paul 1986. "Democrats End Session in Harmony." *Washington Post*, March 9, 1986, A4.

Tolchin, Martin. 1979. "White House Spurs Funds for Florida." *New York Times*, October 7, 1979, p. 27. http://www.nytimes.com/1979/10/07/archives/white-house -spurs-funds-for-florida-grants-reported-expedited-to.html.

Toner, Robin. 1987. "Presidential Race Puzzles the Pundits." *New York Times*, December 11, 1987, A32. https://www.nytimes.com/1987/12/11/us/politics-political -memo-presidential-race-puzzles-the-pundits.html.

Walsh, Edward. 1987. "7 Democrats Ply Hispanic Convention." *Washington Post*, June 29, 1987, A3. https://www.washingtonpost.com/archive/politics/1987/06/29/7 -democrats-ply-hispanic-convention/eac7636e-456f-4037-ad1a-b84f4d9841de/.

Weinraub, Bernard. 1984. "Staff Averts Most Surprises on Mondale's 5 Days in South." *New York Times*, January 9, 1984, B7. https://www.nytimes.com/1984/01/09/us/ staff-averts-most-surprises-on-mondale-s-5-days-in-south.html.

Winebrenner, Hugh, and Dennis J. Goldford. 2010. *The Iowa Precinct Caucuses: The Making of a Media Event*, 3rd ed., 60–63. Iowa City: University of Iowa Press.

Witcover, Jules. 1977. *Marathon: The Pursuit of the Presidency, 1972–1976*, 201–3. New York: Viking Press.

Zeleny, Jeff. 2011. "Will Republican Race's First In Be the First Out?" *New York Times*, July 8, 2011, A15. https://www.nytimes.com/2011/07/08/us/ politics/08pawlenty.html.

Zeleny, Jeff, and Michael D. Shear. 2011. "After Iowa Vote, Republicans Face a New Landscape." *New York Times*, August 15, 2011, A1. https://www.nytimes .com/2011/08/15/us/politics/15repubs.html.

Chapter Seven

The Expanded Party's Influence

Jonathan Bernstein

With the election of Donald Trump, nomination politics—how parties choose their presidential candidates in the United States—has taken on new urgency in the study of American politics. Partisan polarization now appears to ensure that any nominee will win the votes of most partisans and therefore, if conditions are right, the White House, which leaves the question of whether political parties as organizations actively choose their nominees an important one indeed.

Parties in the United States never directly control their own nominations the way that parties in most democracies do. For most U.S. offices, nominations are decided in primary elections, in which formal party organizations by norm and in some cases by law are not free to participate.

Presidential nominations are in some respects even farther removed from simple control. Once upon a time, from the 1830s up through 1968, the national convention determined the nomination, and the delegates to that gathering represented state and local parties who were free to choose those delegates however they wanted—and even free to control their actions at the convention if they could do so. As primary elections were adopted for most other offices early in the twentieth century, some states instituted presidential preference primaries, but most of those were advisory only, rather than a means for selecting delegates. Few states had primaries up through 1968, and they were generally only as important as party insiders took them to be. In 1968, the Democratic convention nominated Vice President Hubert Humphrey, who hadn't entered a single primary election.

Reform after 1968 changed all of that. Beginning in 1972, caucuses and primaries chose the nominees, with the convention mainly playing the role of technically certifying those results and serving as a fail-safe backup in the event that something went wrong.[1] Formal party organizations—the Illinois Republican Party or the Harris County Democratic Party—which had previously dominated the process, no longer had any direct role at all. The delegates are now chosen by voters in a sequential state-by-state process and delegates represent those voters. Or, perhaps more accurately, they serve as little more than tally marks for the candidates the voters have chosen.

Despite plenty of reform commissions, rules tweaks, and technological and political change, the system invented after 1968 is still the system in use today.

This still leaves the question of who exactly chooses the nominees. And that turns out to be a very complicated question. It's true that the voters select the delegates, but the bulk of the research on nomination politics concludes that the voters are autonomous actors to a limited extent: in important ways, they are swayed by the campaign and the hoopla surrounding the campaign. As Cohen et al. (2016) correctly frame the discussion, there are essentially two leading possibilities of who ultimately influences nominations.

The first is, essentially, an argument that the system is ultimately chaotic. Nelson W. Polsby's *Consequences of Party Reform* (1983), looking back at the first three cycles under the new system, describes a process that leaves little or no room for coalition building and party control. Instead, voters in primaries and caucuses will be attracted to seemingly random candidates based on media hype, personality, and factional politics.

For Polsby, the state-by-state gauntlet of primaries required mobilizing a faction, whether it was ideological (2016 examples included democratic socialist Bernie Sanders or moderate conservative John Kasich) or personal (like Donald Trump).[2] Since primaries present voters with several relatively similar contenders without party labels to cue them, the imperative for candidates is differentiating themselves from the others. Only first-choice votes matter; a candidate who wins over a third of the voters in early states at the cost of alienating the other two thirds will survive, while a candidate acceptable to all but first choice of only a handful will be eliminated. There was, in this view of things, nothing to prevent the field winnowing to only two or three of these factional candidates. And that's exactly what happened for Republicans in 2016, as none of the final three candidates standing—Donald Trump, Ted Cruz, and John Kasich—were acceptable to the entire party.[3]

As much as the Trump nomination seemed to confirm Polsby's fears, Trump is also the first case of a clearly factional candidate to win a nomination since Polsby's book. Mitt Romney, John McCain, George W. Bush, Barack Obama, John Kerry, and Al Gore all sought to be and were all widely acceptable to their parties, even if they weren't always the first-choice candidates of all party groups. In fact, they all seemed to fit the idea of coalition candidates.

The explanation advanced by some scholars is that parties have learned to game the system, and that parties have found new ways to fight over and cooperate around nominations (Bernstein 1999, 2004; Cohen et al. 2008).

The case that parties control their nominations rests, to begin with, on the importance of party networks within what I've called "expanded" parties. Party network scholars have found that formal party organizations are not the only, or even necessarily the most important components, of U.S. political parties properly understood. Instead, party actors including politicians, campaign and governing professionals, donors and activists, party-aligned interest groups and the partisan media join with formal party officials and staff to make up the entire party. All of those party actors stick to their own (partisan) side and generally care deeply about the course of the party, even if they also often have personal professional concerns as well—something expanded parties share with formally organized parties, which after all are filled with officials and staff who may combine party and personal goals.

Expanded parties are by their nature decentralized and non-hierarchical in a way that formal organizations cannot be. But they still manage to make decisions, fighting over and then usually agreeing to policy positions and priorities.

And expanded parties can control nominations made by primary elections, too, by giving party-favored candidates important resources such as money, expertise, and publicity. Donor networks can steer money to candidates the party likes, as can websites such as ActBlue, which can help small donors converge on the same candidate (Lerer 2018). Party-loyal campaign and governing professionals can give party-favored candidates know-how to run the best campaigns. And party-aligned media—Fox News and conservative talk radio, MSNBC prime time shows and liberal blogs—can selectively publicize those candidates and can deliver negative information about those candidates who party actors dislike to a partisan audience. Not only that, but the neutral media can use all of this as objective evidence of which candidates are doing well, which generates more favorable publicity for them, which in turn generates more money and other resources.

As long as party-controlled resources are valuable, the Polsby conclusion that coalition building is irrelevant and mobilizing a faction is the clear strategy for candidates in a primary-dominated system no longer holds. A candidate who is everyone's second choice early in the process has real advantages over a candidate with a strong factional base who the rest of the party dislikes.

There's a good deal of empirical evidence that this works in at least some elections. In addition to the material on presidential nominations, see Seth Masket (2009) on how party networks in California are able to control nominations in areas where the formal party organizations are weak and Casey Dominguez (2011) on parties in House nominations.[4]

That said, establishing exactly how these sprawling parties decide in presidential nominations, and exactly how they influence voters, has proven difficult to do. So when Donald Trump comes along and upends everything in exactly the way Polsby predicted, it's easy for people to jump to the conclusion that parties have been irrelevant all along, even as the Hillary Clinton nomination looked a lot more like a party-determined choice. So the questions become these: How did Clinton win? And was Trump a fluke?

THE DEMOCRATS IN 2016

For the Democrats, 2016 was a good example of what essentially, despite plenty of swerves and detours, was a candidate dominating the process. Hillary Clinton, like Ronald Reagan in 1980, George H. W. Bush in 1988, and Al Gore in 2000, was close to the consensus choice of party actors. Reagan in 1980 is probably the closest comparison: a long-time party leader, associated with one party faction but willing to reach out to everyone, who had been a very close runner-up the last time the party's nomination was contested and handled the narrow defeat by mending fences with the winner and his supporters.

The result was an avalanche of endorsements for Clinton from almost every group within the party, which had the effect of discouraging most interested mainstream liberal Democrats from challenging her.

Clinton's party-spanning dominance, easy to see in her biography—she had been associated with a wide range of Democratic groups over the years—and her endorsements, was also demonstrated by her campaign organization.[5]

The campaign manager, Robby Mook, had worked in the 2008 Clinton campaign. But he was less of a Clinton person than a classic party operative. Mook is from Vermont, and his first presidential campaign involvement was Howard Dean's 2004 effort. But instead of returning to Vermont when Dean dropped out, Mook worked on John Kerry's campaign. After Clinton in 2008, Mook was at the Democratic Congressional Campaign Committee, as political director and then executive director. Along the way, he's been involved in a number of other candidate campaigns (Jean Shaheen, Martin O'Malley, Terry McAuliffe) and formal party organizations.

Similarly, the chief strategist and pollster, Joel Benenson, had a strong Clinton connection, having worked on Bill Clinton's reelection effort. But in 2008 (and 2012), he was with Barack Obama's campaign, not Hillary Clinton's. A former reporter, Benenson's first campaign role was as Mario Cuomo's communications director in 1994; as a pollster, he worked for many Democratic candidates. The political director, Amanda Renteria, was a Senate staffer for Dianne Feinstein and Debbie Stabenow for a decade before running unsuccessfully for the House in a California district in 2014. Campaign chair John Podesta had served in the Bill Clinton White House, eventually as chief of staff. After Clinton, Podesta founded the Democratic-aligned think tank, the Center for American Progress (CAP), leaving it eventually for the Obama White House in 2014 and then the Hillary Clinton campaign in 2015. Communications director Jennifer Palmieri had been a House staffer for Leon Panetta, followed him to the Bill Clinton White House, and then became the Democratic National Committee press secretary. She worked on both the 2004 and 2008 John Edwards presidential campaigns, and after some time at CAP wound up at the Obama White House before joining the Hillary Clinton campaign.

That's not to say that there were no long-time Hillary Clinton loyalists in the campaign. The most notable one was Huma Abedin, a one-time intern in the First Lady's office who stayed with Clinton through her Senate career, the 2008 campaign, and at the State Department.

For the most part, however, the campaign was made up of Democratic Party campaign and governing professionals who had worked for a wide variety of Democratic candidates, office holders, formal party organizations, and party-aligned interest groups. In other words, it was a coalition-style campaign, not a factional one. The endorsements from a wide range of Democrats were a consequence of the kind of campaign Clinton was running.

Indeed, only the fringes of the party were excluded from her coalition, so it's not surprising that two of the four challengers who eventually reached the point of declaring their candidacies, Senator Bernie Sanders and former senator Jim Webb, came from the conservative and socialist fringes of the party. Only one mainstream candidate with conventional qualifications, former Maryland governor Martin O'Malley, achieved that stage, and he found no constituency there. The other declared contender, former Rhode Island governor Lincoln Chafee, was more of a vanity campaign than a real effort.[6]

We can't know for sure how many mainstream Democrats were interested in the race—in Josh Putnam's phrasing, were running *for* 2016—but eventually dropped out well short of announcing a formal candidacy at least in part because Clinton was dominant. Surely, there were some, most notably Vice President Joe Biden.[7] What we do know is that no non-incumbent has done a more thorough job of locking up the nomination during the invisible primary period than Hillary Clinton in the 2016 cycle.[8]

The primaries and caucuses that followed appeared to be at least moderately competitive, with Bernie Sanders winning several events, but it's unlikely he ever had any reasonable shot at actually winning the nomination. Clinton never lost her national polling lead, and quickly opened up a large delegate lead.

As for the Sanders campaign, biography and endorsements revealed a candidate with weak ties to the party—after all, Sanders serves as an independent in the United States Senate.[9] And just as the Clinton organization demonstrates her strength within the party, the Sanders effort reveals his weakness. In particular, his campaign manager, Jeff Weaver, was an old Sanders staffer who had dropped out of politics in 2010 and returned for the presidential campaign. While Sanders did add some people with broader links to the party, such as senior advisor Tad Devine, even Devine had previously worked for Sanders. And it's no surprise that for the most part the ties Sanders staffers had were mainly to the very liberal side of the party. It was very much an ideological and personal factional campaign—the kind that hasn't won a Democratic nomination since Jimmy Carter.

The 2016 Democratic nomination certainly is consistent with a "party decides" understanding of presidential nomination politics. It's true that Clinton seemed an obvious choice to most party actors and most voters in the lead-up to the primaries and caucuses, so much so that it's tempting to assume that she would have won regardless of the nomination system. But we don't know that. Voter preferences have proved fickle in the past. Walter Mondale looked unbeatable right up through the Iowa caucuses in 1984—only to suddenly lose the New Hampshire primary to Gary Hart and only narrowly survive to win the nomination. Perhaps a candidate with greater strength within the party than Sanders could have defeated Clinton after all.

Instead, what appears to have happened is that high-profile endorsements and other evidence of her dominant position successfully pre-winnowed the candidate field, pushing most potential candidates to never even show any public interest in a run and those who did, such as Vice President Joe Biden, to back off before reaching the step of announcing a formal candidacy. It's true that Clinton was just a very strong nomination candidate by any measure. Runners-up with a wide appeal to the whole party tend to win the next time, as Reagan did in 1980 and Bob Dole, John McCain, and Mitt Romney all did in later cycles. But that's just to say that despite the seeming randomness of media hype and candidate emergence, the seemingly logical candidate tends to win nominations, which is more evidence that parties are at work. Unless, of course, one of those random candidates actually wins. For that, we turn to the other party.

THE REPUBLICANS IN 2016

While the Democratic side seemed to confirm that parties control nominations, the Republican side certainly did not. Donald Trump won the Republican presidential nomination with virtually no party support at all. He received hardly any endorsements, even fairly late in the process when he had taken a significant delegate lead. His campaign organization, which barely existed in the first place, had hardly any connections with the party network.

What Happened?

There are three basic stories: the effects of changing rules and norms, including media practices; Republican dysfunction; and luck. All of them contributed to help a factional candidate who wasn't very popular and who violated party orthodoxy on numerous issues winning the nomination. And each tells us something important about the presidential nomination system and how parties do and don't control nominations.

It Was the Norms

James Madison explained before mass parties existed that factions were inherent in democratic societies. But how those factions behave depends, as Madison knew, on incentive structures that can be designed into a polity. As Polsby said, coalition building depends on whether the political "system operates by some sort of stable rules giving incentives for factions to undertake strategic behavior" (Polsby 1983, 65). The importance of stable rules is almost certainly even more true of U.S.-style expanded parties, which are composed of both formal organizations and loose networks of other party actors. Because parties of this type are not hierarchical, and therefore require a good deal of sometimes complex coordination among groups spread out across the nation, parties are always going to find it hard to come to agreements no matter what kind of nomination system is employed. And while the McGovern-Fraser reforms that took effect in 1972 wound up being appropriate for expanded parties in that they removed the formal party structure from a central role—appropriate because in most places the formal organizations are not in fact central to what parties do—the reforms did little to make complex coordination easy.

Indeed, even those who believe that parties eventually learned to control new-style nominations agree that it took until the 1980s for party actors to learn enough about how the new system worked to be able to use their influence. When the process is unstable, candidates (or other actors) can win by exploiting the rules, regardless of what the party wants. So George McGovern beat Hubert Humphrey in 1972 even though Humphrey was probably the party's choice because Humphrey didn't realize that entering late was no longer a viable strategy; Jimmy Carter won in 1976 in large part because he contested the newly crucial Iowa caucuses while other candidates waited until New Hampshire or later to get involved.

While there are always small changes in the nominating system—changes in the calendar of primaries and caucuses, or in how money is raised, or in how candidates communicate with voters—the basic process is stable enough that parties know what they have to do to influence the nomination.

That wasn't quite the case in 2016 on the Republican side.

The first big change was the elimination of what had been, since the 1980 cycle, the first big event in Republican nomination politics: the Ames straw poll. That contest had been held in the August before the election year from 1979 through 2011, but it was canceled for 2015 because it had become widely seen as a farce.

Ames was misunderstood by pundits, in part because the event itself was pretty ridiculous. Candidates bought tickets to the event, and then bused in voters to support them in the straw poll portion. There were candidate speeches, and they might have swayed any undecided voters who were there, but to a large extent the straw poll had become an exercise in organizational skill combined with a weird choice about campaign priorities. Ames was also misunderstood because it usually failed to predict the winner of the nomination. More recently, it didn't even do a good job of predicting the winner of the Iowa caucuses. In 2007 Mitt Romney won at Ames but was thumped in the caucuses by Mike Huckabee; in 2011 the winner, Michele Bachmann, finished a poor sixth in the caucuses.[10]

That it was ridiculous and that it failed to predict the nominee, however, was irrelevant to the real usefulness of the Ames straw poll: it provided a bit of structure to the process that everyone involved could count on. That became a critical issue in 2016 because of the nature of the Republican candidate field. An unusually large number of candidates, seventeen, formally declared; no obvious frontrunner emerged; and quite a few candidates had conventional qualifications for the presidency and held orthodox conservative policy positions.

Given those conditions, it's not surprising that party actors were slow to converge on a single candidate. Ames would have helped. Winners—the actual first place finisher and anyone else perceived to have done well—would have received some positive media attention, and perhaps a polling surge. Those perceived to have done badly might well have dropped out, either immediately or after their resources dried up.

And that would have been bad for Trump. Even had he competed in Ames and won (unlikely, since Ames required the kind of organization that Trump's campaign was terrible at), the results would have helped consolidate the field and would have helped party actors who opposed Trump to see him as a genuine threat a whole lot earlier than they did. Had he contested the straw poll and lost, it might have directly hurt him going forward, but even if it didn't, or if he skipped the event, anything that helped the party to settle on a single candidate earlier in the process would have been bad for him.

Perhaps an even more important change in 2016, however, was a major shift in media norms. Previously, media coverage of surging candidates had a recognizable pattern which John Sides and Lynn Vavreck (2013) describe as a "discovery, scrutiny, and decline" pattern. That is, the news media would suddenly begin heavy coverage of one particular candidate, who would then surge in the polls thanks to the additional attention. At first that coverage, in the discovery phase, would be positive, as the media introduced the candidate to voters, but once the surge happened the media would unearth less appealing stories, leading to the end of the polling surge and a decline in media attention to the candidate.

Almost anything can spark media discovery of a candidate—anything from a good moment in a debate to a strong fundraising report to a well-received campaign ad or video. And practically any candidate can benefit from discovery. From the media's perspective, as Sides and Vavreck explain, the point is that the nomination contest doesn't really create a lot of "news," especially during the invisible primary period, and so the media is looking for stories. Discovery-scrutiny-decline is a way of generating them, even from thin material.

It's easy to see how party actors could adapt to a media environment in which discovery-scrutiny-decline is a predictable pattern. To the extent the party has come to agree on a candidate, they can attempt to create "discovery" moments for those they support, and they can either contribute to scrutiny and then decline for those they do not support, or help those they support avoid severe scrutiny and then decline altogether. After all, the media does at least to some extent take cues from party leaders and other party actors. Assuming that voters have very weak attachments (if any) to the various candidates, it shouldn't be difficult for a unified party to get pretty good results from fairly small pushes in the right direction.

What happened in 2016 on the Republican side was completely different. Donald Trump had his discovery. One might even say that he had scrutiny; plenty of negative stories were reported, although there was plenty of positive coverage, mainly focusing on how well he was doing, throughout the nomination process. What was entirely missing was decline. Sides and Vavreck write that "having devoted some time to writing about a particular candidate, the media has a natural incentive to move on and find a storyline that was novel and more exciting. Unless the candidate did something else that was considered newsworthy, his or her news coverage began to decline."

That didn't happen in 2015 and 2016. Instead, Trump dominated coverage of the Republican nomination battle from the day he announced right up through the convention, especially on cable television (for the gory details, see Sides et al. 2018, 50–52). The result was that other candidates were unable to find any footing, and Trump continued to benefit from the extraordinary attention.

Why? Because, I suspect, the news media had learned that finding a new novel and more exciting storyline wasn't the only way to hype the story. Instead, CNN had found, particularly in the story of a missing airplane, that they could sustain a story indefinitely and be rewarded with excellent ratings.

Malaysia Airlines Flight MH370 had disappeared on March 7, 2014, and CNN immediately switched to nonstop coverage of that event. And while the initial story was presumably "news" that was an easy decision to cover, CNN kept pounding away at it for months, even when there were no new events involved and the rest of the media had essentially moved on. It wasn't an on-the-spot decision, exactly; it was part of a thought-out strategy by CNN management (Tyndall 2014; Quest 2016). They had realized that cable news had always done well when there was a major event such as a war or the O.J. Simpson trial. What if, instead of waiting for an event, they just created one by acting as if something was constantly creating breaking news? And it worked, with CNN achieving strong ratings, albeit with a fair amount of media criticism.

This was the context for CNN, followed by other news outlets, deciding to cover politics in 2015 and 2016 as the Trump story, rather than as the election or politics or policy story. On CNN, that was institutionalized by hiring Trump apologists for their panels when it quickly turned out that their normal Republican pundits had no use for the reality show celebrity.[11]

As a result, cues from Republican elites that Trump was unacceptable didn't reach Republican voters, and most of the more acceptable candidates didn't have an opportunity for their moments of discovery. Party actors who might have thought that they could deal with Trump by waiting out the media frenzy over him—in other words, who believed that the strategies that had worked in past nomination cycles would be successful in 2016—found out too late that missing airplane coverage of Trump didn't have any natural expiration date.

At the same time, rival candidates who counted on previous media norms to extinguish Trump without much help made what appeared to be the sensible decision to concentrate their attacks on seemingly more viable candidates. Leading up to Iowa, Jeb Bush attacked Marco Rubio; Rubio attacked

Bush and Ted Cruz; Cruz attacked Rubio (Sides et al. 2018, 66–67). Again, all of this made perfect sense if, at some point, the media was going to get bored of Trump and pick a new candidate to discover. The rules of the game, in particular, had been that whoever beat expectations in Iowa would get a burst of publicity, one that might take someone all the way to the nomination. Preventing Rubio from being that candidate seemed an obvious strategy for most candidates. But the press, it turned out, wasn't playing by the old rules. Even after Trump finished a seemingly disappointing second in Iowa, behind Cruz and only slightly ahead of a surging Rubio, he remained the focus of attention.

The bottom line: when the rules of the game change, it becomes hard for U.S. parties, in all their decentralized and networked complexity, to compete and coordinate over the nomination.

It Was the Broken Republican Party

Picking Trump required more than a flawed process. It certainly helped—that is, hurt the possibilities of healthy competition and successful coordination— that by 2016, the Republican Party had become deeply dysfunctional. It's no surprise that the leading public scholar of that dysfunction, Norm Ornstein, was one of the first observers to take the Trump threat seriously (2015; see generally Mann and Ornstein 2012). Yes, the party had managed to nominate two perfectly ordinary politicians, John McCain and Mitt Romney, in 2008 and 2012. But there were plenty of things for Trump to exploit.

The key to understanding what has gone wrong with the Republicans is that it's not about ideology. They're not simply "too" conservative, whatever that might mean. The problem, instead, is that the normal incentives for political parties—to hold office and to create public policy—appear in many cases to no longer hold for the party as a whole.

That's in part because of the large amounts of money to be made by exploiting the conservative marketplace. Fox News, conservative talk radio, Republican books, and the rest of the marketplace are fueled by resentment, and that works much better when Democrats are in office. The Bill Clinton and Barack Obama presidencies were boom times. That's not to say that Republican-aligned media and others who can make money from that market actively seek the defeat of Republican presidential candidates. It's just that the normal incentives for finding a winner aren't nearly as strong for them as they might otherwise be.

At the same time, the drive to enact party policy positions and priorities is dulled by the positioning of the Republican Party as an ideological force, and one that cares more about purity than pragmatism (Grossmann and Hopkins

2016). What that means is, again, that party actors who care most about the party (and perhaps the party's voters as well) are unlikely to worry a lot about whether their specific preferences can become public policy and are more likely to care about whether the party identifies as conservative.

It may even make them more tolerant of candidates with policy positions that violate party orthodoxy, because what really matters is whether a politician sufficiently proclaims his or her dedication to the conservative cause. The rise of strong levels of negative partisanship may even mean that the real test comes down to whether a candidate strongly opposes (and is strongly opposed by) Democrats and their associated groups (Abramowitz and Webster 2016). Even more bizarrely, it could mean that a highly flawed candidate who (because of those flaws) draws sharp criticisms from Democrats and the neutral media may be able to use those criticisms alone as evidence of his or her strong conservative Republican credentials, regardless of any other evidence of partisan or ideological or policy loyalty.

This tolerance for otherwise inexplicable candidates was evident in a series of "Tea Party" candidates for Senate such as Christine O'Donnell in Delaware, Sharron Angle in Nevada, and Todd Akin in Missouri. Each badly lost contests that a more conventional nominee might have won.[12]

Republican willingness to seriously consider candidates without conventional qualifications goes back well before the Tea Party, however:

- Evangelist Pat Robertson in 1988 won three states, while finishing second in the Iowa caucuses and several other events.
- Pundit Pat Buchanan in 1992 put up a spirited challenge to sitting President George H. W. Bush, peaking at 37 percent of the vote in New Hampshire.
- Buchanan won the 1996 New Hampshire primary and caucuses in three other states, and finished second in overall votes.
- Publisher Steve Forbes in 1996 won two states and finished third in overall votes.
- Forbes tried again in 2000 and finished second in Iowa and Alaska.
- Activist Alan Keyes in 2000 finished third in Iowa; in fact, with activist Gary Bauer finishing fourth in the caucuses, that meant three such candidates finished ahead of eventual runner-up John McCain.
- Business executive and talk show host Herman Cain withdrew before the 2012 primaries, but before he ran into scandal he reached first place in the polling averages for about a month in fall 2011 (HuffPost Pollster 2016).
- While they aren't quite in the same category, both Michele Bachmann and Newt Gingrich made serious runs. Bachmann was a rank-and-file member of the House, and Gingrich, the former Speaker, had resigned from the House in disgrace over a decade earlier.

- In addition to Trump, surgeon Ben Carson and business executive Carli Fiorina both ran in 2016. Carson was second in trial-heat polls in fall 2015 before becoming an also-ran in several caucuses and primaries, and even Fiorina had a brief polling surge in 2015.

The only comparable runs on the Democratic side were activist Jesse Jackson's campaigns in 1984 and 1988.[13] Since then, the only candidate without conventional credentials to even attempt to get anywhere on the Democratic side was activist Al Sharpton, who was a non-factor in 2004.

It is perhaps not surprising that Republicans would be more open to presidential candidates with unconventional backgrounds, especially those from the business world. And yet Republican politicians and others who were concerned about winning rarely embraced these candidates. Indeed, they usually helped to defeat them by supporting those with conventional credentials. Including, to be sure, candidates such as George H. W. Bush, George W. Bush, and Mitt Romney, all of whom had business backgrounds in addition to their political careers.

One way to think of this is that Republican party actors had already either chosen to allow unqualified candidates from contending—or had proven themselves incapable of preventing them from doing so. Either way, it means that Republican voters had long since been trained to consider voting for unconventional candidates. That probably made it harder for those party actors who tried to dissuade them from voting for Trump.

Another possibility is that the cumulative effect of watching Buchanan, Forbes, Cain, and the rest fall short—often after seeming to be real threats to win—was to convince many in the party that such candidates were best left alone until they collapsed on their own.

Granted, this is somewhat speculative. We don't really know exactly why the Republican Party is open to these types of candidates while Democrats are not. But it does seem that there's a big difference between the parties, and it's consistent with the type of diagnosis that Ornstein and Tom Mann, among others, have made concerning what's wrong with the Republican party.

And openness to seemingly unqualified candidates wasn't the only way in which Republican dysfunction helped Trump. They also demonstrated a remarkable inability to compromise over what appear to have been small differences within the party.

In both 2008 and 2012, Christian conservatives were faced with a tough choice. Frontrunners John McCain (in 2008) and Mitt Romney (in 2012) had mixed records on policies that Christian conservatives cared deeply about, and especially in 2008 there was no other strong option—no candidate with conventional qualifications who was broadly acceptable to all other party groups. During the nomination fight in those two cycles, they backed candidates with little appeal to the rest of the party—Mike Huckabee in 2008 and Rick Santorum in 2012—who used that support to win the Iowa caucuses and make a serious bid for the nomination.

During the 2016 cycle, however, they had several reasonable choices, but they eventually settled on Ted Cruz, including an endorsement by a coalition of Christian conservatives in December 2015. Cruz had been in the middle of the back in Iowa polling until October, but support from religious groups pushed him into the top tier and he eventually won the state. The problem was that Cruz was strongly opposed by most of the party. His abrasive style and his leading role in a futile government shutdown in 2013 had alienated a lot of mainstream Republicans nationally, and especially within Washington.

Had Christian conservatives picked, say, Bobby Jindal or Rick Perry or Scott Walker, it's quite possible that Cruz would have never surged, the alternate choice would have either won in Iowa or come close, and the party as a whole would have had their consensus candidate. That almost certainly would have been the case had they chosen Marco Rubio, who finished a close third in Iowa as it was.

A less likely, but still possible option, would have been for the rest of the party to accept Cruz after he won in Iowa. It's true they had good reasons for opposing him, but Cruz did have conventional qualifications for the presidency and orthodox party positions on public policy, and while he had broken norms of civility, those violations were nothing compared to what Donald Trump had done.

Instead, Christian conservatives chose the one candidate acceptable to them who was least likely to gather broad-based support from Republican party actors, and few others were willing to accept him, even at the risk of nominating Trump.[14]

It Was Luck

Trump won—but he hardly dominated the process. He eventually took about 45 percent of the total primary vote, the lowest of any Republican nominee in the modern era; only John McCain in 2012 had failed to reach 50 percent. Trump won only 70 percent of the delegate vote at the convention, the lowest total since 1976.

And even that overstates his win. His delegate lead was so slim that there was still a small but not impossible chance after the primaries were over that he could still be denied a majority on the convention floor, a chance that only disappeared when Republican National Committee chair (and future Trump White House chief of staff) Reince Priebus and delegates loyal to him chose to side with the apparent nominee. Before the RNC tilted toward him at the convention itself, Trump had only captured 1,441 delegates during the primaries and caucuses, just 56 percent of the total, only a bit better than the 1,237 needed for a convention majority.

Granted, unlike the Ford-Reagan contest in 1976 or close Democratic nomination fights such as the Obama-Clinton matchup in 2008, there was no close runner-up—while Trump was a narrow winner, there was no narrow loser, at least not by the convention in Cleveland, to challenge him. Indeed, the last two opponents to be winnowed, Ted Cruz and John Kasich, had dropped out after the Indiana primary on May 3, leaving Trump unopposed in the last several delegate events and at the convention.

Still, his margin of victory was narrow enough that a number of things could plausibly have derailed it. And in fact there were a series of apparently random and unsystematic events on the campaign trail that derailed Trump's opponents and made it possible for him to reach the magic 1,237 delegate number.

Some of those were events that undermined the candidacy of Marco Rubio, who eventually emerged as the (fairly mild) party choice. That included two poorly timed misfires in debates, which slowed his momentum at crucial points during the primaries and caucuses. It also included the decision by Jeb Bush to remain in the race after miserable showings in Iowa and then New Hampshire; it's hardly certain that Rubio would have inherited Bush's support, but it seems likely—especially had Bush, who strongly opposed Trump, endorsed Rubio.

Then there was the bizarre behavior of Ohio governor John Kasich. The long-time conservative made the odd choice of running as a moderate, a strategy that hadn't worked for Republican presidential candidates in decades and one that helped him with a small constituency but eliminated him for the bulk of party actors and Republican voters. He skipped Iowa, another guaranteed-to-lose strategy. After then scoring a weak second place finish in New Hampshire, he chose to stay in the race despite having little chance of winning—and then promptly skipped most of the next states, a strategy that was even less sensible than skipping Iowa.

That wasn't all. After winning in his home state of Ohio and therefore becoming (with Cruz) one of the last two candidates running against Trump, Kasich reacted to Trump's decision to pull out of future debates by also refusing to debate Ted Cruz, thereby losing an opportunity for free publicity. And then after Cruz dropped out after the Indiana primary, Kasich also dropped out, even though the only way any of his strategy made sense was if he was trying to hold Trump under 50 percent of the delegates and then get lucky at the convention; at the point in which Kasich dropped out that unlikely strategy still had a vaguely plausible chance of working, which is all it ever had. By staying in when he should have dropped out, by campaigning the way he did, and then by dropping out when he was the last remaining Trump opponent standing, Kasich constantly disrupted what should have been the normal flow of the campaign, making it harder for the party to mount a coordinated effort for anyone—Rubio, Cruz, or even Kasich (for even more, see Bernstein 2016).

And from Trump's point of view, the fact that Cruz, a candidate who many Republican party actors strongly opposed, was the only viable opponent remaining after Rubio dropped out was essentially luck as well. It's not as if Trump maneuvered that result; it just dropped in his lap. That Cruz had the second-largest pot of delegates was probably a big part of why the party eventually gave up, rather than challenging Trump right up to the end. While Trump had been allotted enough delegates to win, many of the actual people serving as Republican delegates are not slated by the candidates. Given how unconventional Trump was, they might have been willing to oppose him.

A movement to "free" the delegates by changing the convention rules to allow them to vote for the candidate of their choice rather than being bound to vote as the delegates had been allocated was defeated in the convention's credentials committee by a solid margin, and then failed to get a vote on the convention floor. We have no estimate of how such a vote might have gone, but it appears likely that formal party officials and their allies held the balance of power. Their decision to side with Trump prevented any possibility of the chaos of multiple ballots and deadlock at the convention, and ensured his nomination. Would they have done so had Rubio, Bush, Walker, or even Kasich finished in second place instead of Cruz?

Some of these "lucky" events might be interpreted as systematic in some way; perhaps others could be interpreted as consequences of Trump's skills as a candidate. From the point of view of the losing candidates, some of it might just reflect their individual weaknesses: Was it unlucky for Rubio that he "glitched" during the debate before the New Hampshire primary, or did it reflect his shortcomings as a contender? But for the question of why Trump won despite all his own weaknesses and despite the opposition of party actors, a case can be made that each of these things were basically just random events that went Trump's way. And not only that, but given the close margin of victory, it's likely that he needed most, or perhaps even all, of these things to happen for him to show up at Cleveland with enough delegates.

THE LESSONS OF 2016

The 2016 cycle Republican and Democratic contests were only the fifteenth and sixteenth open modern nominations—that is, nominations in which no incumbent was running for that party. We should always remember what a small set of evidence that is, and how likely it remains that any analysis we do is clouded by the quirks of the individual elections we happen to have observed. Nevertheless, it also means that we can still learn things, or at least find evidence to confirm previous suspicions, every four years.

Endorsements Are Not Just Bandwagons

In some nomination cycles, such as 2016 for the Democrats, the party decides well before the voters get involved.[15] But sometimes there's no obvious choice, and multiple candidates have some party support. Then, after the early states vote, the party tends to converge on a candidate who did well in the "cut-out" states, which are allowed early events before the earliest dates allowed for the rest of the sequential process. For the Democrats, that's been Iowa, New Hampshire, Nevada, and South Carolina, while Republicans flip the order and put South Carolina ahead of Nevada.

It has been, unfortunately, difficult to assess what's happening in those cases: Did Democratic party actors rally around John Kerry after he won in Iowa in 2004 because it gave them the key information they had been looking for—that Kerry was acceptable to Democratic voters and that Howard Dean wasn't magic after all, thus giving Kerry the boost he needed to win nationally?[16] Or were those who endorsed Kerry after Iowa merely hopping on the bandwagon?

The 2016 Republican contest provided a good deal of evidence on this question. Republican party actors after Iowa moved to the third-place candidate there, Marco Rubio, and continued moving to him even after he cratered in New Hampshire. Meanwhile, there was basically no bandwagoning at all for Donald Trump. Even as his candidacy moved from a seeming joke to probable nominee, he picked up hardly any high-profile Republican endorsements. At the very least, then, the 2016 results eliminated the possibility that endorsements are nothing more than party actors following the lead of voters.

Early States Matter—In Context

Every four years, reformers complain about the excessive clout of Iowa and New Hampshire. And it certainly is true that winners in those states continue on the trail, while also-rans drop out. And yet 2016 provided another demonstration that the effects of the earliest states are easy to exaggerate. Bernie Sanders finishing in a shocking tie with Hillary Clinton in Iowa on February 1 (Clinton received 49.8 percent of the recorded vote while Sanders had 49.6 percent). Then the Vermont senator clobbered the former secretary of state in New Hampshire by a whopping 22 percentage points. And then—well, not much. Clinton won the other two early states, Nevada and South Carolina, and then moved into an unstoppable delegate lead on Super Tuesday and the other March primaries. Nor was there much evidence that the strong early performances bought Sanders any significant backing from party actors; only three members of Congress endorsed him in February while Clinton added twelve more to her already large total.

That's a big contrast with what happened after Barack Obama won in Iowa in 2008. The difference? The results are mediated through interpretation by both the media and, especially, by the party. Obama demonstrated in 2008 in Iowa that he could win white votes, just as John Kerry showed in Iowa in 2004 that he was viable outside of his home region. Sanders only showed factional strength in Iowa among white liberal activists, a state where that faction is particularly strong.

Similarly, winning in Iowa on the Republican side for a candidate with strong Christian conservative support did relatively little for Mike Huckabee in 2008, Rick Santorum in 2012, and Ted Cruz in 2016. Not nothing—Cruz, for example, was able to eliminate Huckabee and Santorum by beating them there. But relatively little. And regional favorites get the same discount. That's why Sanders got nothing out of winning in next-door New Hampshire, just as Paul Tsongas (from Massachusetts) got little out of it in 1992. The most extreme example of this was from the Democrats in 1992, when Iowa Senator Tom Harkin ran for president and the party and the media reacted to that by pretending that the Iowa caucuses just weren't happening that year.

It works the other way too. John McCain finished fourth in Iowa in 2008, but Republican party actors appeared to discount that poor finish because they knew he wasn't the candidate of Christian conservatives. After Iowa he was able to increase his endorsement lead over Mitt Romney, and once he won in New Hampshire and demonstrated his broad appeal by winning in South Carolina, that lead grew large.

Both the media and the parties do this, but it's probably fair to say that to the extent that parties really control their nominations, the early states are only as important as party actors think they are.

The Force of Plebiscitary Democracy

As Julia Azari writes in chapter 8, parties may find themselves opposing pressure for direct forms of democracy; indeed, she has argued that one problem for parties is that the efforts of party actors to control nominations can clash with notions of legitimacy derived through elections (see also Azari 2018).

Both parties have, whether deliberately or not, developed backstop systems that allow party actors to overturn narrow victories at the convention if someone they find unacceptable is about to be nominated. For Democrats, it's the superdelegates—automatic delegates who can support any candidate. Regular Democratic delegates are not formally bound, but since they are slated by the candidates (who naturally choose their strongest supporters for the job), it's extremely unlikely any significant number will defect. On the Republican side, some wiggle room is provided because many delegates are not slated by candidates; instead, while delegate allocation is determined by primaries and caucuses, actual delegate selection proceeds in many states on a separate track, meaning that some delegates allocated to a candidate do not in fact support that candidate.[17] Republican rules mandate that those delegates must vote for the candidate for whom there are allocated, but since there is no higher authority in either party than the convention itself, the delegates are always free to overturn those rules.

None of this had ever been put to the test until Donald Trump won just over half the Republican delegates in 2016 while failing to win much support at all from Republican party actors. As discussed above, party leaders chose to oppose the effort to "free" delegates. While the motive might have been fear of a chaotic convention that would severely harm the party (up and down the ballot) in November or even just continuing fear that Ted Cruz would be the nominee, it certainly seems likely that part of the reason was concern that a convention-imposed nominee who hadn't won (or perhaps even competed in) the primaries and caucuses would seem illegitimate.

Convention backstops might still be useful in other circumstances—if two candidates wind up essentially tied after the final primaries, or if a single candidate is a clear plurality winner but needs help reaching a majority. But for now at least, 2016 demonstrated that the wiggle room provided for by the process and the rules is unlikely to be used to overturn the results of the primaries and caucuses as long as they produce even a narrow majority winner. And the Democrats confirmed that interpretation by changing the rules to prevent the supers from doing so, as Josh Putnam explains in chapter 5.

Party Control

One reasonable way of looking at the outcomes in 2016 is to conclude that the party decided on the Democratic side but that it did not on the Republican side, and then go back and count up how well the parties have done overall. One could conclude, as Cohen et al. do, that "the force of Polsby's 'mobilize your faction' argument looks stronger today than at any time since he published it" (2016, 703). For them, the evidence for party control is weaker in the several recent cycles than it had been from 1980 through 2004.

To some extent, I disagree—other than Trump, I think parties have been perfectly happy with the outcomes—but I think the more important point is about how to best think about the question.

It's certainly true that, as they point out, "it should be unsurprising that co-alitions sometimes come apart in the course of making high stakes presiden-tial nominations." In fact, it's important to remember that party nominations are about both cooperation and conflict; every nomination, and especially presidential selections, are occasions for all party actors to attempt to rene-gotiate the terms of the party coalition in their favor. That's easy to see on policy, or when newly mobilized demographic groups begin to assert them-selves within the party. It also can happen with other questions of party man-agement, even in sprawling expanded parties composed in part of informal networks. Tea Party Republicans have pushed against the influence of formal parties and elected politicians; more recently, some Democrats have tried to curb the importance within the party of campaign professionals.

We can read those kinds of conflict between various party components as primarily about policy—and they often are understood that way by the party ac-tors involved—but they may have other important implications as well. A party dominated by its formal party bureaucracy is apt to act very differently from one in which party-aligned interest groups are central to the party.[18] Indeed, one of the reasons the Republican Party appears to be dysfunctional is, as discussed above, the important influence won in the party by aligned media and others who appear to have a financial stake in Republican electoral failure.

But in another sense, answering the question of whether or not the parties choose the nominees may be not quite the way to go about this. Political par-ties as collective organizations, after all, have two main objectives when they nominate candidates for the presidency: They want to maximize the chances of winning in November, and they want to ensure that if their candidate wins that he or she will carry out their policy preferences and priorities.

They do that in conditions of both electoral uncertainty and internal policy competition. So assessing whether the party is controlling nominations re-quires keeping in mind that they may be collectively uncertain about exactly what they want and which candidate would best achieve it—especially early in a campaign cycle.

On questions of electability, for example, it appears that in 2004 many Democratic party actors were genuinely intrigued by Howard Dean's abil-ity to raise money and generate enthusiasm. Dean appeared to be using new electioneering technologies and also recasting policy interests in ways that might have been foolish for the party to ignore. Once he failed to turn that into votes in Iowa, however—Dean finished third there—party actors quickly moved to a more conventional candidate, John Kerry, although the evidence of antiwar sentiment from Dean's early surge probably helped moved the party consensus on the Iraq War (Bernstein 2004).

In 2008, on the other hand, Democratic party actors appeared to be content to let the primaries and caucuses determine whether Barack Obama or Hillary Clinton would be the nominee after Obama demonstrated his broad electoral appeal in Iowa. Of course, individual party actors had their favorite candidate. But Obama and Clinton both appeared to be safely committed to being loyal to the party if they became president (a commitment that both of them fulfilled after the election). In other words, by narrowing the field down to two acceptable candidates, the party "decided" just as effectively as it would have had it successfully attempted to impose one of those candidates on Democratic voters.

Again, the way that 2016 played out when a party did not get its way shows clearly the contrast between a real party failure and party nominations such as those of the Democrats in 2004 and 2008 and complicated Republican nominations in 2008 and 2012.

On to 2020

Parties adapt (Masket 2016). In the U.S. system, they have to adapt constantly, in large part because there are so many anti-party forces constantly trying to keep parties from doing what they want to do. On top of that, technology and social change makes doing things the same way a good formula for chaos. The modern presidential nomination system, in which networked, informal parties must find ways to compete and cooperate in a process originally designed without any of that in mind, certainly challenges the capacity of party actors. Every four years they can find that what previously seemed like hard-and-fast rules of the game are now as outmoded as nineteenth-century stalking horses and favorite sons.

And yet we should be careful about assuming that any particular change will be inherently difficult once the parties have a chance to assimilate it. For example, Cohen et al. note that the invisible primary has become a lot more visible these days. As a consequence, while once a breakout candidate like Gary Hart in 1984 was launched with early success in the primaries and caucuses, more recent upstarts such as Dean in 2004 and Sanders and Trump in 2016 were able to attract wide support well before voters went to the polls. Part of that is about a political press that has learned to pay attention to the contest earlier and earlier; part of it is the much easier availability of large sums of money raised relatively easily and inexpensively.

The questions going forward are these: How well can the parties work to absorb these changes? They, too, have resources. The partisan press is far more extensive in the twenty-first century than it was in the twentieth century. Once upon a time, party leaders had to meet in person to work out deals. Later, communications improved enough that they could arrange things in advance—even sending out signals, in the form of endorsements and other statements by high-profile leaders, in the media. Now communications through the partisan press is possible. But that doesn't guarantee success, as the total failure of a special issue of *National Review* attacking Donald Trump made clear (*National Review* editors 2016). Can the parties learn to use the partisan press to their advantage—without empowering them in dysfunctional ways?

Similarly, while Internet-based fundraising appears to allow candidates access to an important campaign resource unmediated by parties, it turns out that the stamp of approval by partisan websites and signaling through partisan media may in fact be a critical piece of how money in politics is organized. Once again, it's an open question of whether parties can harness the new technologies and organization styles to enhance their ability to coordinate—again, without making the list-holders and the gateway minders too influential.

And Democrats in 2020 will certainly need to be concerned about the possibility that CNN or other neutral news outlets may intervene by choosing a candidate to organize the election story around in the way that they did for Donald Trump in the 2016 Republican nomination contest. In the early going, it appears that Democrats have at least avoided, whether through coordination or by luck, having a celebrity candidate without any political experience. But surely no candidate this time around will assume that any media-favored surge will automatically burn out by itself.

The bottom line is that neither the (mainly healthy) forces driving parties to coordinate and the (generally destructive) structure and the incentives pushing toward chaos in the modern nomination system are going anywhere. So while the parties have usually managed to overcome the obstacles and wind up with reasonably electable candidates who will behave as partisan presidents if elected, the threat of party failure is not going away any time soon.

NOTES

1. The chief functions of conventions now are to facilitate the party network with an in-person gathering—the same as regular national conventions for any organization—and to kick off advertising for the general election.

2. One can certainly argue that Trump's support was an ideological extension of xenophobic strains within the party. Overall, however, I think it's best to see his campaign as essentially personal; it was the personal dimension that captivated the news media, and while he did draw votes from anti-immigration Republicans and bigots who thought he was on their side, in large part his support was based on his (supposed) business expertise. See McCarty (2018).

3. Thanks to high levels of partisan polarization in the electorate, Trump was able to win in November anyway—but with only 46 percent of the vote in a contest with no prominent third-party candidate.

4. See also Hans Hassell (2018), who emphasizes the role of national party organizations in congressional nominations but accepts that larger party networks play a part as well.

5. Campaign operative information from Ballotpedia's compilation of key campaign staffers and their political histories (Ballotpedia 2019a, 2019b). The main campaign operative pages for each candidate are backed up by the individual Ballotpedia pages for the various staffers. It's not clear how comprehensive these records are, nor is it certain that Ballotpedia's choices of which staffers to feature are in fact the most important ones. However, the differences between the Clinton and Sanders campaigns in the available data are wide, and the staff story is consistent with endorsements and other information. The advantage of the campaign staff data is that they demonstrate that Clinton's candidacy was itself essentially a party, or at least a party-connected, operation, while the Sanders candidacy was both factional and personal.

6. Those are the major candidates; there are always plenty of minor candidates for both parties' nominations. Perhaps the most notable Democrat in 2016, other than perennial favorite Vermin Supreme, was campaign finance activist Lawrence Lessig. Neither lasted long.

7. Biden didn't ever do much in the way of campaigning and never formally entered, but he did publicly talk about the possibility of seeking the presidency up until finally withdrawing in October 2015, citing the recent death of his son as the reason for passing on the opportunity. As usual in these cases, it's impossible to say to what extent Biden's decision was influenced by the reactions of party actors to his early testing of the waters, but it's not hard to imagine him beginning a declared candidacy had he received more encouragement—and if Clinton's position wasn't as strong.

8. Both Al Gore and George W. Bush had strong endorsement records, but neither was quite as successful at either the range or the number as Clinton (Bernstein and Dominguez 2003; Bycoffe 2016).

9. It's not clear how much the refusal by Sanders to call himself a Democrat outside of the context of his presidential campaign really matters. Despite being an independent, he caucuses and works closely with the Democrats in the Senate, and one might say he's functionally a Democrat in all but name. Still, his independent status clearly bothered many Democrats, and its hard to argue it wasn't at least to some extent a sign of distance from the party he sought to lead.

10. For more on Ames, with a somewhat less forgiving view, see chapter 6.

11. It's not clear to what extent that was a deliberate choice, either by CNN or the other networks, or just an evolution in media norms. Some of it was surely a reaction

to strong audience response to Trump stories. It was at least consistent with, however, a general CNN strategy of creating long-run news events, whether or not they set out to make Trump into one at the outset of his campaign.

12. It's true that some seemingly similar candidates, such as Ron Johnson in Wisconsin, did just fine. It's not so much that Republicans have deliberately nominated terrible candidates; it's that nominating candidates without conventional qualifications is highly risky.

13. Jackson won several states in 1984 and did even better the second time. While Jackson had never been elected to political office before, he had been a prominent national leader for years; whether that's different than a Steve Forbes or Pat Buchanan campaign is a complicated question. At any rate, after 1988 the Democrats have never had another significant candidate without conventional political experience.

14. As it turned out, at least through Trump's first two years in the White House, Christian conservatives couldn't have been happier with Trump's judicial nominations and policy decisions. While as a group they never supported Trump during the nomination phase, it's likely that his public lists of potential judges were critical in keeping them from working harder to defeat him late in the nomination process. Even in a cycle where the party really did not choose the nominee, at least one party faction, then, was able to intimidate a candidate into toeing their line during the campaign and then to continue that loyalty once in office.

15. Even in those years, voters matter. Clinton's early, extremely strong poll numbers—in other words, what voters said about her at the time—surely contributed to the enthusiasm party actors showed for her, and many party actors have other ways to informally assess what voters think of a candidate.

16. Dean's surprising grass roots organizing and fundraising in 2003 had, in this interpretation, intrigued many Democratic party actors. What if the former Vermont governor really had tapped into some new message and method (using the then-newfangled internet) that the party would be foolish to ignore? As soon as the Iowa results revealed that Dean was more hype than reality and that Kerry was viable, the party turned to the Massachusetts senator. See Bernstein (2004).

17. It's far from clear that either party did it deliberately. On the Democratic side, the superdelegates were above all a way to allow party elites to go to the convention without having to go through the normal delegate selection process, although some reformers probably wanted to give formal parties additional clout. See David Price (1984), *Bringing Back the Parties*. For Republicans, the separation of delegate selection and delegate allocation was probably just a consequence of inertia, since (unlike Democrats) they never established a national set of rules on delegate selection to impose on the states.

18. Bawn et al. (2012) essentially believe that interest groups and their policy demands are inherently central to political parties, but I've argued (Bernstein 1999) that any group of party actors can be dominant.

REFERENCES

Abramowitz, Alan I., and Steven Webster. 2016. "The Rise of Negative Partisanship and the Nationalization of U.S. Elections in the 21st Century," *Elections Studies* 41 (1): 12–22.

Azari, Julia. 2018. "Will New Rules Make the Democratic Party Stronger?" Mischiefs of Faction. July 16, 2018. https://www.vox.com/mischiefs-of-fac tion/2018/7/16/17576702/new-rules-democratic-party.

Ballotpedia. 2019a. "Hillary Clinton Presidential Campaign Key Staff and Advisors, 2016." https://ballotpedia.org/Hillary_Clinton_presidential_campaign_key_staff_ and_advisors,_2016.

———. 2019b. "Bernie Sanders Presidential Campaign Key Staff and Advisors, 2016." https://ballotpedia.org/Bernie_Sanders_presidential_campaign_key_staff_ and_advisors,_2016.

Bawn, Kathy, Marty Cohen, David Karol, Seth Masket, Hans Noel, and John R. Zaller. 2012. "A Theory of Political Parties: Groups, Policy Demands and Nominations in American Politics." *Perspectives on Politics* 10 (3): 571–97.

Bernstein, Jonathan. 1999. "The Expanded Party in American Politics." PhD diss., University of California, Berkeley.

———. 2004. "The Rise and Fall of Howard Dean and Other Notes on the 2004 Democratic Presidential Nomination." *The Forum* 2 (1): Article 1. doi:10.2202/1540-8884.1029.

———. 2016. "John Kasich Is Wrecking the Republican Party." Bloomberg View. March 18, 2016. https://www.bloomberg.com/opinion/articles/2016-03-18/john -kasich-is-wrecking-the-republican-party.

Bernstein, Jonathan, and Casey Dominguez. 2003. "Candidates and Candidacies in the Expanded Party," *PS: Political Science and Politics* 36, no. 2 (April): 165–69.

Bycoffe, Aaron. 2016. "The Endorsement Primary." *FiveThirtyEight*. June 7. https:// projects.fivethirtyeight.com/2016-endorsement-primary/

Cohen, Marty, David Karol, Hans Noel, and John Zaller. 2008. *The Party Decides: Presidential Nominations before and after Reform*. Chicago: University of Chicago Press.

Cohen, Marty, David Karol, Hans Noel, and John Zaller. "Party versus Faction in the Reformed Presidential Nominating System." *PS: Political Science and Politics* 49, no. 4 (October 2016): 701–8.

Dominguez, Casey B. K. 2005. *Before the Primary: Party Elite Involvement in Congressional Nominations*. PhD diss., University of California, Berkeley.

Dominguez, Casey B. K. 2011. "Does the Party Matter? Endorsements in Congressional Primaries." *Political Research Quarterly* 64 (3): 534–44.

Grossmann, Matt, and David A. Hopkins. 2016. *Asymmetric Politics: Ideological Republicans and Group Interest Democrats*. New York: Oxford University Press.

Hassell, Hans J. G. 2018. *The Party's Primary: Control of Congressional Nominations*. New York: Cambridge University Press.

HuffPost Pollster. 2016. "2016 National Republican Primary." https://elections.huff ingtonpost.com/pollster/2016-national-gop-primary.

Lerer, Lisa. 2018. "ActBlue, the Democrats' Not-So-Secret Weapon." *The New York Times.* November 16.

Mann, Thomas E., and Norman J. Ornstein. 2012. *It's Even Worse Than It Looks: How the American Constitutional System Collided with the New Politics of Extremism.* New York: Basic Books.

Masket, Seth E. 2009. *No Middle Ground: How Informal Party Organizations Control Nominations and Polarize Legislatures.* Ann Arbor: University of Michigan Press.

Masket, Seth E. 2016. *The Inevitable Party: Why Attempts to Kill the Party System Fail and How they Weaken Democracy.* Oxford: Oxford University Press.

McCarty, Timothy Wyman. 2018. "The Trumpism Phenomenon." In *The New Authoritarianism, Vol. 1: A Risk Analysis of the U.S. Alt-Right Phenomenon,* edited by Alan Waring, 105–136. Stuttgart: Ibidem Press.

National Review editors. 2016. "Against Trump." *National Review,* January 22, 2016.

Ornstein, Norman J. 2015. "Maybe This Time Really Is Different." *The Atlantic.* August 21, 2015. https://www.theatlantic.com/politics/archive/2015/08/maybe-this-time-really-is-different/401900/.

Polsby, Nelson W. 1983. *Consequences of Party Reform.* New York: Oxford University Press.

Price, David. 1984. *Bringing Back the Parties.* Washington, DC: CQ Press.

Quest, Richard. 2016. "The Vanishing of Flight MH370: The Inside Story of CNN's Coverage." *Flying.* April 15. 2016. https://www.flyingmag.com/vanishing-flight-mh370-inside-story-cnns-coverage.

Sides, John, and Lynn Vavreck. 2013. *The Gamble: Choice and Chance in the 2012 Presidential Election.* Princeton: Princeton University Press.

Sides, John, Michael Tesler, and Lynn Vavreck. 2018. *Identity Crisis: The 2016 Presidential Campaign and the Battle for the Meaning of America.* Princeton: Princeton University Press.

Tyndall, Andrew. 2014. "What CNN Sacrificed for Missing-Plane Ratings." *The Hollywood Reporter.* April 23, 2014. https://www.hollywoodreporter.com/news/what-cnn-sacrificed-missing-plane-692704.

Chapter Eight

Are Parties Inherently Conservative?

Julia Azari

The elections of 2016 brought the phrase "party elites" into the popular lexicon. At the height of the primary season, the *New York Times* reported on the friction between former GOP presidential nominees John McCain and Mitt Romney, who sought to undermine Donald Trump's insurgent candidacy, and the Republican primary voters who remained determined to give the reality TV star their support. Writing of the anti-elite campaigns waged by both Trump and Vermont senator Bernie Sanders, historian Julian Zelizer (2016) suggested, "rather than simply think of ways to stifle these insurgencies, the parties should take a closer look at themselves and their approach to government." These tensions highlighted some questions in American politics: what exactly are political parties, and what do they do? What exactly are the insurgents pushing back against?

FORMAL PARTY ORGANIZATIONS

Recent research in political science suggests that formal party organizations serve as a moderating force against the more extreme demands of activists. Ray LaRaja and Brian Schaffner observe that "historically, we know that pragmatists and purists have fought for domination. In the modern era, the policy-demanding purists have pursued a variety of rules and regulations to weaken the influence of party pragmatists" (LaRaja and Schaffner 2015, 19). The argument in this chapter takes this logic a step further, suggesting that in the United States, parties are not only pragmatic, but intrinsically conservative. I define this conservatism in three ways: the expression of preservationist ideology; risk averse behavior in coalition formation; and resistance to plebiscitary reforms, such as open primaries. The focus in this chapter is on how the dynamics of institutional conservatism inform presidential nomination processes.

A popular refrain in the Trump era concerns the failure—or potential—of institutions to "save" American democracy from illiberal leadership. Institutions, in the words of Douglass North, "constrain behavior" (North 1997). They are assumed to be the root of political stability, a necessary condition for democracy to thrive. However, that instability can have different normative implications depending on your perspective. Institutions preserve the status quo, often protecting hierarchies and inequities long past their de jure expiration date. Parties are especially challenging yet crucial sorts of institutions to assess through this lens. When we hear the phrase "conservative party," we tend to think of a political party that embraces whatever we define as a conservative ideological agenda. But parties are also involved in making choices about how new ideas will be received and incorporated, about whether to adopt new policy positions that might alter the status quo, and about how to manage internal competition.

Both Democrats and Republicans struggled to resolve internal competition in 2016, and the 2020 election offers new challenges. For Democrats, the imminent 2020 nomination season brings questions of whether established party leaders will resist the influence of a vocal left faction within the party, particularly as it promotes candidates who embrace the once-taboo label of socialist. For Republicans, a different set of questions emerges. Despite the inability of the GOP to coordinate and stop Trump—a candidate with no elite support—there are early signs that the party may close ranks around the incumbent, forestalling a challenge from what was once the establishment wing of the party. I also consider the role of preservationist ideology in both parties—the extent to which elected officials express the impulse to preserve, revere tradition, and learn from the past, rather than to look forward, embrace change, and work toward progress.

For 2020 and beyond, the Democrats have a wide range of candidates who might seek the nomination. To some degree, Trump's election has opened up possibilities about the kind of person who might compete—entertainers, business leaders, and even less experienced politicians (mayors, members of the House of Representatives). The prospect of a crowded field is likely in 2020, and if not then, then in the near future.

Although the possible scenarios for the Republican side are fewer, Trump's unusual presidency, low approval ratings, and brewing scandals have invited speculation about whether he might face a primary challenge from the so-called "NeverTrump" wing of the party. The disruptive and plebiscitary process by which Trump won the party nomination over a field of elite-endorsed candidates puts the Republican Party in an especially tricky position. Closing ranks around the president risks exacerbating the very tensions that brought him to power in the first place; conceding that loyalty to Trump is now the animating logic of the party may be further than party leaders want to go.

While parties may be inherently conservative institutions, they operate in an environment of strong partisan polarization. The strength of partisan identity as a predictor of other behaviors (Margolis 2018; Mason 2018) as well as policy attitudes (Layman and Carsey 2014) has become a commonplace characterization of the state of American politics. How partisan attitudes influence the shape of party coordination is a more complicated matter. Hans Noel (2016) observes that within each party there exists a pragmatic wing, oriented toward compromise and governance, alongside an ideological wing. He further suggests that the balance between these wings is different within the Republican party, which has a stronger ideological wing, and the Democratic party where pragmatism reigns. Others have argued that the differences between the two parties run deeper, finding a fundamental asymmetry between the ideological character of Republicans and the group-interest orientation of the Democrats (Grossmann and Hopkins 2015). The argument about parties and inherent institutional conservatism presented here has implications for the debate over asymmetry and the relationship between partisanship and party structures. In particular, some recent research on American political parties suggests a tension between party structure and parties' linkages to change-oriented social movements (Schlozman 2015), and to efforts to make them ideologically cohesive, distinct, and "responsible" (Rosenfeld 2017).

THE STRUCTURE OF POLITICAL PARTIES

Why do political parties in the United States have a seemingly intrinsic tendency to be conservative? Some of the answer lies in their structure. The outsized parties produced by a two-party system, especially one that has historically been decentralized and geographically diverse, have a strong incentive to maintain a coalition. Preservationist ideology also motivates many of the foundational theories in American political development and thought. Affirmation of constitutional values is a constituent element of reconstructive leadership in Stephen Skowronek's political time typology. Presidents who seek to break with the old order or remake the polity often do so in a way that connects to founding values, couched in the suggestion that the old order has strayed from these anchoring principles. In other words, political actors are charged with the task of responding to new problems and addressing society's evolving needs. But American politics seems to demand that these efforts be couched in terms that affirm the past and its values, connecting to Constitutional tradition and not to fundamental transformation of the system.

PRESERVATIONIST IDEOLOGY

One source of American party conservatism is the persistent embrace of a preservationist agenda—political appeals based on preserving the nature and values of American society from threat or transformation. Preservationist ideology has a long history in the American political tradition. John Gerring identifies such a strain among Jeffersonian Democrats (1828–1892), whose rhetoric explicitly rejected calls for progress in government or economic development. Gerring quotes the address of the 1840 Democratic convention, which expressed concern that, "our Republican institutions, though they might preserve their form, would not long retain their purity, their simplicity, or their strength" (Gerring 1998, 177). Populism on the right in the United States is associated with claims to "make America great again," by restoring traditional industries, and traditional hierarchies of gender and race.

Preservation is also linked to populism on the left and the right. J. Eric Oliver and Thomas Wood (2018) also describe "restoration" as a defining element of populist claims, arguing that it was central to Trump's appeals and yet less crucial to Bernie Sanders's rhetoric than his reputation as a populist would suggest. The application of this concept to Donald Trump and other populists on the right is even more straightforward.

In order to measure the role of preservationist ideology in 2016, I developed an index of preservation and progress in political rhetoric. Preservation rhetoric included words like "restore," "tradition," "founders," and "threat." Progress rhetoric included words such as "transform," "failed," and "outdated." (See the appendix at the end of this chapter for a full list of the custom dictionaries.) Using a computer-assisted text-analysis program (Diction 7.1.3), I was able to analyze the use of preservation and progress rhetoric in all 2016 candidates' announcement speeches and from major party national convention addresses since 1980.[1] Then, a "preservation index" was created by subtracting progress rhetoric from preservation rhetoric.

National convention addresses provide insight into the intersection between candidate and party values. As Mary Stuckey (2005) writes, "During the campaign, candidate and party hope to speak with a united voice, providing a clear and convincing image of their joint understanding of the American past, their vision for the American future, and their definition of the national self." Stuckey's assessment of the 2004 Republican convention message is consistent with the Diction analysis of Bush's acceptance speech; she highlights the combination of past values in the convention messages with the assertion of "forward momentum" based on core principles.

Figures 8.1–8.4 illustrate where the 2016 nominees fall in relation to their competitors for the party nod in 2016 and to their predecessors in the party. In figure 8.1, we see that Trump's now-famous June 2015 announcement speech stands out from other 2016 Republican contenders for its heavy tendency toward preservationist rhetoric. Similarly, Trump's 2016 RNC speech stands out and is an especially stark contrast with Mitt Romney's 2012 convention speech. In 2012, Romney spoke of the American dream and the failure of the Obama administration to deliver promised change. Trump's 2016 address featured lines such as "The attacks on our police, and the terrorism in our cities, threaten our very way of life" (Trump, RNC, July 21, 2016). Viewed alongside other nomination acceptance speeches, the uniqueness of Trump's preservationist claims is evident. Of the eleven speeches included in the analysis, six placed a greater emphasis on progress than preservation. Mc-Cain's 2008 address comes second to Trump's in its balance on preservation, but it is a distant runner up.

Turning to candidate announcement speeches, Trump's address once again stands out. Several other candidates stressed preservationist themes in their announcement speeches, including the ultra-conservative Ted Cruz and constitutional libertarian Rand Paul. However, as with the RNC acceptance speech, Trump's ratio of preservationist language was in a class by itself,

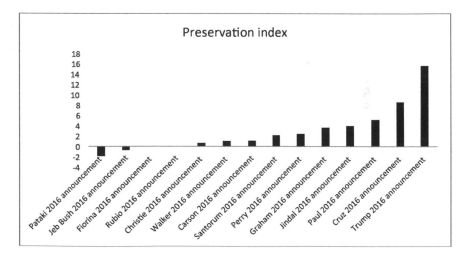

Figure 8.1. Preservation vs. progress rhetoric, 2016 Republican announcement speeches. Graph shows "preservation" words minus "progress" words per speech.
Source: Original analysis by the author using Diction 7.1.3. Speeches collected from The American Presidency Project. https://www.presidency.ucsb.edu

and preservation themes, while more common among 2016 candidacy announcement speeches than acceptances overall, were nevertheless far from
the rhetorical norm. Among the 2016 candidate field, the preservation index
corresponds somewhat with ideology among the more conventional candidates, with cultural conservatives like Cruz and Jindal and libertarian Paul
on the more preservationist end of the scale. Trump, whose absence of a
political record and intermittent embrace of government strength made his
difficult to classify ideologically, displayed an unambiguous commitment to
preservation.

That Trump would stand out in this way is largely unremarkable; his subsequent general election campaign and presidency have also reflected the
importance of these themes to his overall political project. However, debates
remain about the extent to which Trump's unusual candidacy represents a
genuine departure from Republican positions and perspectives. While the
electorate may have been more focused on race and immigration in 2016 than
in previous years, race has long been a central cleavage in American politics,
perhaps even forming the backbone of partisan-ideological sorting in the
twentieth century (Carmines and Stimson 1989; Schickler 2016). Evidence
also suggests that Trump's support may have come from Republican primary
voters who were especially "hawkish on immigration" while being liberal on
economic issues.

However, the analysis of Trump's announcement speech next to the others illustrates how his candidacy stood out. While not the most conservative

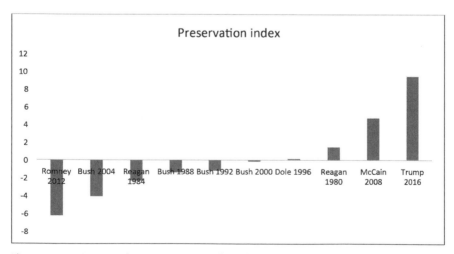

**Figure 8.2. Preservation vs. progress rhetoric, Republican nomination acceptance
speeches, 1980–2016.**
Source: Original analysis by the author using Diction 7.1.3. Speeches collected from The American Presidency Project. https://www.presidency.ucsb.edu

candidate in the field on every dimension, Trump's candidacy represented a turn to the past that broke with most of his competitors as well as many previous Republican nominees. At the same time that Trump embraced preservationist ideas about the substance of politics, his approach to government was avowedly disruptive. This approach included the violation of campaign norms, such as delivering personal insults to his opponents and calling for their imprisonment.

Hillary Clinton's 2016 rhetoric stands out much less. Figure 8.4 shows the preservation indexes for Democratic presidential candidates' convention speeches. It is notable that the Democrats do not look much different from the Republicans in this regard (with the exception of Trump)—candidates vary in their balance of preservation and protection rhetoric, with a trend toward more preservationist rhetoric after 2000. Clinton's Philadelphia speech falls on the preservationist end of the spectrum, but in the middle rather than at an extreme. That honor instead belongs to Obama, whose 2008 speech talked about threats to the American promise, and likened contemporary victims of the recession to past Americans. In 2016, Clinton talked about America's promise as well, and linked the country's history to her central campaign themes: "That's why 'stronger together' is not just a lesson from our history, it's not just a slogan for our campaign, it's a guiding principle for the country we've always been and the future we're going to build, a country where the economy works for everyone, not just those at the top."

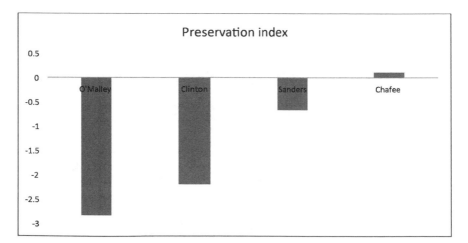

Figure 8.3. Preservation vs. progress rhetoric, 2016 Democratic announcement speeches.
Source: Original analysis by the author using Diction 7.1.3. Speeches collected from The American Presidency Project. https://www.presidency.ucsb.edu

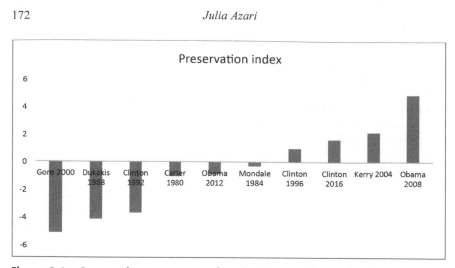

Figure 8.4. Preservation vs progress rhetoric, Democratic nomination acceptance speeches, 1980-2016.
Source: Original analysis by the author using Diction 7.1.3. Speeches collected from The American Presidency Project. https://www.presidency.ucsb.edu

However, her 2016 campaign "kick-off" remarks—delivered about two months after the release of her April 2015 video announcement—illustrate the Democrats' dilemma regarding preservation. The kick-off speech emphasized progress and moving forward to adapt to new problems and realities. Indeed, her announcement speech placed a stronger emphasis on progress relative to preservation than the announcement speech of Bernie Sanders, despite his promises to reject large swaths of the status quo. Both Democratic contenders, however, gave announcement speeches that emphasized progress (as did fellow hopeful Martin O'Malley). Not unexpectedly, this is different from Republican candidates in the same year. It also leaves us unable to clearly classify Clinton as either a candidate of preservation or of progress. Democratic presidential candidates must be able to articulate the ways in which their ideas are innovative, yet grounded in the country's political tradition and values.

Signs point to the possibility that this dilemma will factor into the Democrats' task in selecting a 2020 candidate. Recent findings by Sides, Tesler, and Vavreck (2018) suggest that ideological divisions within the Democratic Party are overstated. However, the likely scenario facing 2020 is a fairly crowded and competitive field, with a number of ideologically similar candidates attempting to carve out a distinct niche. A few high-profile primaries in 2018 demonstrate how reconciling progress and preservation might pose a challenge. Ayanna Pressley, a Massachusetts politician who defeated long-term incumbent Mike Capuano, made "change can't wait" a key message of her campaign, and pointed to generational and style factors as the main distinctions between herself and her incumbent. "I was running on bold, visionary, activist leadership as I have said repeatedly since Tuesday one week ago today, that I think our victory was less a referendum against hate and more a mandate for hope," she told WBUR-Boston a few days after her surprise victory. In a similar race—in which a young, progressive candidate defeated a multi-term incumbent—Alexandra Ocasio-Cortez has become a national figure in the party. She has also received pushback for her stances that depart from existing political traditions; conservative media obsessively covered her criticism of the Electoral College on October 6, 2018 (Chasmar 2018). (Ocasio-Cortez joins 62 percent of Americans, as well as former president Jimmy Carter, in her criticism of the institution.) Ocasio-Cortez and her ideas have also drawn some criticism from other Democrats, including Rep. Alcee Hastings, who remarked "meteors fizzle out" (Lillis 2018), and House Minority Leader Nancy Pelosi suggested that the party remained a "big tent" and not necessarily a national movement toward the left or, specifically, toward "democratic socialism" (Resnick 2018). To be sure, many of these criticisms can be linked to sexism, ideological disagreements, or even sour grapes. They also reveal the risk aversion and orientation toward the status quo that coexists with progressive ideology in the Democratic Party.

Risk Aversion

Party actors can also demonstrate conservatism by balking at the adoption of new positions that might appeal to new constituencies but also alienate traditional ones. This tradeoff has been especially sharp when new policy positions involve challenging traditional power structures—embracing civil rights for minority groups (Baylor 2017; Frymer 1999) or women's rights (Wolbrecht 2000). Parties adjust their positions on these issues in response to considerable pressure from organized interests (Karol 2009). Party coalitions inevitably encompass actors who obstruct change. As Paul Frymer explains, historically marginalized groups are especially vulnerable to electoral capture, leaving powerful political actors with little incentive to expend political capital on remediating oppressive situations (Frymer 1999, 212). For Democrats, these questions cut in multiple directions. After self-described democratic socialist Alexandra Ocasio-Cortez defeated a long-term incumbent in a Congressional primary in 2018, House minority leader Nancy Pelosi denied the idea that "socialism is ascendant" in the Democratic Party. Other Democratic leaders have expressed reservations about moving too far to the left. At the same time, institutional conservatism and risk aversion may also affect Pelosi's own leadership profile as the first woman to serve as Speaker of the House.

Anti-Plebiscitary Politics

Finally, party conservatism can come in the form of anti-plebiscitary politics. Broadening the electorate or embracing plebiscitary moves (the adoption of primaries or the direct election of senators) can be strategic moves by political actors. Parties can also oppose these changes, either adopting stances against expanding public participation in a specific process, or stances against a more open and inclusive electoral system in general. Historically, the parties have sometimes been internally split on these questions, with reformist factions favoring more open and plebiscitary processes and others putting the brakes on these changes. This internal tension still defines Democrats in the twenty-first century, with disputes over the role of "superdelegates," open primaries, and elite influence over nominations. When it comes to issues of inclusion in the electorate, clearer partisan lines have been drawn. These issues include voter identification laws, voter registration practices (such as purging old voter lists), and more controversial public policies like felon disenfranchisement. With regard to internal procedure, Republicans have fewer disputes of the nature and magnitude of those facing Democrats. However, the crowded field in 2016 and the competition for prime-time debate slots did introduce questions about intraparty democracy (Azari and Masket 2017), and struggles between the Tea Party movement and "establishment" Republicans were evident before Trump and Trumpism became part of the party (Blum 2016).

Beyond nominations, the politics of voting rights has become highly contentious in the twenty-first century (this development fits a long-standing pattern in American history; see, for example, Rhodes 2017). The introduction of voter identification laws was explicitly linked with Republican politics, as were unfounded accusations of voter fraud after the 2016 and 2018 election, some of which came directly from President Trump. Harkening back to the country's problematic history of voting rights protection, controversies erupted in North Dakota and Georgia over policies that disproportionately affected Native American and African American citizens, respectively. Yet, while voting rights have become a partisan issue, bipartisan majorities have occasionally emerged, such as the overwhelming passage of Florida's Amendment 4, which restores the right to vote for those with some kinds of felony convictions.

The increasingly antagonistic conflicts over voting provide the context for controversy over plebiscitary politics within the parties. One site of such controversy in the Democratic Party is over closed primaries. Jeff Weaver, campaign manager for Bernie Sanders, pointed out in an CNN op-ed that independent voters in New York would have to switch party registration eight months in advance in order to vote in the 2016 Democratic presidential primary (Weaver 2018). A 2016 poll found that six in ten Democrats preferred the idea of an open primary in which all registered voters would be eligible to participate over one limited to registered Democrats only (Gass 2016). The Democratic National Committee altered its rules to limit the influence of "super delegates"—elected officials not bound by the results of a state primary or caucus, in a nod toward giving more influence to the voters rather than elites. It is worth noting, as well, that factions within parties will design rules—from Bernie Sanders's supporters pushing for open primaries (Kilgore 2018) to moderate Democrats urging the adoption of a South-oriented Super Tuesday—in order to enhance or consolidate their power (Norrander 1992, 27).

WHAT HAPPENED IN 2016?

The Republican nomination in 2016 was undeniably unusual in both process and outcome. Party elites first failed to coordinate on a candidate, leaving the putative favorites to languish in the polls and compete to define the conservative standard. This left the party vulnerable to an outsider challenge, and Donald Trump became the nominee despite little elite support, considerable elite opposition, and a number of Republican voters who were displeased with the party's nomination of a reality TV star without any political experience.

Trump's nomination also highlights the ways in which different aspects of party institutional conservatism can be in tension. In the spring of 2016, as Trump began to win primaries, it became evident that party leaders were unprepared for their process to deviate from the expected—elite-dominated—script. As it became apparent that Jeb Bush's poll numbers would not likely improve, elite endorsements gradually slid to Marco Rubio, particularly after his close third finish in the Iowa caucuses after Ted Cruz and Donald Trump. Voters did not follow suit. Party elites were slow to adapt to their new reality. A few members of Congress endorsed Trump during the primary season, including Jeff Sessions as the sole Senate primary endorsement, and a few governors. House Speaker Paul Ryan endorsed Trump's candidacy a few weeks after he was declared the party's presumptive nominee, and RNC chair Reince Priebus assured CNN that he wasn't "pouring Bailey's on my cereal" and said in April that he thought Trump's nomination would "probably be good for the party" (Milbank 2016).

Just as the party lacked the informal mechanisms to coordinate and narrow the field early in the season, it also lacked both formal and informal capacities to challenge Trump's nomination later on. Importantly, the Republican Party in 2016 lacked the "superdelegate" provisions that might have allowed Democrats to overturn a primary victory, at least in theory. Even after Trump passed the delegate threshold for the nomination, there were rumblings about the possibility of a convention challenge. One Colorado GOP delegate pushed for a change in the convention rules to allow a "conscience vote" that would allow delegates to defy their pledges to state primary or caucus results (Jaffe 2016). Other elites deferred to the rules of the process, such as Speaker Ryan, who noted that "Trump won fair and square" (East 2016). The decision not to pursue measures that would allow delegates to select another nominee illustrates that while this approach was technically possible under the rules, going against the choice of the party's primary electorate did not appear to be the best option.

WHAT WILL HAPPEN IN 2020?

Obviously, no one knows. On the Republican side, there exists much speculation about whether Trump will face an internal challenger. It is, of course, unusual for a sitting president to face a nomination challenge in the modern era. The two most recent incumbents in this position, Jimmy Carter and George H. W. Bush, both lost their reelection campaigns. They also made decisions in their first terms that made them relatively easy targets for their parties' respective ideological bases; Ted Kennedy's challenge to Carter focused on healthcare, while Pat Buchanan tried to capitalize on both Bush's broken promises (such as no new taxes) and his lack of favorability with social conservatives. In both years, economic woes fueled the challenges as well.

As is so often the case, with Trump the situation is more complicated. The left-leaning academic and journalistic worlds may envision a challenger who fits some definition of "moderate," which would defy the recent pattern. On the other hand, many conservatives who criticized Trump during the 2016 nomination season did so on the grounds that he failed to uphold conservative orthodoxies, not that he took them too far. Potential 2020 challengers like John Kasich and Nikki Haley (who denies that this is in her plans, at the time of this writing) are very conservative but have developed media reputations as relative moderates due to their demeanor and establishment ties (Bennett 2018; Rahn 2018).

In other words, the potential for a Trump challenge in 2020 already illustrates his uncomfortable relationship with traditional conservatism, in contrast with the usual dynamic of a primary challenge. Risk-averse party leaders have several considerations. It seems likely (though not certain) that a possible challenger to Trump would be perceived as more moderate, in temperament at least. However, faced with the possibility of an unstable situation that might threaten Trump's reelection chances and divide the party, the logical approach for party leaders is to try to prevent such a challenge from materializing. This response is what we would expect—party leaders rarely relish a challenge to a sitting leader, even one who has proven as unpopular and unpredictable as Trump.

As the analysis in the beginning of this chapter suggests, the Democrats have a built-in dilemma that hinges on several factors related to parties' institutional conservatism. Democratic contenders for the nomination will likely include both those who place a high value on affirming norms and past practices and values, and those who advocate for more fundamental change in American political economy and society.

The contours of this particular tension could take several forms. Of course, it is possible that the conventional process of winnowing will work as it has in past years, narrowing the field to a single favorite (as in 2000 and 2016) or a few top contenders (as in 2004 and 2008). Given the large number of politicians (and other figures!) engaging in exploratory activity (Bacon 2018), and the growth of the antiestablishment mood within the party, these scenarios seem less likely than a more crowded and chaotic field. I explore these two possibilities through the lens of the preservation dilemma and questions about how the party will balance new directions and constituencies with the impulse to preserve the traditional Democratic coalition. In this scenario, the Democrats would experience something similar to the Republican field in 2016, with a number of candidates vying for mainstream positions, plus a few stray ideologues and at least one celebrity candidate. The challenge in this case for Democrats is to narrow a wide field of candidates with similar credentials and ideological profiles, and to prevent a less-experienced candidate with high name recognition, or an extreme candidate, from scratching out a plurality victory.

However, a different kind of field could emerge, with a handful of top contenders lasting through the initial stages of the contest. This more closely resembles the kind of nomination battle of the post-McGovern-Fraser, pre-2016 period in which a strong invisible primary would narrow the field to a few top contenders. One potential lesson of the 2016 race for the Democratic nomination is that the party can effectively winnow its conventional candidates but is limited in its ability to respond to an unexpected challenge that resonates with primary voters. The Democrats could end up with a group of traditionally qualified candidates whose fortunes are sorted out over the course of a protracted primary season, as we saw with Hillary Clinton and Barack Obama. But it seems at least somewhat likely, at this juncture in time, that even a small field might include a few candidates who, like Bernie Sanders or the more moderate Tim Ryan, have positioned themselves as relative outsiders. Depending on the level of antagonism expressed toward the party's leadership and institutional structure during the nomination contest, it is possible that such a contest could once again lead into a tense convention and a nomination that some party adherents see as evidence of an illegitimate and unduly powerful national party.

In either case, however, the Democrats have some consistency between substance and process; the segment of the party that most strongly favors heading away from traditional practices in terms of policy and rhetoric also tends to be more critical of party practices that preserve power among elites, like superdelegates and big money in politics. The more mainstream candidates, who have been slower to adopt positions favoring radical policy change, are also party "insiders" likely to garner substantial elite support.

FiveThirtyEight.com writer Perry Bacon identifies several serious candidate activities: travel to early primary states, writing a book, sitting down with a journalist for a magazine profile, and campaigning for a Senate or gubernatorial candidate. Of the candidates who have done these most in 2018, the roster is mainly Democratic officeholders who would make fairly conventional presidential candidates—governors, senators, former cabinet members, and Los Angeles mayor Eric Garcetti. However, in 2014, the Republican field might have looked rather similar, with a robust list of qualified hopefuls, and a highly unconventional candidate waiting in the wings. Indeed, Trump had begun some groundwork—such as meeting Newt Gingrich in Iowa in early 2015—for his 2016 bid well advance of his 2015 announcement.

The next section looks at how each facet of institutional conservatism might shape the questions facing the two parties in 2020, both in their internal nomination battles and in their struggles to define their brands, mobilize their voters, and remain nationally competitive.

Preservation

Republicans

The roster of possibilities for a Republican bid to beat Trump includes Ohio governor John Kasich, former Arizona senator Jeff Flake, Nebraska senator Ben Sasse, and former UN ambassador (and South Carolina governor) Nikki Haley. The ways in which each of these candidates has publicly criticized the president has rested heavily on policy issues. Haley broke with the administration on a number of key policy issues, such as the timing of the announcement of sanctions against Russia and the administration's sometimes belligerent status toward U.S. alliances. From this group of high-profile dissenters,

John Kasich has perhaps offered the most consistent and wide-ranging policy critique of the Trump administration. Kasich has publicly broken with the administration in the areas of trade, immigration, and his approach to international alliances.

The theme of preservation highlights a key tension for mainstream Republicans and the forty-fifth president. One set of possible critiques includes a set of objections to the president's break with treasured American values. Senator John McCain (R-AZ) referred to Trump's "half-baked, spurious nationalism" (Elbaum and AP 2017); Trump's comments about blame on "both sides" after a violent white nationalist rally in Charlottesville, Virginia, drew criticism in this general vein as well. In other words, there is a preservationist argument against Trump. Objections to the administration's disruptive approach to international trade and alliances fit into this formulation as well. Such claims are about the preservation of a more immediate past and a set of shared liberal values—commitment to Cold War–era values like open trade, anti-racism, and peace through international alliances—rather than a more culturally rooted idea of preservation.

Sasse (R-NE) is perhaps the most overtly invested in preservationist appeals; his work as a senator has included several books about how America has changed, and not for the better. He has written about the "vanishing American adult" as well as a glorified past in which towns unified around high school sports, invoking some of the same simplified, and implicitly racialized, notions of American nostalgia that inform the rhetoric of the president he opposes. Such visions of American identity have a long history in Republican rhetoric and played a key role in Ronald Reagan's communication strategy; his signature "Prouder, Stronger, Better" campaign spot in 1984 featured scenes from small town life, removed from urban concerns and largely devoid of people of color (Lopez 2013). In other words, Republicans seeking to challenge Trump in 2020 have a series of rhetorical choices about how to frame conservative opposition to the president. The former approach—an emphasis on preserving the pre-Trump status quo and its values, rather than a more nostalgic framework—might emerge as a strategy for an anti-Trump movement aimed at peeling off moderate voters and even centrist Democrats. But the prospects for such a movement, especially in a Republican primary, appear limited.

An alternative is for Republicans to contest Trump on preservation grounds. Religious, cultural populism from Pat Buchanan to Mike Huckabee to Rick Santorum has proven a potent mix, but until Trump it was inadequate to win the presidential nomination. At the same time, Trump's personal electoral brand has almost certainly been exaggerated in the popular imagination. It is possible that a candidate who embraces culturally nostalgic appeals could pose a substantial challenge to Trump, destabilizing his coalition even if not denying him renomination.

Democrats

As the analysis above suggests, preservationist ideas are not the exclusive domain of Republicans. Even change-oriented candidates like Bernie Sanders and Barack Obama have invoked the glory of the country's past and couched their arguments for change in arguments about how the country has strayed from its best qualities. Some of the party's themes in the 2018 midterms, however, challenge the possibility for a past-oriented and preservationist set of arguments. The Democratic delegation to the 116th Congress is a more diverse group of representatives than in the past, and within the party's modest but vocal Progressive Caucus, there may be energy for new directions in the areas of environmental policy, economic inequality, and Medicare for all.

These policies and the legislators who support them—a group that includes more representatives of non-white, non-Christian, and LGBT identities than in any previous Congress—might represent a unique turn in the history of the Democratic Party. Perhaps a focus on both new economic policies and the relatively recent turn toward social liberalism will remake the party in a way that is incompatible with familiar preservationist themes.

On the other hand, the substance of the new economic plans suggests that there may not be anything new under the sun. A "green New Deal" and a federal jobs program both come straight from the mid-century Democratic playbook. As with potential Republican challengers, Democratic challengers in 2020 may compete with Trump on preservationist terrain, offering a message of change that is mixed with ideas about recapturing core American values.

Anti-Plebiscitary Politics

Republicans

Debates about who should vote and how open and participatory politics should be have changed a great deal. Contemporary norms favor mass enfranchisement and popular participation in decisions. However, during and after the 2018 midterms, Republicans at the state level have run into a number of controversies surrounding enfranchisement, voting rights, and respect for election results. Voting rights controversies began before the election, with new voter identification laws in North Dakota and serious delays in registration processing in Georgia, where the secretary of state responsible for overseeing voter registration was also a (successful) candidate for governor. An instance of vote suppression in one North Carolina congressional district led to the decertification of the election, and investigation into missing absentee ballots in several counties. Perhaps most controversially, Republicans in Wisconsin and Michigan faced accusations of not respecting the outcome of the process because they introduced bills to limit the power of newly elected officials. Wisconsin Republicans sought to curb early voting in the state as well. In sum, the subject of voting rights and expansion of participation may have become a partisan question.

Democrats

In contrast with Republicans, where no clear intraparty division is evident, Democrats may be facing internal disputes about the nature of nomination contests. After cutting back the influence of superdelegates in the nomination process in an August 2018 decision, the party still faces a variety of choices about open primaries, closed primaries, and caucuses. While the stakes of these decisions may be lower than the more fundamental questions facing Republicans, they have more potential to solidify internal divisions, and lend themselves to jockeying among presidential contenders for advantageous institutional arrangements. Candidates whose messages favor openness may find themselves performing better in caucuses or closed primary states. In principle, Democrats may be divided among themselves over how open the party's processes should be. In practice, these process preferences can shift as candidates try out different venues for consolidating support and winning delegates. These fights are likely to be low-salience outside of party activists and highly engaged voters; however, they will have implications both for who wins the presidential nomination in 2020, and whether a distinct cleavage forms within the party between activists who favor more open processes and establishment stalwarts who seek to slow them down—a dichotomy that may be in fact be more complex under the surface. These preferences and interests may not be so easily aligned.

Risk Aversion

Republicans

What will risk aversion look like for Republicans in 2020, particularly if there is evidence of party splintering? The 2018 midterms return a set of GOP senators, representatives, and governors who are closer to the president's style and policy positions (Binder 2018; Mudde 2018). At the same time, the president's low approval ratings, coupled with the Russia investigation, may make him a political liability going into a reelection campaign. If a challenger emerges to contest the nomination, Republican elites and officials will face a decision about how much to close ranks around President Trump or to take a hands-off approach. Parties are in an ambivalent position, as national organizations are expected to be neutral in nomination contests. Yet, when the party controls the White House, it effectively becomes a political arm of that White House. Boris Heersink (2018) notes that Trump has gained considerable influence over the RNC and that the organization is likely to support his reelection as the RNC did for George H. W. Bush in 1992, despite the two presidents' very different histories with their party prior to taking office.

Democrats

Risk averse elements of the Democrats coalition have already emerged. The question of how to maintain internal diversity has shaped the party's entire history. The debates about whom to nominate in 2020 are no exception, despite the party's transformation into a more uniformly liberal party heavily populated by historically marginalized groups. Put bluntly, presidential nominations have very rarely deviated from selecting a white, Protestant man to head the ticket. The electoral risks of doing so remain unclear. Despite handwringing about the possibilities for a "Tom Bradley effect" in 2008, and concerns about whether rural whites would be willing to cast a vote for Barack Obama, the Illinois senator became the first Democratic presidential candidate to win a popular vote majority since 1976. A different set of questions emerged for the party after Hillary Clinton's 2016 loss. Some postelection narratives pointed to excess focus on "identity politics"—although the activism and candidacies of women and people of color in 2018 may belie this point. Few have put it as bluntly as attorney Michael Avenatti (who briefly considered a 2020 bid), who argued that the 2020 nominee "better be a white male" in order to have the best chance at beating Trump (Watkins 2018). Others have suggested that winning back white working-class voters in the Midwest may be the key to defeating Trump. The party's perception of electoral risk and reward is likely to influence the type of nominee it recruits, as well as the ways in which it approaches the existing coalition.

CONCLUSION: ASYMMETRIC INSTITUTIONS?

One of the characteristics of the 2016 nomination contests was the rift revealed between party voters and party leadership. This division took divergent forms in each party, with different consequences. Democrats nominated an unquestionably establishment candidate, stirring backlash against the party's processes. Emphasis on the representation of new demographic groups led to post-election recriminations about over-reliance on "identity politics" to the detriment of the party's traditional coalition. For Republicans, institutional safeguards disintegrated as primary voters selected a nominee outside of the elite mainstream. However, elements of historical preservation permeated Republican rhetoric even more than in the past.

In 2020, the parties are likely to face different kinds of challenges regarding their institutional conservatism. Trump's preservationist rhetoric and tendency to undermine the legitimacy of the electoral process have increasingly become the party brand. The party as an institution has demonstrated itself to be neither especially resistant to change nor invested in maintaining a broad coalition. For Democrats, change-oriented messaging may clash with elite institutional conservatism. Does this mean that parties are inherently conservative? Their demonstrated dynamism and permeability suggests that such conservatism may not be ironclad. Yet forces within parties have strong incentives to be risk averse, preservationist, and sometimes anti-plebiscitary. These forces may not always win out, but they do appear to have some structural advantages when it comes to internal party competition.

Recent political scholarship has seized on the idea that American political parties are fundamentally asymmetrical, responding to different imperatives within their distinct coalitions. According to a 2016 study, Republicans are more ideological while Democrats coalesce around a sense that their party is good for distinct groups in American society. The analysis in this chapter focuses on three aspects of institutional conservatism that have characterized American political parties in the long term. These facets have manifested differently in the two parties. Risk aversion, in the service of coalition maintenance, has historically been central to Democrats. As the party diversifies and moves to the left, these practices increasingly cause tension between party elites and their electorate. Republicans have typically been the party that is more cautious and skeptical about expanding the franchise and popular participation in decision making. The contemporary GOP is no exception, and as a result, voting rights issues have become polarized. Both parties demonstrate recent tendencies toward preservation, though with the rise of Trump, Republicans have taken a clear turn toward a specific definition of national preservation. In other words, neither party has tended to have a monopoly on institutional conservatism in the past. But this is changing, with different pressures bearing down on each party. The very nature of what parties are and what parties do has become contested, altering each party's trajectory and fueling the competition between them.

Appendix

Words used to develop index of "preservation" and "progress" in presidential candidate speeches

Preservation

Abandoned
Again
Attack
Back
Becoming
Changing
Constitution
Defend
Desert
Disrupt
Faith
Founders
Founding
Invaders
Maintain
Outside
Past
Perpetuate
Preserve
Protect
Radical
Reclaim
Restore
Restraint
Return
Safeguard
Safety
Shelter
Shield
Strengthen
Surrender
Threat
Tradition
Uphold
Used
Values

Progress

Adapt
Advance
Breakthrough
Contemporary
Development
Diversity
Failed
Forward
Future
Growth
Modern
Movement
New
Old-fashioned
Open
Outdated
Progress
Strides
Tomorrow
Transform
Transition

NOTE

1. Texts for announcement speeches for some candidates, including John Kasich and Jim Webb, were not available on the American Presidency Project.

REFERENCES

Azari, Julia, and Seth Masket. 2017. "Intraparty Democracy and the 2016 Election." In *Conventional Wisdom, Parties and Broken Barriers in the 2016 Election*, edited by Jennifer Lucas, Christopher Galdieri, and Tauna Starbuck Sisco, 137–162. Lanham, MD: Lexington Books.

Bacon, Perry, Jr. 2018. "Who's Behaving Like a 2020 Presidential Candidate?" FiveThirtyEight.com, October 11, 2018. https://fivethirtyeight.com/features/whos-behaving-like-a-2020-presidential-candidate/.

Barbaro, Michael, Ashley Parker, and Jonothan Martin. "Rank and File Republicans Tell Party Elites: We're Sticking with Donald Trump." *New York Times*, March 4,

2016. https://www.nytimes.com/2016/03/05/us/politics/donald-trump-republican-party.html.

Baylor, Christopher. 2017. *First to the Party: The Group Origins of Political Transformation*. Philadelphia: University of Pennsylvania Press.

Bennett, Grace. 2018. "Mainstream Media are Trying to Spin Nikki Haley as a Moderate," MediaMatters.com, October 10, 2018. https://www.mediamatters.org/blog/2018/10/10/mainstream-media-are-trying-spin-nikki-haley-moderate/221636.+

Blum, Rachel. 2016. *The Tea Party: A Party within a Party*. PhD diss (Georgetown University).

Burns, Alexander, and Maggie Haberman. "Donald Trump's Presidential Run Began in an Effort to Gain Stature." *New York Times*, March 12, 2016. https://www.nytimes.com/2016/03/13/us/politics/donald-trump-campaign.html.

Carmines, Edward, and James Stimson. 1989. *Issue Evolution: Race and the Transformation of American Politics*. Princeton: Princeton University Press.

Carsey, Thomas and Geoffrey Layman. 2014. "Our Politics Is Polarized on More Issues Than Ever Before." *Washington Post*. January 17.

Chakrabarti, Meghna. 2018. "'Change Can't Wait': Ayanna Pressley on Primary Win, Bid for Congress." *WBUR*, September 11, 2018. https://www.wbur.org/onpoint/2018/09/10/ayanna-pressley-democratic-nominee-massachusetts.

Chasmar, Jessica. 2018. "Alexandria Ocasio-Cortez: We Must 'Eliminate the Electoral College.'" *The Washington Times*, October 8, 2018. https://www.washingtontimes.com/news/2018/oct/8/alexandria-ocasio-cortez-we-must-eliminate-the-ele/.

Duncan, Charles, and Maayan Schechter. 2018. "SC Republicans Could Forgo 2020 Primary to Protect Trump." TheState.com, December 18, 2018. https://www.thestate.com/news/state/south-carolina/article223302340.html.

East, Kristin. 2016. "Ryan Dismisses Convention Challenge: Trump Won 'Fair And Square.'" Politico. June 11, 2016. https://www.politico.com/story/2016/06/paul-ryan-donald-trump-convention-224224.

Elbaum, Rachel, and Associated Press. 2017. "McCain Condemns Half-Baked, Spurious Nationalism in Speech," NBC.com, October 17, 2017. https://www.nbcnews.com/news/us-news/mccain-condemns-half-baked-spurious-nationalism-speech-n811361.

Frymer, Paul. 1999. *Uneasy Alliances: Race and Party Competition in America*. Princeton, NJ: Princeton University Press.

Frymer, Paul. 2010. *Uneasy Alliances: Race and Party Competition in America*. Princeton: Princeton University Press.

Gass, Nick. 2016. "Poll: 6 in 10 Democratic Voters Want Open Primary Process." Politico, June 7, 2016. https://www.politico.com/story/2016/06/poll-democrats-open-primary-223981.

Gerring, John. 1998. *Party Ideologies in America, 1828–1996*. New York: Cambridge University Press.

Grossmann, Matthew, and David A. Hopkins. 2015. "Ideological Republicans and Group-Interest Democrats." *Perspectives on Politics* 13 (1): 119–39.

Heersink, Boris. 2018. "Trump and the Party in Organization: Presidential Control of National Party Organizations." *Journal of Politics* 80 (4): 1474–482.

Jaffe, Alexandra. 2016. "Campaign to Dump Trump at Republican Convention Emerges." NBC News, June 17, 2016. https://www.nbcnews.com/politics/2016 -election/campaign-dump-trump-republican-convention-emerges-n594766.

Karol, David. 2009. *Party Position Change in American Politics: Coalition Management.* Cambridge: Cambridge University Press.

Kilgore, Ed. 2018. "Open Primaries Are a Double-Edged Sword for Progressives," *New York Magazine,* March 21, 2018. http://nymag.com/intelligencer/2018/03/ open-primaries-are-a-double-edged-sword-for-progressives.html.

LaRaja, Ray, and Brian Schaffner. 2015. *Campaign Finance and Political Polarization: When Purists Prevail.* Ann Arbor: University of Michigan Press.

Lillis, Mike. 2018. "Ocasio-Cortez Draws Ire from Democrats: 'Meteors fizz out.'" The Hill, July 17, 2018. https://thehill.com/homenews/house/397333-ocasio cortez-draws-ire-from-democrats-meteors-fizz-out.

Lopez, Ian Haney. 2015. *Dog Whistle Politics: How Coded Racial Appeals Have Reinvented Racism and Wrecked the Middle Class.* New York: Oxford University Press.

Margolis, Michele. 2018. *From Politics to the Pews.* Chicago: University of Chicago Press.

Mason, Lilliana. 2018. *Uncivil Agreement: How Politics Became Our Identity.* Chicago: University of Chicago Press.

Milbank, Dana. 2016. "Reince Priebus Is in Over His Head," *Washington Post,* April 11, 2016. https://www.washingtonpost.com/opinions/reince-priebus-is-in-over -his-head/2016/04/11/73555864-0024-11e6-9d36-33d198ea26c5_story.html.

Mudde, Cas. 2018. "Don't Be Fooled. The Midterms Were Not A Bad Night for Trump." *The Guardian,* November 7, 2018. https://www.theguardian.com/com mentisfree/2018/nov/07/midterms-not-a-bad-night-for-trump.

Noel, Hans. 2018. "The Activists Decide: The Preferences of Party Activists in the 2016 Presidential Nominations." *Journal of Elections, Public Opinion and Parties* 28 (2): 225–44.

Norrander, Barbara. 1992. *Super Tuesday: Regional Politics and Presidential Primaries.* Lexington: University Press of Kentucky.

North, Douglass. 1997. "Institutions." *Journal of Economic Perspectives* 5 (1): 97–112.

Oliver, J. Eric, and Thomas Wood. 2018. *Enchanted America: How Intuition and Reason Divide Our Politics.* Chicago: University of Chicago Press.

Rahn, Will. 2018. "Believe It or Not, John Kasich Matters." CBSNews.com, March 15, 2018. https://www.cbsnews.com/news/commentary-believe-it-or-not-john-ka sich-matters/.

Resnick, Gideon. 2018. "Nancy Pelosi Disagrees That Alexandria Ocasio-Cortez's Win Means Democratic Socialism Is on the Rise." The Daily Beast, June 27, 2018. https://www.thedailybeast.com/nancy-pelosi-dismisses-ascendent-left-after -democratic-socialist-alexandria-ocasio-cortez-wins-primary.

Rhodes, Jesse. 2017. *Ballot Blocked: The Political Erosion of the Voting Rights Act.* Stanford, CA: Stanford University Press.

Rosenfeld, Sam. 2017. *The Polarizers: Post-War Architects of Our Partisan Era.* Chicago: University of Chicago Press.

Schickler, Eric. 2016. *Racial Realignment: The Transformation of American Liberalism, 1932–1965.* Princeton: Princeton University Press.

Schlozman, Daniel. 2015. *When Movements Anchor Parties: Electoral Alignments in American History.* Princeton: Princeton University Press.

Sides, John, Michael Tesler, and Lynn Vavreck. 2018. "Hunting Where the Ducks Are." *Journal of Elections, Public Opinion and Parties* 28 (2): 135–56.

Skowronek, Stephen. 2011. *Presidential Leadership in Political Time: Reprise and Reappraisal.* Lawrence: University Press of Kansas.

———. 1997. *The Politics Presidents Make: Presidential Leadership from John Adams to Bill Clinton.* Cambridge, MA: Harvard Belknap.

Stuckey, Mary. 2005. "One Nation (Pretty Darn) Divisible: National Identity in the 2004 Conventions." *Rhetoric and Public Affairs* 8 (4): 639–56.

Watkins, Eli. 2018. "Michael Avenatti to *Time*: 2020 Democratic Nominee 'Better Be a White Male.'" CNN.com, October 25, 2018. https://www.cnn.com/2018/10/25/politics/michael-avenatti-time/index.html.

Weaver, Jeff. 2018. "Democrats Need to Fix Their Own Voter Suppression Problem." CNN, July 20, 2018. https://www.cnn.com/2018/07/19/opinions/democrats-need-reform-new-york-primary-weaver/index.html.

Wolbrecht, Christina. 2000. *The Politics of Women's Rights: Parties, Positions, and Change.* Princeton, NJ: Princeton University Press.

Zelizer, Julian. 2016. "Trump and Sanders: How Party Elites Fueled Them." CNN, April 4, 2016. https://www.cnn.com/2016/04/04/opinions/wisconsin-tests-both-parties-zelizer/index.html.

Chapter Nine

The System Evolves

Changes in the Presidential Selection Process, 1792–1824

William G. Mayer

One of the most striking features of the presidential selection process set forth in Article II of the Constitution is how little apparent resemblance it bears to the process we are familiar with today.[1] To be sure, the constitutional text does make provision for an Electoral College (though that term is never actually used in the Constitution), but each elector is instructed to vote for *two* presidential candidates, not a president and a vice president. Moreover, there is no allowance for political parties, and no reference to or requirement for popular voting. So how did we go from the text of Article II to the system we know today?

The answer centers on four important developments that took place largely or entirely in the years between 1792 and 1824:

1. The Framers had hoped that the process they created would eliminate or at least greatly diminish the role of political parties in presidential selection. To the extent that a formal "nomination process" was needed, it would be performed by the Electoral College itself. If no presidential candidate received a vote from a majority of the electors, the House of Representatives would make the final decision, with the important stipulation that they had to choose from among the top five finishers in the Electoral College voting. The Electoral College would thus narrow what might otherwise be a long and unwieldy list of presidential possibilities to a final five.

   In fact, right from the start, party-like groups (whether and when they became full-blown parties is a matter of some dispute) sought to rally their forces around their preferred presidential and vice presidential candidates, and then get like-minded people chosen for the Electoral College. The essential precondition for this sort of activity, of course, was for the group to reach agreement on which candidates to support. In the earliest presidential elections, this task was achieved by informal consultations among group leaders. From 1800 to 1816, the most frequently used method for making presidential and vice presidential nominations was the congressional caucus, a meeting of a party's members in the U.S. Senate and House of Representatives. In 1832, both of the embryonic major parties first used a method that would soon become standard practice and is still employed today: a national convention composed of delegates selected by the state parties.

2. Article II specifies that every member of the Electoral College would cast two undifferentiated votes for president, not separate votes for president and vice president. The top finisher in the Electoral College voting, if he received a vote from a majority of the electors, would become president. The second-place finisher, regardless of how many votes he received, would be elected vice president. This system never worked the way it was supposed to, instead leading to a good deal of mischief and one near-constitutional crisis. The result was the adoption of the Twelfth Amendment in 1803–1804, which required the members of the Electoral College to cast "distinct" votes for president and vice president.

3. Though the evidence on this point is not exceptionally rich, the Framers of the Constitution probably expected the members of the Electoral College to be "free agents." They would gather together in their respective states without prior promises or commitments, deliberate upon the various presidential possibilities, and then cast their votes according to their own best judgments. As parties began to play an active role in the presidential selection process, however, electors were chosen with the clear expectation that they would cast their votes for the presidential and vice presidential candidates of the party that had nominated and elected them. The Electoral College, in short, was transformed from an independent deliberative body to a rubber stamp.

4. In Article II, state legislatures were given the discretion to select the members of the Electoral College in any manner they chose. In the first presidential election held under the Constitution's aegis, the states, not surprisingly, used that discretion in a variety of ways. Some states allowed the voters to choose the electors; some state legislatures performed the task themselves; still others used mixed systems.[2] That sort of diversity continued up through at least 1820. By 1836, however, every state except South Carolina had opted for a single method for selecting electors: one in which members of the Electoral College were chosen *by popular vote on a statewide, plurality-winner basis*. In other words, whichever candidate got the most popular votes in a state would get all of its electoral votes.

A popular vote thus went from being just one among many options to the all-but-exclusive method by which members of the Electoral College were chosen.

Add all four of these developments together, and by the early 1830s the presidential selection process looked very different from the one the Framers had envisioned—and was recognizably similar to the one we know and suffer with in the early twenty-first century. In particular, the process had become both more partisan and more participatory. Though they had no legal status at this time, political parties were clearly central to the whole system, defining the range of effective choice and thereby helping transform almost every other component of the process. And ordinary voters, who played only a minor role in the first presidential election, were now a major player, directly electing the members of the Electoral College who were, in turn, expected to register the voters' preferences without exercising any discretion or independent judgment. The purpose of this chapter is to examine these four changes and how and why they took place.

THE EMERGENCE OF THE FIRST PARTY SYSTEM

Of the four changes just listed, the emergence of political parties was clearly the most consequential. It was parties that were the driving force in converting the Electoral College into a rubber stamp and that made the dual-vote system so plainly unworkable. Parties also played a role in pushing states to choose their presidential electors via statewide popular vote.

Historians disagree about when the first American political parties came into existence. Some scholars see them present as soon as the Constitution went into effect—indeed, as an extension of the two broad coalitions that had previously been fighting about whether or not to ratify the Constitution.[3] Noble Cunningham, in a highly regarded monograph on Thomas Jefferson and his adherents, concluded that "political parties were beginning to take form in 1792."[4] William Nisbet Chambers, in another often-cited study of early American politics, stated, "We may speak of a Federalist party proper by the late months of 1793 and the early months of 1794." The Jeffersonian Republicans took a little longer to coalesce but had attained "reasonably full development" by 1795 or 1796.[5] John Hoadley, looking primarily at congressional roll call votes, found a sharp increase in party "polarization" in the 4th and 5th Congresses (1795–1799; Hoadley 1986). At the other end of the spectrum, Ronald Formisano has argued that the Federalists and Republicans *never* achieved many important attributes of political parties and that the first American party "system" did not come into being until the 1830s and 1840s.[6]

The dispute here, at least as I read it, is less about the facts of history—who was doing what and when—and more about matters of definition. Just what kinds of things must a group be doing, and on what kind of scale, before it can meaningfully be called a "political party"? For the purposes of this study, there is, fortunately, no need to settle this argument. It is enough to note that, from the very beginning, groups of political activists, in and out of government, began to perform at least some of the tasks that are generally ascribed to parties: in particular, nominating presidential and vice presidential candidates (with varying degrees of formality) and then working to ensure that people were chosen for the Electoral College who were likely to be supportive of those choices. Through the rest of this chapter, I will often call these groups parties because that is simpler and less awkward than referring to them as "party-like groups."

By 1792, the once highly charged debate over the Constitution had been effectively settled. North Carolina and Rhode Island, the two states that had refused to ratify in 1787–1788, had both finally joined the union. A Bill of Rights had been appended to the original document, but no additional specific limitations on the powers of Congress had been agreed to. But the resolution of one momentous question did not inaugurate an extended era of peace and harmony in the new nation. It merely meant that Americans turned their attention to a different issue: what policies should this new and more powerful national government adopt? Put another way, what kind of country would we become? Answering this question was partly a matter of deciding how to interpret the sometimes vague, compromise-riddled document that had just been ratified, even more a matter of choosing from among several different visions of the national future.

In a story that has often been told, a series of policy disagreements quickly cumulated into a persistent and increasingly bitter division between two broad clusters of national political leaders. In the beginning, the disagreements centered around a series of reports on economic matters that Alexander Hamilton, the first secretary of the treasury, had sent to Congress, recommending (among other things) the assumption of state debts by the national government, the payment of all past debts at full value, the creation of a governmentally subsidized but privately run Bank of the United States, and a vigorous effort to promote American manufactures. After 1792, during George Washington's second term as president, the two proto-parties also disagreed about foreign policy—in particular, about whether the United States should have been more sympathetic to and supportive of Great Britain or France. The congressional opposition to these policies was led by James Madison, then a representative from Virginia; but its titular and spiritual leader was another member of Washington's cabinet, Secretary of State Thomas Jefferson. Though President Washington tried to govern above parties, almost all historians today agree that Washington's decisions sided more often with Hamilton than with Jefferson. Hamilton and his followers are usually referred to as the *Federalists*; Jefferson and his adherents are most often called *Republicans*. (To distinguish the latter group from the Republican Party that was created in the 1850s, historians sometimes call them the Jeffersonian Republicans or the Democratic Republicans, though neither label was in widespread use at the time.)

Table 9.1 shows the various methods that these two parties used to nominate their presidential tickets from 1792–1824. As indicated, in the earliest elections, the two parties made nominations by informal consultations among party leaders. In 1792, for example, the consensus choice for president, favored by both Hamilton and Jefferson, was George Washington. The two camps disagreed, however, about the best person to serve as vice president. Federalists were content to support John Adams, the current occupant of that office, who had cast some thirty-one tie-breaking votes in support of administration positions. Even Alexander Hamilton, who was endlessly scheming about one thing or another, preferred Adams to any of the alternatives. Many Republicans, however, had developed a distinct distaste for Adams, partly because of his behavior in office, even more because of a series of controversial positions he had taken in his book *A Defence of the Constitutions of the United States*, published in 1789.

For reasons of geographic balance, there seems to have been a general understanding that the Republican vice presidential nomination had to go to a northerner. The most obvious possibility was George Clinton, recently

Table 9.1. Methods Used to Make Presidential and Vice Presidential Nominations, 1792–1824

Year	Republican Party	Federalist Party
1792	Informal consultation among party leaders	Informal consultation among party leaders
1796	Informal consultation among party leaders	Informal consultation among party leaders
1800	Congressional caucus	Congressional caucus
1804	Congressional caucus	Informal consultation among party leaders
1808	Congressional caucus	National convention
1812	Congressional caucus	National convention
1816	Congressional caucus	None made
1820	None made	None made
1824	Congressional caucus	None made

Source: Compiled by the author.

reelected governor of New York, who had also been touted by some anti-Federalists as a vice presidential candidate in the first presidential election in 1789. In late September 1792, John Beckley, the clerk of the House of Representatives and an important early Republican manager, was sent to New York to confer with that state's Republican leaders. What Beckley did in New York or whom he met with is not known, but several days later two prominent New York Republicans wrote a letter to Rep. James Madison and Sen. James Monroe, both of whom were then in Virginia, saying that most Empire State Republicans actually preferred Aaron Burr for the vice presidential slot. Both Monroe and Madison reacted quite negatively to this recommendation, thinking Burr to be too young (he was then thirty-six) and inexperienced and uncertain that he was really a Republican. Eventually, they sent a letter back to the New Yorkers that strongly endorsed Governor Clinton—but before the letter arrived, a meeting of Pennsylvania and New York Republicans had decided to "exert every endeavor for Mr[.] Clinton, and drop all thoughts of Mr[.] Burr."

However unsystematic these consultations might seem to twenty-first-century eyes, they served their intended purpose. Of the 132 electoral votes that were cast in 1792 for someone besides George Washington, virtually all of them went to either Adams (77) or Clinton (50).

The best-known nomination method used during these years was the congressional caucus, but as table 9.1 shows, it was nowhere near as dominant as some histories of the presidential nomination process have suggested. The first congressional caucus was held by the Federalist Party in 1800—but they never held another. The Republican Party held a congressional caucus in every presidential-election year between 1800 and 1816, held an abortive meeting in 1820 that adjourned without making any nominations, then held a final, hotly criticized caucus in 1824, whose presidential nominee finished a distant third in the Electoral College balloting. The bottom line, however, is that in every presidential election between 1800 and 1816, the person nominated by the Republican congressional caucus was subsequently elected president.

As its name implies, the congressional caucus was a meeting of a party's U.S. senators and representatives, usually held in the late winter or early spring of a presidential-election year, to nominate candidates for the presidency and vice presidency. The two 1800 caucuses were both held in secret, though they were mentioned in private correspondence. The other Republican caucuses were held openly in the House or Senate chamber and were reported on in contemporary newspapers. Though most reports on these caucuses were rather sketchy, it appears that they were brief, businesslike affairs. There were no nominating speeches, no debates about the relative merits of the candidates. Though reliable attendance numbers are not available for the

1800 caucuses, in later years the caucuses were attended by between 60 and 80 percent of the Republican members of Congress.

The principal attraction of the congressional caucus for the early American parties was that it was almost the only practical way to bring together a group of party members who could plausibly be described as nationally representative. Given the primitive state of the country's transportation and communication facilities, the logistics of assembling a truly national convention would have been quite daunting. The experience of the Constitutional Convention in 1787 is instructive in this regard. That convention was supposed to start on May 15—but it wasn't until May 25, ten days later, that a seven-state quorum was achieved. The 1st U.S. Congress had an even worse experience. Scheduled to commence proceedings on March 4, 1789, the House of Representatives did not achieve a quorum until April 1; the Senate took until April 6.

After 1800, the Federalist Party entered into a period of substantial, long-term decline from which they never recovered. By 1804, the Federalist contingent in Congress had shrunk so much that a Federalist congressional caucus could no longer be portrayed as a national gathering. In the 8th Congress (1803–1805), Federalists held only about a quarter of the seats in the House and Senate. More than a third of the states had no Federalist in either chamber. The Federalists responded to this situation in 1808 and 1812 by holding what historians have called the first national nominating conventions in American history.[7] Both conventions were held in secret, so our knowledge about them is fragmentary. The 1808 conclave was held in New York in late August and was attended by about twenty-five to thirty delegates from eight states. The 1812 convention also took place in New York, though in September, and was attended by about seventy delegates from eleven states. There is no direct evidence as to how these delegates were selected, but it is unlikely that there was any systematic effort to assess or incorporate the opinions of the grassroots, rank-and-file party adherents. As the eminent historian Samuel E. Morison has concluded, both conventions "were representative only of the party leaders."[8] By 1816, the Federalist Party had declined even further, to the point where it no longer made sense for the party to nominate a presidential or vice presidential candidate.

At a time when Americans of all stripes were critical of political parties, Republicans tolerated the first two congressional caucuses only because the Federalist Party was seen as such a threat to republican institutions and because unity among Federalist opponents was seen as essential to victory. As the Federalists' electoral strength continued to decline, however, many Republicans became convinced that the opposition party no longer had a serious prospect of winning a national election. The result, not surprisingly, was that the congressional caucus came under increasingly heavy criticism. With little or no Federalist opposition, many critics said that the caucus had, in effect, taken away the voters' power to choose the president. An even more common complaint was that the congressional caucus violated the spirit and maybe even the letter of the Constitution. Allowing the members of the legislature to choose the chief executive was seen as a breach of the separation of powers and (perhaps) of the provision in Article II that stated that "no Senator or Representative . . . shall be appointed [a presidential] Elector." By the time the 1824 election was settled by a second contingency vote in the House of Representatives, it was clear that whoever decided to challenge John Quincy Adams in the 1828 election would seek an alternative method of nomination.

THE END OF THE DUAL-VOTE SYSTEM

The most bitter and divisive presidential election held during the first thirty-five years under the Constitution was unquestionably the election of 1800. As is well known, the campaign for electoral votes that year was a smear job on both sides. John Adams, the incumbent president, was attacked as a wannabe monarchist; Thomas Jefferson, the Republican nominee, was depicted as an atheist and a Jacobin. To make matters worse, the contest did not end when the electoral votes were finally counted in February 1801. Unlike the Federalists, the Republicans had neglected to make sure that one of their electors voted for their presidential candidate but not for their vice presidential nominee, Aaron Burr. The result was that Jefferson and Burr each received seventy-three votes, thereby invoking for the first time the contingency procedure set forth in Article II of the Constitution, which required the House of Representatives to choose between the two, with each state given one vote, no matter how many representatives it had. Balloting would continue until one candidate received a vote from a *majority* of the states.

On the first House ballot, the Republicans all supported Jefferson while the Federalists supported Burr, with the result that Jefferson received eight votes and Burr six with two states equally divided between the two and thus not voting. Jefferson, in short, had a plurality of the votes, but not a majority. And so it continued for thirty-four more ballots over the next six days, each ballot producing an 8-to-6-to-2 vote stalemate. Finally, on February 17, a handful of Federalists decided not to prolong the agony. Federalist representatives from Maryland and Vermont "retired" from the chamber and thus allowed their Republican counterparts to cast their states' votes for Jefferson. When the Federalist members from Delaware and South Carolina decided to cast blank ballots, the final result was ten votes for Jefferson, four for Burr, and two abstentions.

How close did the country come in early 1801 to a serious constitutional crisis? The answer depends on an issue that was difficult to assess at the time and is even more elusive for twenty-first century observers: the likelihood that various political actors would have been willing to adopt certain risky or unpopular political strategies—or to put it more bluntly, how reckless one thinks the Federalists were. Had Burr succeeded in acquiring nine state votes in the House of Representatives and thus been elected president, many Republicans would have been disappointed, but they almost certainly would have gone along with the result. As Jefferson himself said, "Had [the House balloting] terminated in the election of [Mr.] Burr, every republican would have acquiesced in a moment; because, however it might have been variant from the intentions of the voters, yet it would have been agreeable to the constitution."[9]

If the House had been unable to make a choice, however, the remaining options were not just problematic, but potentially disastrous. One possibility that was floated at the time said that if March 4 came with no properly elected president, Article II allowed the Congress, most of whose members were Federalists, to confer the presidency by law on someone else. Had the Federalists attempted such a move, Republicans would have almost unanimously regarded it as an act of "usurpation"[10] and resisted it in ways well beyond the realm of "politics as usual." Several weeks after Jefferson's inauguration, for example, Thomas McKean, the Republican governor of Pennsylvania, told Jefferson that in the event of "an appointment, of any other person than one of the two elected by the Electors," he had framed a "proclamation . . . enjoining obedience" to Jefferson and Burr from "all officers civil [and] military and the citizens of this State." In addition,

> The [Pennsylvania] Militia would have been warned to be ready, arms for upwards of twenty thousand were secured, brass field-pieces [etc.] and an order would have issued for the arresting [and] bringing to justice every member of Congress, or other person found in Pennsylvania, who would have been concerned in the treason.[11]

Virginia Governor James Monroe was thinking along the same lines. "The intimation of such a projected usurpation," he informed Jefferson in mid-January, had excited "much alarm" within the state legislature and "a spirit fully manifested not to submit to it." More ominously, Monroe had sent Thomas Mann Randolph to spy on the federal arsenal in New London, Virginia, to see how many guns it held and how much ammunition, and whether there were any signs that such weaponry might be moved farther north to Harpers Ferry, where a national army would have easier access to it.

All of which suggests that there is considerable wisdom in the recent conclusion of historian James Roger Sharp:

> Viewed from the perspective of the twenty-first century, the electoral crisis might seem to have been almost comically overblown. Yet the electoral deadlock of 1801 stands as one of the two great political and constitutional crises of our nation's history. The participants believed that they were staring into an awful abyss and that all of the fruits of the American Revolution and the many accomplishments in its aftermath were in danger of being swept away in a civil war and a dismemberment of the Union.[12]

Overblown or not, the electoral deadlock of 1801 was enough to convince most politically attentive Americans of the need to do away with the constitutional provision that required members of the Electoral College to cast two undifferentiated votes for president. This provision had been recognized as a "defect" in the Constitution while the first presidential election was still in progress and had never really functioned as intended.

As detailed in an earlier article, the dual-vote system was included in Article II partly as a sop to small-state concerns, even more as a response to the parochialism of the new nation's inhabitants.[13] Particularly if the president were popularly elected, many delegates at the Constitutional Convention argued, the people "will generally vote for some man in their own state, and the largest State will have the best chance for the appointment."[14] As an elite group, the members of the Electoral College would hopefully approach their duties from a more cosmopolitan perspective, but to make sure that they didn't succumb to the same vice, the Convention gave each elector two votes, along with the stipulation that at least one of the votes had to be cast for someone who "shall not be an Inhabitant of the same State with themselves." Thus, an elector from New Hampshire or Georgia could still cast one vote for some third-rate, home-state favorite, and then give his second vote to an established national contender such as Washington, Adams, or Jefferson.

In fact, the electors turned out to be much less parochial than many Convention delegates had feared. Even in 1789, when only the most primitive party-like creatures made any attempt to organize the presidential voting, most electors cast both of their votes for candidates who had some pretensions to national stature: Washington, Adams, John Jay, and John Hancock. Of the 138 electoral votes cast in 1789, I have calculated that a maximum of 18 were cast for home-state candidates with no plausible claim to national office—and many of these 18 were only thrown away in order to make sure that Adams wasn't inadvertently elected president. By the same criterion, there was one "home-state vote" cast in 1792, 5 (out of 276) in 1796, and zero in 1800.

Besides overestimating the parochialism of the presidential electors—or underestimating the operation of countervailing institutions such as parties—the Framers more egregiously failed to anticipate all the ways that the dual-vote system could be manipulated and all the problems that could result if this were done. In sum, the dual-vote procedure was a reminder that the Framers of the Constitution, for all their gifts and talents, were still fallible—which is why the Constitution also included a procedure for enacting amendments.

The Twelfth Amendment made four major changes to the provisions of Article II.

- First and most conspicuously, it provided that presidential electors would cast "distinct ballots" for president and vice president, rather than two un-differentiated presidential votes. In the congressional debates of the time, this was known as the principle of *designation* or *discrimination*.
- If no presidential candidate received a vote from a majority of the electors appointed, the final decision would again be made by the House of Representatives, voting by state. But where Article II had allowed the House to choose from among the top *five* finishers in the Electoral College voting, the Twelfth Amendment limited the House's choice to the top *three* finishers.
- The original Constitution made no provision for what would happen if the House were unable to reach a decision: that is, if after repeated balloting no candidate was able to win the support of a majority of the states. The Twelfth Amendment tried to fill this void by declaring that if the House had not chosen a president by March 4 (the by-then traditional date for presidential inaugurations), "then the Vice-President shall act as President."[15]
- Under the terms of Article II, no minimum vote percentage was required for the vice presidency; the vice president was simply the second-place finisher in the presidential voting, no matter how many votes he received. But now that the vice president would be elected separately, the Twelfth Amendment stipulated that, just like the president, he needed to receive a vote from "a majority of the whole number of electors appointed." If no candidate received a majority, the final decision would be made by the Senate, which had to choose from among the top *two* finishers in the Electoral College's vice presidential voting.

This text was drafted by the Senate and approved on December 2, 1803, by a 22–10 vote, just barely over the two-thirds threshold required by the Constitution. Having sent the proposed amendment to the House, a number of Republican senators left Washington, thus leaving House members with two effective options: accept the amendment exactly as the Senate had written it, or force the country to use the dual-vote system in (at least) one more election. On December 9, the House narrowly chose to accept the Senate version; the vote was 84–42. In both houses, the vote split almost entirely along party lines, with every Federalist voting against it and almost every Republican supporting it.

The proposed amendment was then sent to the state legislatures and moved swiftly toward ratification. By late July 1804, it had been ratified by the requisite thirteen (of seventeen) states. It had been rejected only in the stalwart Federalist states of Delaware, Massachusetts, Connecticut, and (maybe) New Hampshire.[16] In March 1804, Congress had passed a law stating that if presidential electors had not received word of ratification when they met on the first Wednesday of December, they were to cast two sets of votes, one using the old dual-vote procedure, the other in which they cast distinct ballots for president and vice president. Only the votes consistent with the state of the Constitution on the day the electors met would be opened and counted (Kuroda 1994, 159). As it turned out, however, this precaution was unnecessary. On September 24, Secretary of State James Madison sent out a circular letter to the nation's governors, informing them that the Twelfth Amendment had been properly ratified and was now part of the Constitution.

The passage of the Twelfth Amendment remedied a major defect in the original constitutional provisions concerning presidential selection. Less obviously, it also made the parties' work a lot easier. Under the dual-vote system, the parties had had to perform a delicate balancing act. They had to give their vice presidential candidate *some* votes. Otherwise, he and his followers might feel shabbily treated (a la Adams in 1789 and Burr in 1796) or the party might wind up with a vice president of the opposite party (as happened to the Federalists in 1796). But they couldn't give their second candidate *too many* votes, as this might produce an Electoral College tie (as in 1800) or even lead to the vice presidential nominee being elected president. Especially in an era of poor national communications, diverting just the right number of votes was an enormously difficult task.

Once the Twelfth Amendment was in place, however, the parties could go all-out for both of their national candidates without worrying about all these complicated scenarios. Each party's presidential candidate was clearly marked out, so was its vice presidential candidate, and never the twain shall meet. A lot of strange and unexpected things have happened in American presidential elections since 1804, but there has never been a case where a person nominated as vice president threatened to win the presidential election. Outside the realm of political fiction, it is difficult to imagine how such a thing could ever happen again.

THE EVOLUTION OF A RUBBER STAMP

While all this was going on, another important change was taking place in the American presidential election process: The Electoral College was being transformed from an independent deliberative body to a rubber stamp. The men who wrote and ratified the Constitution did not say a great deal about how the presidential electors who met in each state were to function; but the few clues they did leave strongly suggest that they expected the electors to be a deliberative body. In particular, Alexander Hamilton, writing in Federalist No. 68, said that the electors would be the sort of people "most capable of analyzing the qualities adapted to the station [i.e., the presidency] and acting under circumstances favorable to *deliberation*."[17] This is, at best, a partially accurate description of what took place during the first presidential election in 1789—and it became less and less accurate in the following decades.

Even in the first presidential election, the political elites and activists who took part in that contest understood that the presidential election process involved more than just finding a suitable number of people who possessed (to quote Hamilton again) "the information and discernment requisite to so complicated an investigation."[18] To judge by the characteristics of the first set of presidential electors, special knowledge, training, and experience were seen as very important.[19] But so, too, were the electors' political ideas and values. Those who had supported the adoption of the Constitution frequently expressed the desire to elect what they called "federal electors": men who were committed to giving the new government a fair trial and opposed the desire for amendments that would radically diminish its powers. The Constitution's opponents also made some effort to secure the selection of electors who wanted immediate amendments and would elect a vice president sympathetic to that goal. So far as I can determine, however, there was not a single elector candidate or group of candidates who announced in advance of their selection which presidential or vice presidential candidate they intended to vote for. Nor did anyone else publicly demand that they commit themselves prior to their selection.[20]

The result was an election that seems to have been characterized by a pervasive sense of uncertainty, even after the electors were chosen. Yes, there were lots of federal electors and hopefully (but not certainly) they would all give one vote to George Washington. But who would get their other vote—Adams, Hancock, Henry Knox? It was precisely because no one knew the answer to this question that Alexander Hamilton and others made an effort to divert a significant number of votes away from John Adams and thus make sure that he did not inadvertently finish ahead of Washington.

By 1796, however, just seven years later, the process of choosing presidential electors had become significantly more transparent. There was, as one historian has observed, a "growing tendency of electoral candidates [i.e., candidates for the Electoral College], in states where they were popularly chosen, to declare for whom they would vote."[21] For example, the November 2–5 issue of the *Washington Gazette* included the following notice:

> To the Voters of the Second District composed of the Counties of Prince George and Montgomery.
>
> GENTLEMEN,
>
> As a decided friend to the election of MR. JEFFERSON to fill the Office of President of the United States I offer myself as a Candidate at the ensuing election for the appointment of an Elector to vote for a President and Vice President of the United States.
>
> JOHN T. MASON

The same issue of this paper contained an announcement by Mason's opponent:

> I make no hesitation in declaring that, from all I can learn of the conduct of John Adams in the worst situation of American affairs, as well as in more prosperous times, I sincerely believe him to be a true Republican and a sound politician, as well as a decided friend to our Government, and, that if Elected I shall vote for him as President, unless it should be made appear, that he has by some conduct to which I am a stranger, deserved to forfeit the confidence, and is no longer intituled [*sic*] to the gratitude of his country.
>
> FRANCIS DEAKINS[22]

Perhaps because the political mores of the time frowned on efforts at political self-promotion, some elector announcements read as if made by a candidate's supporters.

> We are authorized to inform the freemen of the 5th district, that Mr. Duvall will serve as an elector of the President and Vice-President, if elected. This district comprehends Anne-Arundel county (including the city of Annapolis) and Baltimore-town. Mr. Duvall is decidedly in favour of Mr. Jefferson, as president of the United States.[23]

Newspapers published in Maryland and Virginia contain numerous statements of this kind.[24] Yet there are also indications that as of 1796, the role of presidential elector was still being defined. Note, for example, the hedging at the end of Francis Deakins's statement. He will vote for John Adams—unless he learns some new, disqualifying information. Such caveats appear in a number of elector announcements; some electors, it appears, were unwilling to renounce completely the idea that presidential electors were supposed to think for themselves.[25]

All of the declarations just quoted were made by elector candidates in states like Maryland and Virginia, which used a *district* system to choose their presidential electors. In a typical district system (there were many variations), a state was first divided into districts, each of which elected one person to serve as a presidential elector. Elector candidates therefore ran as individuals and consequently had to make individual declarations of vote intention. In states that used the *general ticket* system, such as Pennsylvania, the usual practice was for each party to convene a state legislative caucus which then nominated a full slate of elector candidates. Local mass meetings would later be held to endorse and ratify these tickets.

Pennsylvania Republicans proudly proclaimed which candidate their electors were pledged to support. One handbill that was circulated throughout the state read,

> Citizens attend! On [November 4] the important question is to be decided, whether the Republican JEFFERSON, or the Royalist ADAMS, shall be the President of the United States. Subjoined is a list of fifteen good Republicans, friends of the people, who love Liberty, hate Monarchy, and will vote for a Republican President.

Two Republican mass meetings took an even more direct approach, labeling the slate of electors they endorsed as the "Jefferson ticket."[26]

With John Adams under attack as an advocate of monarchy and aristocracy, Federalists were more reticent in describing their elector candidates. A Federalist meeting in Philadelphia called the electors they supported the "Federal and Republican Ticket." An address adopted by that meeting promised to "choose electors who have uniformly evinced an approbation of his [Washington's] conduct," but John Adams's name was never mentioned.[27]

The fact that elector candidates said in advance whom they intended to vote for would have been of little value if the electors didn't follow through on their commitments. There is, however, ample evidence that they did follow through. The overwhelming majority of electors voted for the presidential and vice presidential candidates of the party that had nominated them.

A member of the Electoral College who votes for a different candidate than the ones nominated by his or her party is today called a "faithless elector." (So far as I can determine, this term was never used in the early 1800s.) In the first three presidential elections, especially in 1789 and 1796, it is difficult to get a meaningful count of the number of faithless electors. In the former year, John Adams was never formally nominated as the vice presidential candidate of the pro-Constitution side, though an informal understanding was reached among some leading Federalists; and many pro-Constitution electors were later urged to vote for someone besides Adams in order to make sure that he didn't become president in place of Washington. In 1796, there is some doubt as to whether Aaron Burr actually was the Republican vice presidential nominee. For every election since then, however, we can readily count the number of electoral votes, for president and vice president, where either (a) the votes were cast for someone who was not nominated by either the Federalist or Republican Party; or (b) a Federalist elector voted for a Republican nominee, or vice versa. These results are shown in table 9.2.

In the six elections examined in this table, there are virtually no faithless electoral votes for president. In 1808, I have counted the six presidential votes cast for George Clinton as faithless, even though New York Republicans were divided that year between supporters of James Madison and supporters of George Clinton, and the New York electors were apparently selected without determining their presidential preferences or extracting a promise that they would vote for Madison, who had earlier been nominated by that year's congressional caucus. So it is at least possible that this set of electors was always regarded by the electors themselves as a compromise slate and

Table 9.2. Number of "Faithless" Electoral Votes Cast in Early Presidential Elections, 1800–1820

		Votes for President		Votes for Vice President	
	Total Number of Electoral Votes	Number of Faithless Votes	Percentage Presidential Votes	Number of Faithless Votes	Percentage of Vice Presidential Votes
1800	138	0	0	1	0.7
1804	176	0	0	0	0
1808[a]	175	6	3	15	9
1812	217	0	0	3	1
1816[b]	217	0	0	12	6
1820	232	1	0.4	14	6
Totals	1,155	7	0.6	45	4

a. One elector from Kentucky did not vote in 1808.
b. Counting Rufus King as the Federalist presidential candidate and John Howard as that party's vice presidential candidate.
Source: Compiled by the author.

that the six who voted for Clinton thought they were not violating a previous commitment. But even counting these votes as faithless, less than 1 percent of all presidential electoral votes can be classified this way. Faithless electoral votes were a bit more common in the vice presidential voting. Yet even here, only 4 percent of the votes were cast in a faithless manner.

The upshot is nicely summed up in two quotations from the end of this period. Both quotations, it will be noted, are descriptive rather than prescriptive in nature. The two quotations, that is to say, purport to describe how the Electoral College actually functioned at this time, not to argue how it ought to have worked.

The first quotation comes from a speech in the U.S. Senate made by James Barbour of Virginia in 1819:

> [The Elector] has but one insulated duty to perform, that of voting for the character his constituents prefer, as President, and of whom a pledge is always required, and indeed given, before he is supported by the people. So that, in effect, it is of little consequence who is selected, as he serves only as an organ, to convey the wishes of his constituents to the Electoral College. He furnishes the only requisite, by the pledge he previously gives of supporting the man of their choice.[28]

The second quotation is taken from a Report of the Select Senate Committee on the Resolutions Proposing Amendments to the Constitution, issued in January 1826:

> It was the intention of the Constitution that these electors should be an independent body of men, chosen by the People from among themselves, on account of their superior discernment, virtue, and information; and that this select body should be left to make the election according to their own will, without the slightest control from the body of the People. That this intention has failed of its object in every election, is a fact of such universal notoriety, that no one can dispute it. . . . [Electors] are not the independent body and superior characters which they were intended to be. They are not left to the exercise of their own judgment; on the contrary, they give their vote, or bind themselves to give it, according to the will of their constituents. They have degenerated into mere agents, in a case which requires no agency, and where the agent must be useless, if he is faithful, and dangerous, if he is not.[29]

THE TRIUMPH OF THE GENERAL TICKET SYSTEM

Article II of the Constitution allowed the states to choose their presidential electors "in such Manner as the Legislature thereof may direct." Table 9.3

shows how states used this discretion in the presidential elections from 1789
to 1836. Specifically, I have divided the methods states used for choosing
their presidential electors into five categories.

1. *Legislative Selection.* Many state legislatures decided that the legislature
   itself would choose the state's presidential electors, an option that would
   seem to have been allowed by the wording of Article II but that became
   increasingly controversial during the years examined here.
2. *District Systems.* As used here, a district system is any selection procedure
   that divided a state into a number of distinct districts and then allowed the
   voters within each district to elect one or more presidential electors. States
   that used this system also sometimes allowed two electors to be selected
   by statewide popular vote.[30]
3. *General Ticket System.* This is the procedure that the vast majority of
   states use today to select their members of the Electoral College. Electors
   are chosen through a statewide, plurality-winner, popular vote.[31]
4. *Mixed Systems.* A small number of states devised procedures for selecting electors in which the voters and the state legislature both played some
   significant role. In Massachusetts in 1789, for example, a popular election
   was first held within each of the state's congressional districts. The state
   legislature then chose an elector from among the top two finishers in each
   district. The legislature also chose two "at-large" electors. In New Hampshire that same year, a statewide popular election was held, in which all
   eligible voters were allowed to vote for five persons. Any person receiving a vote from a majority of the voters automatically became an elector.
   If five persons were not elected in this way, the remainder of the elector
   slots would be filled by the state legislature, choosing from among the top
   finishers in the popular vote.
5. *Other.* There are, finally, a few state selection systems that are sufficiently
   idiosyncratic as to defy easy classification. In the first presidential election, the New Jersey legislature allowed the governor and his privy council
   to select that state's presidential electors. Perhaps the strangest system was
   the one employed by Tennessee in 1796 and 1800. The legislature first
   divided the state into three districts, and then appointed three electors from
   each county in a district. The electors for each district then met and chose
   one presidential elector.

One pattern jumps out from the data in table 9.3. The general ticket system grew from a device used by only two states in the first four presidential
elections to the all-but-exclusive method that states used for selecting their
presidential electors. By 1836, every state except South Carolina chose its

Table 9.3. Changes to the Number (and Percentage) of States Using the General Ticket System as a Method for Choosing Presidential Electors

	Legislative	District	General Ticket	Mixed	Other
Number of States Using Each Method					
1789	3	2	2	2	1
1792	9	2	2	1	1
1796	7	4	2	2	1
1800	10	3	2	0	1
1804	6	4	7	0	0
1808	7	4	6	0	0
1812	9	4	5	0	0
1816	9	3	7	0	0
1820	9	6	9	0	0
1824	6	6	12	0	0
1828	2	4	18	0	0
1832	1	1	22	0	0
1836	1	0	24	0	0
Percentage of Total Electoral Votes					
1789	26	20	25	20	8
1792	47	18	18	12	4
1796	34	34	14	16	2
1800	61	19	18	0	2
1804	30	22	48	0	0
1808	41	22	38	0	0
1812	44	24	32	0	0
1816	44	14	42	0	0
1820	31	25	45	0	0
1824	27	20	53	0	0
1828	5	26	69	0	0
1832	4	4	93	0	0
1836	4	0	96	0	0

Source: Information on the methods states used to select their presidential electors is taken primarily from Charles O. Paullin, *Atlas of the Historical Geography of the United States* (Washington, DC, and New York: Published jointly by the Carnegie Institution and the American Geographical Society, 1932), 88–89; and "A New Nation Votes," https://elections.lib.tufts.edu. Where these sources disagreed or did not provide complete information, I have examined state laws, legislative records, and contemporary news reports.

electors by a statewide, plurality-winner, popular vote. (South Carolina didn't abandon legislative selection until after the Civil War.)

The trend shown in table 9.3 is actually the result of two separate developments. The first was the growing belief that the people should elect the president—if not directly, then at least indirectly. Though those who took this position often claimed that they were only being faithful to the intentions of the Framers, the evidence to substantiate this assertion is fairly sparse.[32]

The men who designed and approved the Electoral College procedure were primarily concerned to have a presidential selection process that made the president independent of the legislature and that was insulated from corruption and intrigue. They also wanted to give a little extra weight to the votes and preferences of small states. All that accomplished, their feelings about the value of popular participation were rather mixed, with some convention delegates hoping to give the presidency a broad popular base and others wondering if the voters were capable of choosing a chief executive wisely. The Framers of the Constitution were not the raging anti-democrats they have sometimes been accused of being, but neither were they at the forefront of the movement to expand American democracy. Perhaps the most revealing indication of the Framers' views was the provision in Article II that allowed the state legislatures to select the electors in any way they wanted. So the states *could* allow the presidential electors to be popularly elected—but they weren't *required* to do so.

That checkered history notwithstanding, as early as 1791, just two years after the new government began operations, two members of the U.S. House of Representatives asserted that the Constitution forbade the state legislatures from choosing the electors themselves. As the *Annals of Congress* reported the comments of one of these members:

> MR. GILES said, that he conceived but one mode of choosing Electors was contemplated by the Constitution. The State Legislatures he thought ought not to choose them; they ought to be chosen by the people. He adverted to the Constitution; the words are:
> "That each State shall choose," [etc.]
> This plainly implies that the Legislatures are not authorized to exercise that power themselves. Congress has a power to say when they shall be chosen; this imposes a necessity for one mode, and that the mode should be uniform, and be by the people; for the Legislatures, from the different circumstances of the States, must meet at different periods. He wished this point to be settled. He thought the people ought to choose the Electors.[33]

Though this reading of the Constitution strikes me as highly contrived and clearly contradicted by the plain wording of Article II,[34] it found a remarkable number of adherents in succeeding years, even among some of the most die-hard Federalists.[35] Moreover, even those who didn't argue that the Constitution *required* presidential electors to be chosen by popular vote often claimed that this was the preferred method and/or the one intended by the men who had written Article II. Every time thereafter that Congress debated the mechanics of presidential selection, one or more members could be counted on to make this argument:

David Thomas (NY), 1806: "[H]e always did think, and still thought, that the mode of choosing Electors for the Chief Magistrate of this country, ought to be by the people . . ."

James Barbour (VA), 1816: "God forbid, said he, that the power of electing a President of the United States should be lodged in any other hands than those of the people themselves."

Nathaniel Macon (NC), 1816: "Of all the elections affecting the nation, none, he said, so nearly touched its great interests as the election of the great office of President; and if in any case the public voice should be heard more distinctly than another, it was in that election."

Ezra Gross (NY), 1821: "It is, then, of the greatest importance that the election of President of the United States, should be the effect of the free, unbiassed, and unbought will of the people."

Samuel Smith (MD), 1824: "He believed it was in the spirit of the Constitution that the President should be elected by the people of the United States."[36]

The push to have presidential electors popularly elected was just one aspect of a larger movement to make the American political system more democratic, which took place between 1790 and the early 1850s (Wilentz 2005; also Pessen 1978; Watson 2006). Probably the most prominent manifestation of this trend was the attack on property and taxpaying requirements for voting, which by the 1850s had produced something close to universal white male suffrage (Williamson 1960; Keyssar 2000). But these years also saw an effort (only partially successful) to bring about a more equal apportionment of seats in state legislatures; the widespread shift from viva voce voting to paper ballots; the democratization of many state judiciaries, first by shortening judicial terms and then by having judges popularly elected;[37] and, as documented earlier, the insistence that presidential electors vote for the candidates nominated by the party that elected them, rather than act as independent decision makers. Though some of these changes were brought about by ordinary legislation or by changes in public norms and expectations, many required changes in the state constitutions. As Alexander Keyssar has pointed out, "Between 1790 and the 1850s, every state . . . held at least one constitutional convention, and more than a few held several."[38]

If there was so much sentiment for popular election, why did it take so long to have an effect on state election practices? As table 9.3 shows, not until 1820 did legislative selection surrender its title as the predominant method of choosing presidential electors. One reason for the delay, of course, was that state legislatures were not just the entity that selected the electors in many states; they were also the body that would have to approve any changes in state election laws. Not unexpectedly, the legislators were reluctant to give up this power. Partisan considerations also played an important role. If one party had a clear majority in the legislature, why take a chance that those crazy, unpredictable voters would elect a slate of electors nominated by the other party? Keeping the choice in the state legislature's hands was much the safer course.

A particularly glaring example of this took place in New Jersey in 1812. Like many other states during this period, New Jersey held several different elections during the year, depending on the office at stake. The state legislature was to be elected in October; the balloting for presidential electors was scheduled for November. In the legislative elections, Republican candidates received a majority of the votes; but because these votes were concentrated in two northern counties, it was the Federalists, aided by the supporters of DeWitt Clinton, who won a narrow majority of seats in both houses of the New Jersey legislature. When the new legislature convened, just a week before the presidential voting was to take place, the Federalists decided to change the election law so that the legislature itself would choose the state's electors. The result was that New Jersey's eight electoral votes were cast for Clinton, whereas a general ticket election would very likely have given them to Madison (Risjord 1971).

Eventually, however, the democratic tide that was establishing universal white manhood suffrage and rewriting state constitutions also transformed the character of presidential elections. But the growing sentiment for popular presidential elections is only a partial explanation for the trend in table 9.3. If presidential electors were to be selected by popular vote, why not use a district system?

From the early 1800s to the late 1820s, there were repeated attempts to adopt a constitutional amendment that would have required all states to choose their presidential electors by a popular-vote-based district system. Indeed, on four different occasions—in the 12th, 15th, 16th, and 17th Congresses—the Senate passed a districting amendment by the requisite two-thirds majority. In every case, however, the amendment stalled in the House. Opposition to the amendment came primarily from the large states, who thought that the district system would reduce their power in presidential elections. If large states were allowed to use the general ticket system, a state like New York could deliver thirty-six election votes to its favored candidate (in the elections of 1824 and 1828). If they were forced to use the district system, the New York electoral vote might split 19–17, meaning that the state's preferred candidate would only receive a net electoral vote of just two.

Without an amendment that would have imposed a uniform national standard, both large and small states eventually decided to adopt a law that maximized their own power—namely, the general ticket system. By 1824, half of the states were using the general ticket system; by 1836 it had become the all-but-exclusive method for choosing presidential electors.

CONCLUSION

By 1824, as we have seen, the era of the congressional caucus was at an end. Not until 1832 would the supporters of Andrew Jackson and Henry Clay (neither entity was then sufficiently crystallized to deserve being called a political party) hold a national convention to make their presidential and vice presidential nominations. In most respects, however, the presidential election process of 1824 was at least recognizably similar to the one we know today. Most members of the Electoral College were chosen by popular vote—virtually all would be by 1836. And those electors would then dutifully vote for the candidate nominated by their party. A system that many critics have accused of being set up to shield the presidential election process from popular input would soon become the high point of American political participation.

Moreover, all of the changes examined in this chapter had the effect of making the presidential nomination process more important. The Twelfth Amendment, as noted earlier, allowed the parties to go all out for both their presidential and vice presidential nominees. No longer did they need to worry that the vice presidential candidate might somehow get elected in place of their presidential nominee. If the Electoral College had served as an independent decision maker, party nominations would have been much less important. Finally, the general ticket system, more than the district system or selection by the state legislatures, compelled not just a nomination by the national parties, but also a slate of electors nominated by each state party.

NOTES

1. This chapter is the third in a series of articles examining the origins and development of the American presidential nomination process. For the first two entries in the series, see William G. Mayer, "What the Founders Intended: Another Look at the Origins of the American Presidential Selection Process," in *The Making of the Presidential Candidates 2008*, edited by William G. Mayer (Lanham, MD: Rowman & Littlefield, 2008), 203–34; and Mayer, "Theory Meets Practice: The Presidential Selection Process in the First Federal Election, 1788–89," in *The Making of the Presidential Candidates 2012*, edited by William G. Mayer and Jonathan Bernstein (Lanham, MD: Rowman & Littlefield, 2012), 159–202.

2. For a listing of the specific methods used in 1789, see Mayer, "Theory Meets Practice," box 7.1, p. 166.

3. This argument is most closely associated with Charles A. Beard; see his *Economic Origins of Jeffersonian Democracy* (New York: Macmillan, 1915), especially chapters 1–4. Mary P. Ryan, in an analysis of voting patterns in the first four Congresses, found "the emergence in the first session of the United States Congress of two voting blocs which remained remarkably stable in the eight sessions that fol-

lowed. . . . Most members of the first American congresses quickly identified with one of two voting blocs and maintained this affiliation throughout the period." Ryan does not indicate, however, whether these two voting blocs are the same as the two that battled over the adoption of the Constitution. See Ryan, "Party Formation in the United States Congress, 1789 to 1796: A Quantitative Analysis," *William and Mary Quarterly* 28 (October 1971), 531–32.

4. Noble E. Cunningham, Jr., *The Jeffersonian Republicans: The Formation of Party Organization, 1789–1801* (Chapel Hill: University of North Carolina Press, 1957), 22. John C. Miller reached a similar conclusion: "In 1792, the conflict between the ideas and economic interests personified by Hamilton and Jefferson began to crystallize in the form of political parties." See Miller, *The Federalist Era: 1789–1801* (New York: Harper & Row, 1960), 99.

5. See William Nisbet Chambers, *Political Parties in a New Nation: The American Experience, 1776–1809* (New York: Oxford University Press, 1963), 50, 85.

6. See Ronald P. Formisano, "Deferential-Participant Politics: The Early Republic's Political Culture, 1789–1840," *American Political Science Review* 68 (June 1974): 473–87; and Formisano, "Federalists and Republicans: Parties, Yes—System, No," in *The Evolution of American Electoral Systems*, edited by Paul Kleppner, Walter Dean Burnham, Ronald P. Formisano, Samuel P. Hays, Richard Jensen, and William G. Shade (Westport, CT: Greenwood Press, 1981), 33–76.

7. The following discussion draws on Samuel E. Morison, "The First National Nominating Convention, 1808," *American Historical Review* 17 (July 1912): 744–63; and John S. Murdock, "The First National Nominating Convention," *American Historical Review* 1 (July 1896): 680–83.

8. Morison, "First National Nominating Convention," 754.

9. See Thomas Jefferson to Thomas McKean, March 9, 1801, in *The Papers of Thomas Jefferson*, edited by Julian P. Boyd and others (Princeton: Princeton University Press, 1950–2017), 33:229. The same opinion is expressed in Thomas McKean letter to Thomas Jefferson, March 21, 1801, in ibid., 391.

10. The words "usurp" and "usurpation" are used over and over again in contemporary Republican writings to describe this sort of scenario, by such prominent party leaders as Thomas Jefferson, James Madison, James Monroe, Albert Gallatin, and even Aaron Burr. See, respectively, Thomas Jefferson letter to Thomas McKean, March 21, 1801, in *Papers of Thomas Jefferson*, 33:230; James Madison letter to Thomas Jefferson, February 28, 1801, in ibid., 33:100; James Monroe letter to Thomas Jefferson, January 18, 1801, in ibid., 32:482; Albert Gallatin letter to Hannah Gallatin, January 15, 1801, in Henry Adams, *The Life of Albert Gallatin* (Philadelphia: J.B. Lippincott, 1879), 254; and Aaron Burr letter to Albert Gallatin, February 12, 1801, in ibid., 246.

11. See Thomas McKean letter to Thomas Jefferson, March 21, 1801, in *Papers of Thomas Jefferson*, 33:391.

12. James Roger Sharp, *The Deadlocked Election of 1800: Jefferson, Burr, and the Union in the Balance* (Lawrence: University Press of Kansas, 2010), 132.

13. See Mayer, "What the Founders Intended," 218–20.

14. Roger Sherman in Max Farrand, ed., *The Records of the Federal Convention of 1787* (New Haven: Yale University Press, 1937), 2:29.

15. Though the original Constitution stipulated that Congress meet at least once a year "on the first Monday in December, unless they shall by Law appoint a different Day," no date was established for presidential inaugurations. George Washington was sworn in as the first president on April 30, 1789, but Congress chose to date his term as starting on March 4, the date assigned for the first Congress to meet. (In fact, neither the House nor the Senate achieved a quorum until early April.) But Washington in 1793, Adams in 1797, and Jefferson in 1801 all took the oath of office on March 4, a date that was then given constitutional status by the Twelfth Amendment.

Having resolved one ambiguity, the Twelfth Amendment promptly created two new ones. First, what would happen on March 4 if *both* the House and the Senate were stalemated—that is, if there was neither a president nor a vice president? Second, suppose that a vice president became president in this way, and a while later the House finally resolved its stalemate and one presidential candidate managed to receive a vote from a majority of the states? Did that person now become president, or did the (former) vice president continue to "act as president"? The first of these questions was actually raised by opponents of the amendment, but never definitively answered.

Both issues would remain unresolved until the adoption of the Twentieth Amendment in 1933.

16. In New Hampshire, both houses of the state legislature voted in favor of the amendment, but New Hampshire Governor John Gilman then vetoed the ratification resolution. Both houses then attempted to muster the two-thirds vote necessary to override that veto, but were unable to do so. This raised a constitutional question which had never at that time been addressed: Do state governors have any role in ratifying constitutional amendments, or should the provision in Article V that requires ratification by three-fourths of the state "Legislatures" be read more narrowly so as to require only legislative approval? Fortunately for advocates of the Twelfth Amendment, thirteen other states unambiguously ratified the amendment, so it wasn't necessary to litigate this question. In *Hawke v. Smith*, 253 US 221 (1920), the Supreme Court seemed to adopt the position that "legislature" should be interpreted in the narrow sense, but the decision is not entirely conclusive on this issue.

17. Alexander Hamilton, "Federalist No. 68," in Alexander Hamilton, James Madison, and John Jay, *The Federalist Papers*, edited by Clinton Rossiter (New York: New American Library, 1991 [1788]), 410 (emphasis added).

18. Hamilton, "Federalist No. 68," 410.

19. My analysis of the 1789 election draws on Mayer, "Theory Meets Practice." The qualifications and experience of the first set of presidential electors are discussed on pages 189–90.

20. These statements are based on a close reading of all the relevant materials in Merrill Jensen, Robert A. Becker, Gordon DenBoer, and Lucy Trumbull Brown, eds., *The Documentary History of the First Federal Elections*, 4 vols. (Madison, WI: University of Wisconsin Press, 1976–1984).

21. Cunningham, *Jeffersonian Republicans*, 94. The same trend in noted in Jeffrey L. Pasley, *The First Presidential Contest: 1796 and the Founding of American Democracy* (Lawrence: University Press of Kansas, 2013), 317; and Malcolm C. Clark, "Federalism at High Tide: The Election of 1796 in Maryland," *Maryland Historical Magazine* 61 (September 1966), 218.

22. Both statements are in *Washington Gazette*, November 2–5, 1796.

23. *Maryland Gazette*, October 20, 1796.

24. In addition to the announcements referred to elsewhere in this section, see also the statements by: John Lynn, in *Washington Spy*, October 26, 1796; Josiah Riddick, *Gazette of the United States*, November 7, 1796; and John Archer, *Federal Gazette and Baltimore Daily Advertiser*, November 3, 1796.

25. For two other examples, see the statement by Charles Simms, *Federal Gazette and Baltimore Daily Advertiser*, October 4, 1796; and the statement by William Deakins, *Federal Gazette and Baltimore Daily Advertiser*, October 20, 1796.

26. Two such meetings are described in *Claypoole's American Daily Advertiser*, November 1, 1796.

27. A report on this meeting, including the address, was published in both *Federal Gazette and Baltimore Daily Advertiser*, November 3, 1796; and *Gazette of the United States*, November 4, 1796.

28. Speech by Senator James Barbour, *Annals of Congress*, 15th Congress, 2nd session (Washington, DC: Gales and Seaton, 1854), 153. [In future citations from the *Annals of Congress*, *Annals* is followed by two numbers, separated by a hyphen. The first number is the number of the Congress from which the material is drawn; the second number is the number of the session. For example, *Annals* 8-1 refers to the *Annals* volume(s) covering the 8th Congress, 1st session.]

29. Report of the Select Committee, in the Senate, on the Resolutions Proposing Amendments to the Constitution, January 19, 1826, *Register of Debates in Congress*, 19th Congress, 1st session, appendix, 121.

30. Also included in this category was the system New York state used in 1828, in which the voters selected thirty-four electors on a district basis; these electors then chose two more "at-large" electors.

31. For inclusion in this category, all three of these attributes were necessary. In 1792, New Hampshire state law called for choosing presidential electors by a statewide popular vote, but required successful candidates to receive a vote from a *majority* of the voters. If the requisite number of electors did not receive a majority—which was, in fact, the case—a second statewide election would be held among the top finishers in the first-round voting. Though this procedure undeniably selected the New Hampshire presidential electors via statewide popular vote, I do not include it in this category because it was not a *plurality-winner* system. It was instead coded as "other" (category 5).

32. The analysis in this paragraph draws on Mayer, "What the Founders Intended."

33. William Branch Giles, January 14, 1791, *Annals* 1-3, 1868. Shortly before Giles's speech, Daniel Carroll of Maryland had also declared, "For his part, he was fully convinced that this power [of choosing the electors] is exclusively vested in the people by the Constitution." Ibid., 1867.

34. This is not merely my own opinion. Immediately after Giles's speech, two other House members, James Jackson and Benjamin Goodhue, said that the power to choose presidential electors "was left discretionary with the State Legislatures." See *Annals* 1-3, 1868.

35. See, in particular, the comments of Rufus King in his letter to Charles King, September 29, 1823, in Charles King, *The Life and Correspondence of Rufus King* (New York: G.P. Putnam's Sons, 1894–1900), 6:532–34. For other expressions of the same opinion, see Eligius Fromentin, March 20, 1816, *Annals* 14-1, 224; Mahlon Dickerson, January 13, 1819, *Annals* 15-2, 143; Ezekiel Whitman, January 25, 1821, *Annals* 16-2, 967; John Holmes, February 13, 1823, *Annals* 17-2, 231; and Thomas Hart Benton, February 3, 1824, *Annals* 18-1, 170 and 172.

36. Quotations are taken from, respectively, David Thomas, March 29, 1806, *Annals* 9-1, 895; James Barbour, March 20, 1816, *Annals* 14-1, 213; Nathaniel Macon, March 20, 1816, *Annals* 14-1, 219; Ezra Gross, January 25, 1821, *Annals* 16-2, 963; and Samuel Smith, March 18, 1824, *Annals* 18-1, 362.

37. Both trends are discussed in Jed Handelsman Shugerman, *The People's Courts: Pursuing Judicial Independence in America* (Cambridge: Harvard University Press, 2012), chaps. 2–5.

38. Keyssar, *Right to Vote*, 26–27.

REFERENCES

Adams, Henry. 1879. *The Life of Albert Gallatin*. Philadelphia: J.B. Lippincott.

Beard, Charles A. 1915. *Economic Origins of Jeffersonian Democracy*. New York: Macmillan.

Boyd, Julian P. 1950-2017. *The Papers of Thomas Jefferson*. Princeton: Princeton University Press.

Chambers, William Nisbet. 1963. *Political Parties in a New Nation: The American Experience, 1776–1809.* New York: Oxford University Press.

Clark, Malcolm C. 1966. "Federalism at High Tide: The Election of 1796 in Maryland," *Maryland Historical Magazine* 61.

Cunningham, Jr., Noble E. 1957. *The Jeffersonian Republicans: The Formation of Party Organization, 1789–1801.* Chapel Hill: University of North Carolina Press.

Farrand, Max. 1937. *The Records of the Federal Convention of 1787*. New Haven: Yale University Press.

Formisano, Ronald P. 1974. "Deferential-Participant Politics: The Early Republic's Political Culture, 1789–1840." *American Political Science Review* 68 (June): 473–87.

———. 1981. "Federalists and Republicans: Parties, Yes—System, No," in *The Evolution of American Electoral Systems*, edited by Paul Kleppner, Walter Dean Burnham, Ronald P. Formisano, Samuel P. Hays, Richard Jensen, and William G. Shade. Westport, CT: Greenwood Press.

Hoadley, John F. 1986. *Origins of American Political Parties, 1789–1803.* Lexington: University Press of Kentucky.

Jensen, Merrill, Robert A. Becker, Gordon DenBoer, and Lucy Trumbull Brown, eds. 1976–1984. *The Documentary History of the First Federal Elections*, 4 vols. Madison, WI: University of Wisconsin Press.

Keyssar, Alexander. 2000. *The Right to Vote: The History of Democracy in the United States* New York: Basic Books.

King, Charles. 1894–1900. *The Life and Correspondence of Rufus King*. New York: G.P. Putnam's Sons.

Kuroda, Tadahisa. 1994. *The Origins of the Twelfth Amendment: The Electoral College in the Early Republic, 1787–1804.* Westport, CT: Greenwood Press.

Mayer, William G. 2008. "What the Founders Intended: Another Look at the Origins of the American Presidential Selection Process." In *The Making of the Presidential Candidates 2008*, edited by William G. Mayer, 203–34. Lanham, MD: Rowman & Littlefield.

———. 2012. "Theory Meets Practice: The Presidential Selection Process in the First Federal Election, 1788–89," in *The Making of the Presidential Candidates 2012*, ed. William G. Mayer and Jonathan Bernstein, 159–202. Lanham, MD: Rowman & Littlefield.

Miller, John C. 1960. *The Federalist Era: 1789–1801.* New York: Harper & Row.

Morison, Samuel E. 1912. "The First National Nominating Convention, 1808." *American Historical Review* 17 (July): 744–63.

Murdock, John S. 1896. "The First National Nominating Convention." *American Historical Review* 1 (July): 680–83.

Pasley, Jeffrey L. 2013. *The First Presidential Contest: 1796 and the Founding of American Democracy*. Lawrence, KS: University Press of Kansas.

Pessen, Edward. 1978. *Jacksonian America: Society, Personality, and Politics*, rev. ed. Homewood, IL: Dorsey Press.

Risjord, Norman K. 1971. "Election of 1812." In *History of American Presidential Elections, 1789–1968*, edited by Arthur M. Schlesinger, Jr., Fred L. Israel, and William P. Hansen. New York: Chelsea House.

Rossiter, Clinton, ed. 1991. *The Federalist Papers*. New York: New American Library.

Ryan, Mary P. 1971. "Party Formation in the United States Congress, 1789 to 1796: A Quantitative Analysis." *William and Mary Quarterly* 28 (October): 531–32.

Sharp, James Roger. 2010. *The Deadlocked Election of 1800: Jefferson, Burr, and the Union in the Balance*. Lawrence: University Press of Kansas.

Shugerman, Jed Handelsman. 2012. *The People's Courts: Pursuing Judicial Independence in America*. Cambridge: Harvard University Press.

Watson, Harry L. 2006. *Liberty and Power: The Politics of Jacksonian America*. New York: Hill and Wang.

Wilentz, Sean. 2005. *The Rise of American Democracy: Jefferson to Lincoln*. New York: Norton.

Williamson, Chilton. 1960. *American Suffrage: From Property to Democracy, 1760–1860.* Princeton: Princeton University Press.

Index

About the Contributors

Julia Azari is associate professor of political science at Marquette University. Her current research focuses on the relationship between weak parties and strong partisanship. She is the author of *Delivering the People's Message: The Changing Politics of the Presidential Mandate* (Cornell, 2014) and writes regularly for FiveThirtyEight.com and for the Mischiefs of Faction on Vox.com.

Linda Beail is professor of political science at Point Loma Nazarene University in San Diego, where she teaches courses on gender and race politics, U.S. elections, and feminist theory and served as the founding director of the Margaret Stevenson Center for Women's Studies. She is the author of *Framing Sarah Palin: Pit Bulls, Puritans and Politics* (with Rhonda Kinney Longworth, 2013) and coeditor of *Mad Men and Politics: Nostalgia and the Remaking of Modern America* (with Lilly J. Goren, 2015), and served as guest editor for a special issue of *Visual Inquiry* (7:2, Fall 2018) on gender, nostalgia, and twenty-first-century Disney culture. She has contributed several chapters to books on the politics of popular culture and presented her work at national and international conferences. She currently chairs the American Political Science Association's section on politics, literature, and film and has served as an NGO delegate to the United Nations Commission on the Status of Women. Professor Beail holds a PhD from the University of Iowa.

Jonathan Bernstein is a columnist for Bloomberg Opinion. He previously wrote A Plain Blog on Politics. His academic research has focused on parties, elections, and democracy, and he was coeditor of *The Making of the Presidential Candidates 2012.*

Casey B. K. Dominguez is a professor of political science and international relations at the University of San Diego. She teaches courses about the presidency, war powers, campaigns and elections, voting, and political parties. Her research focuses on the relationships between political parties and interest groups, and on the evolution of Constitutional war powers in the United States. Her research has appeared in *American Politics Research, Congress and the Presidency, Political Research Quarterly,* and *PS: Political Science and Politics.* She and her colleagues have a biweekly podcast about American politics called *A Few Reasonable Words.*

Lilly J. Goren is professor of political science and global studies at Carroll University in Waukesha, Wisconsin. She teaches American government, the presidency, politics and culture, gender studies, politics and literature, and political theory. Her research often integrates popular culture and literature as means to understanding politics. Her published books include *Mad Men and Politics: Nostalgia and the Remaking of Modern America* (coedited with Linda Beail, 2015); *Women and the White House: Gender, Popular Culture, and Presidential Politics* (coedited with Justin Vaughn, 2012)—winner of both the 2014 Susan Koppelman Book Award and the 2014 Peter C. Rollins Book Award; *You've Come a Long Way, Baby: Women, Politics, and Popular Culture* (2009); and *Not in My District: The Politics of Military Base Closures* (2003), as well as articles in *Politic & Gender*; *Society*; *Political Research Quarterly*; *White House Studies*; and *The Forum: A Journal of Applied Research in Contemporary Politics,* and she served as guest editor, with Justin Vaughn, for a special issue of *White House Studies* on the presidency and popular culture in 2010. Goren has twice served as chair of the American Political Science Association's politics, literature, and film section, and she is currently serving as a member of the executive board for the APSA's presidents and executive politics section. She is an elected member of the governing committee of the Association for Political Theory, where she served as conference committee cochair for the APT annual meeting in 2015. Goren was elected to the governing council of the American Political Science Association in August 2017, and is currently serving a three-year term on the APSA. Goren was a Fulbright Fellow to the University of Bonn in the summer term, 2018. Professor Goren earned her AB in political science and English from Kenyon College and has an MA and a PhD in political science from Boston College, and is a regular contributor to local, national, and international media.

William G. Mayer is a professor of political science at Northeastern University in Boston. He is the author or coauthor of ten books, including *The*

Front-Loading Problem in Presidential Nominations (2004), *The Making of the Presidential Candidates 2016* (2016), and *The Swing Voter in American Politics* (2008). He has been called "the nation's leading academic authority" on the presidential nomination process. He has also written numerous articles on such topics as voting, public opinion, and media and politics. Most importantly, he is married to Amy Logan and the father of Natalie and Thomas.

Mary A. McHugh is the executive director of the Office of Civic and Community Engagement and adjunct faculty member in the political science department at Merrimack College in North Andover, Massachusetts, where she teaches a variety of classes in U.S. politics and American political institutions. McHugh earned an MA in political science from Boston College, a BA in government and history from Colby College, and is currently working on her dissertation. Her research interests include civic engagement, political humor, the presidency, and Congress.

Josh Putnam is author of Frontloading HQ (http://frontloading.blogspot.com/), a widely cited website that tracks both parties' presidential nomination rules. He has taught political science at a number of North Carolina universities and colleges since receiving his PhD from the University of Georgia.

Patrick Rose (BA, Temple University, 2015) is a PhD student in the political science department at Louisiana State University. His interests include news media and political psychology. He is currently working on a coauthored article investigating the effects of mobile screen size on the processing of fake news.

Kathleen Searles (PhD, Washington State University, 2011), assistant professor, holds a joint appointment in the Manship School of Mass Communication and the Department of Political Science at Louisiana State University. Her interests include news media, campaign advertising, and political psychology. During the last presidential election, she received several grants to support her research using eye-tracking technology, part of a broader agenda that influenced the advertising landscape of the 2016 presidential election. Her work has appeared in *Public Opinion Quarterly*; *The Journal of Computer Mediated Communication*; *Political Research Quarterly*; *Political Communication*; *Journal of Experimental Political Science*; *American Political Research*; and *Political Psychology*. She is currently working on a coauthored book manuscript that investigates the effects of mobile devices on information processing. She also serves on the editorial board for WomenAlsoKnowStuff.com, a website designed to amplify the voice of women political scientists in public discourse and decrease the gender imbalance in media representation of experts.

John Sides is professor of political science at George Washington University. He is an author of *Identity Crisis: The 2016 Presidential Campaign and The Battle for the Meaning of America* (with Michael Tesler and Lynn Vavreck, 2018); *The Gamble: Choice and Chance in the 2012 Election* (with Lynn Vavreck, 2013); and *Campaigns and Election: Rules, Reality, Strategy, Choice* (with Daron R. Shaw, Matthew Grossman, and Keena Lipsitz, 2014).

Michael Tesler is associate professor of political science at UC Irvine. He is author of *Post-Racial or Most Racial? Race and Politics in the Obama Era* (University of Chicago Press, 2016), co-author with David O. Sears of *Obama's Race: The 2008 Election and the Dream of a Post-Racial America* (University of Chicago Press, 2010), and co-author with John Sides and Lynn Vavreck of *Identity Crisis: The 2016 Presidential Campaign and the Battle for the Meaning of America* (Princeton University Press, 2018).

Lynn Vavreck is the Marvin Hoffenberg Professor of American Politics and Public Policy at UCLA, a contributing columnist to "The Upshot" at the *New York Times*, and a recipient of the Andrew F. Carnegie Prize in the Humanities and Social Sciences. She is the author of five books, including the "most ominous" book on the 2016 election: *Identity Crisis: The 2016 Presidential Campaign and the Battle for the Meaning of America* and *The Gamble: Choice and Chance in the 2012 Presidential Election*, described as the "definitive account" of the 2012 election. Political consultants on both sides of the aisle refer to her work on political messaging in The Message Matters as "required reading" for presidential candidates. Her research has been supported by the National Science Foundation, and she has served on the advisory boards of both the British and American National Election Studies. At UCLA she teaches courses on campaigns, elections, public opinion, and the 1960s. Professor Vavreck holds a PhD in political science from the University of Rochester and held previous appointments at Princeton University, Dartmouth College, and The White House.